*Danger was a part of him.*
*Not like a coat that*
*one gets rid of from time to time,*
*but like skin.*
*One dies with it.*

Graham Greene

D1571578

# HUNGARIAN RHAPSODY

THE ADVENTURES OF MAX FRIEDMAN

HUNGARIAN RHAPSODY

Written and illustrated by Vittorio Giardino
Translation by Jeff Lisle
Edited by Bernd Metz

Published by Catalan Communications
43 East 19th Street
New York, NY 10003

© 1986 by Vittorio Giordino. Rights managed by
Norma Agency/Barcelona

English language edition © 1986 by Catalan
Communications

ISBN 0-87416-033-2
Dep. L. B-38.399-86

Printed in Catalonia (Spain) by JTV Publishing Services.

First Printing December 1986

# VITTORIO GIARDINO

# HUNGARIAN RHAPSODY

**catalan communications**
new york

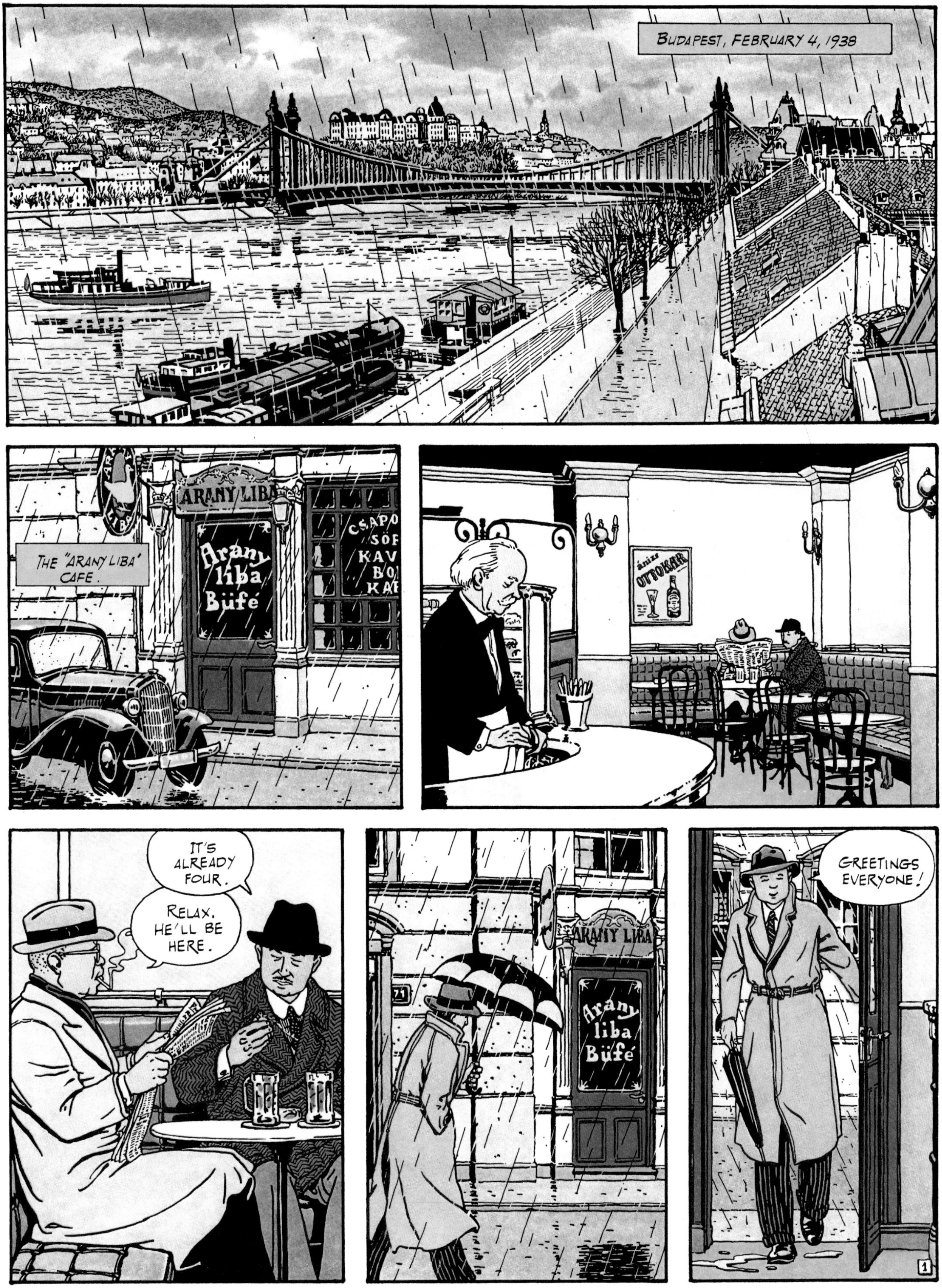

BUDAPEST, FEBRUARY 4, 1938
THE "ARANY LIBA" CAFE.
ARANY LIBA
Arany liba Büfé
ánizs OTTOKAR
IT'S ALREADY FOUR.
RELAX. HE'LL BE HERE.
ARANY LIBA
Arany liba Büfé
GREETINGS EVERYONE!
1

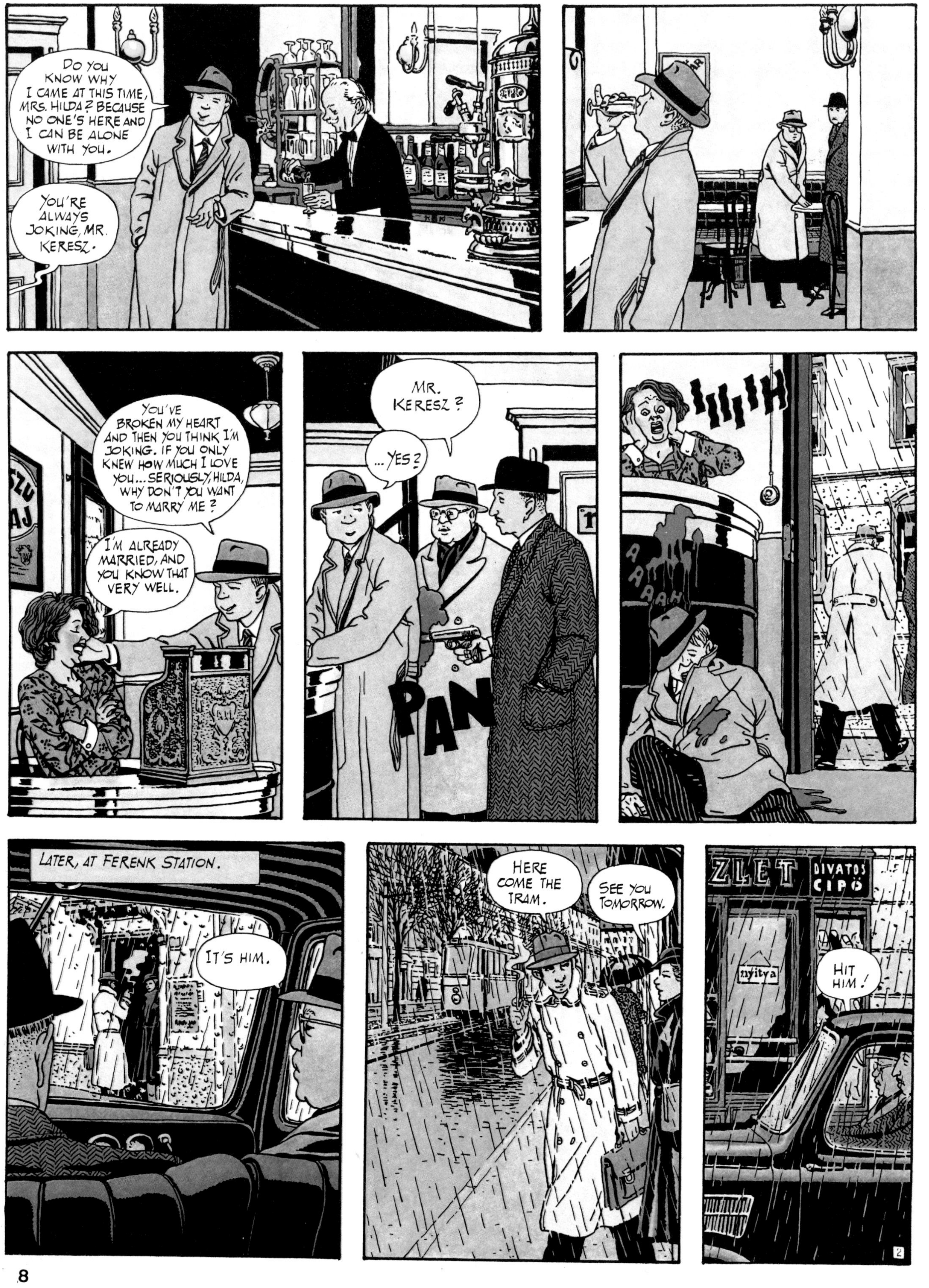

DO YOU KNOW WHY I CAME AT THIS TIME, MRS. HILDA? BECAUSE NO ONE'S HERE AND I CAN BE ALONE WITH YOU.
YOU'RE ALWAYS JOKING, MR. KERESZ.
YOU'VE BROKEN MY HEART AND THEN YOU THINK I'M JOKING. IF YOU ONLY KNEW HOW MUCH I LOVE YOU... SERIOUSLY, HILDA, WHY DON'T YOU WANT TO MARRY ME?
I'M ALREADY MARRIED, AND YOU KNOW THAT VERY WELL.
MR. KERESZ?
...YES?
PAN
IIIIIH
AAAAAH
LATER, AT FERENK STATION.
IT'S HIM.
HERE COME THE TRAM.
SEE YOU TOMORROW.
ZLET
DIVATOS CIPŐ
nyitva
HIT HIM!

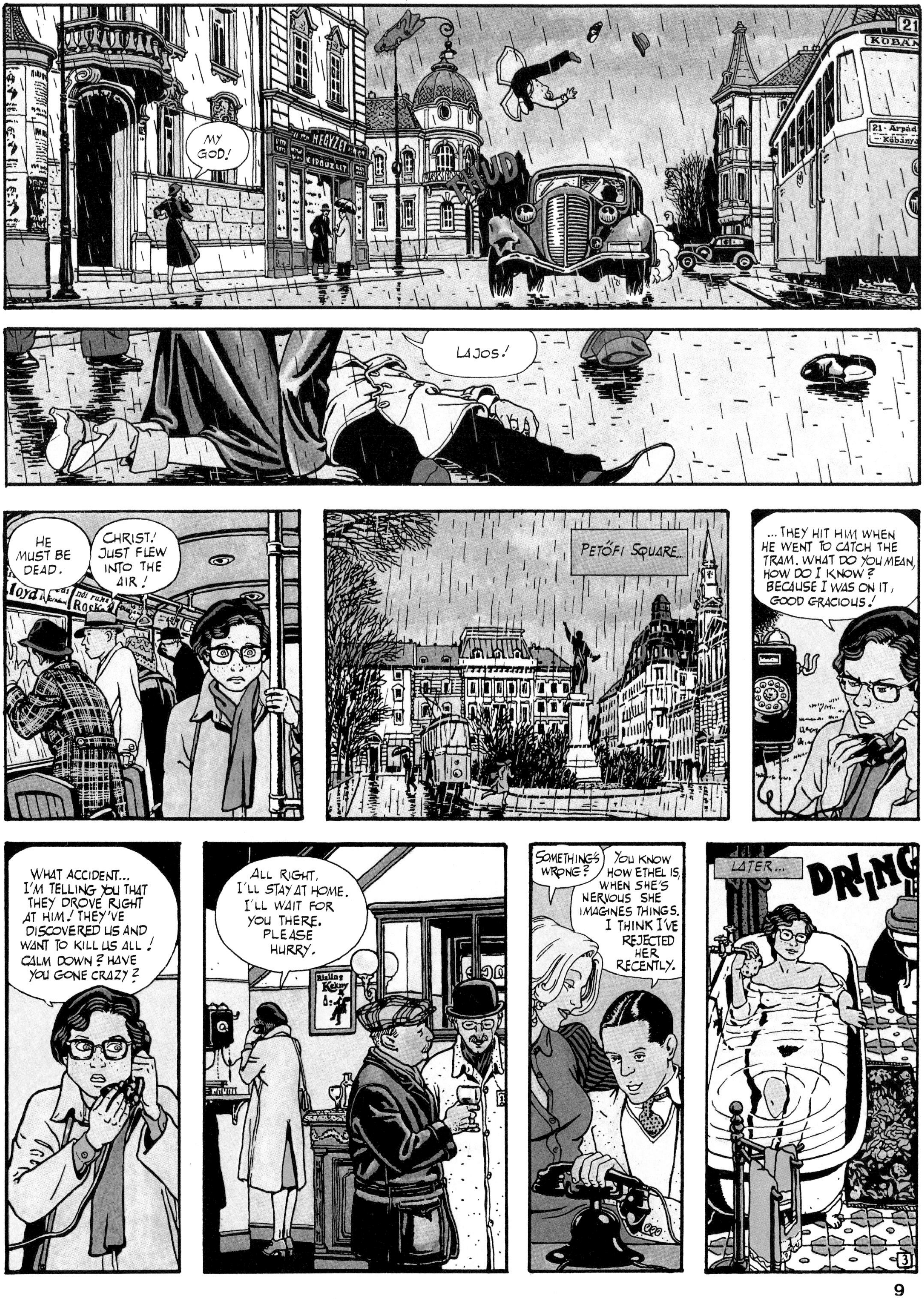

MY GOD!
THUD
LAJOS!
HE MUST BE DEAD.
CHRIST! JUST FLEW INTO THE AIR!
PETŐFI SQUARE...
...THEY HIT HIM WHEN HE WENT TO CATCH THE TRAM. WHAT DO YOU MEAN, HOW DO I KNOW? BECAUSE I WAS ON IT, GOOD GRACIOUS!
WHAT ACCIDENT... I'M TELLING YOU THAT THEY DROVE RIGHT AT HIM! THEY'VE DISCOVERED US AND WANT TO KILL US ALL! CALM DOWN? HAVE YOU GONE CRAZY?
ALL RIGHT, I'LL STAY AT HOME. I'LL WAIT FOR YOU THERE. PLEASE HURRY.
SOMETHING'S WRONG?
YOU KNOW HOW ETHEL IS, WHEN SHE'S NERVOUS SHE IMAGINES THINGS. I THINK I'VE REJECTED HER RECENTLY.
LATER...
DRING

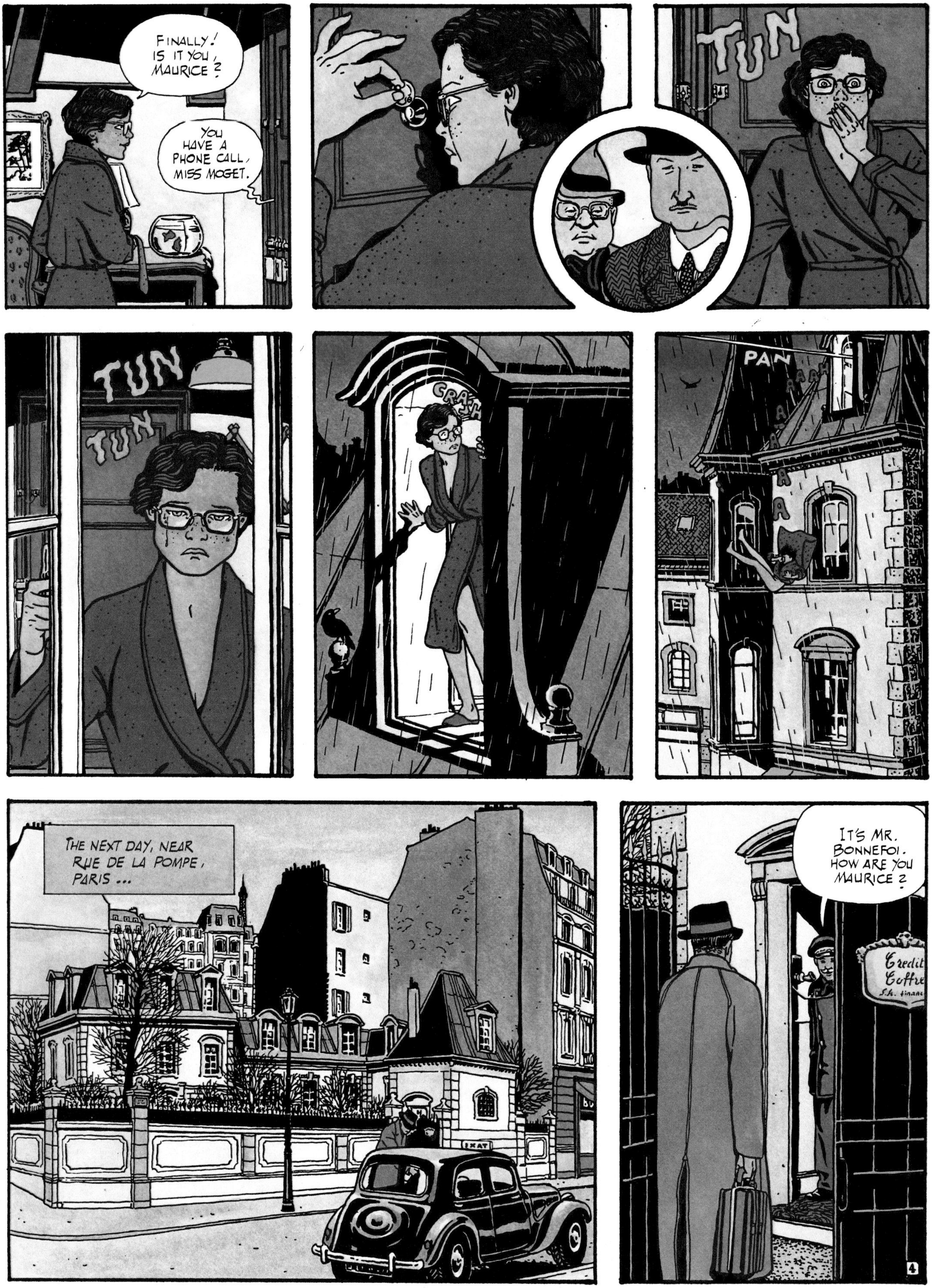
FINALLY! IS IT YOU, MAURICE?
YOU HAVE A PHONE CALL, MISS MOGET.
TUN
TUN
TUN
CRASH
PAN
THE NEXT DAY, NEAR RUE DE LA POMPE, PARIS ...
IT'S MR. BONNEFOI. HOW ARE YOU MAURICE?

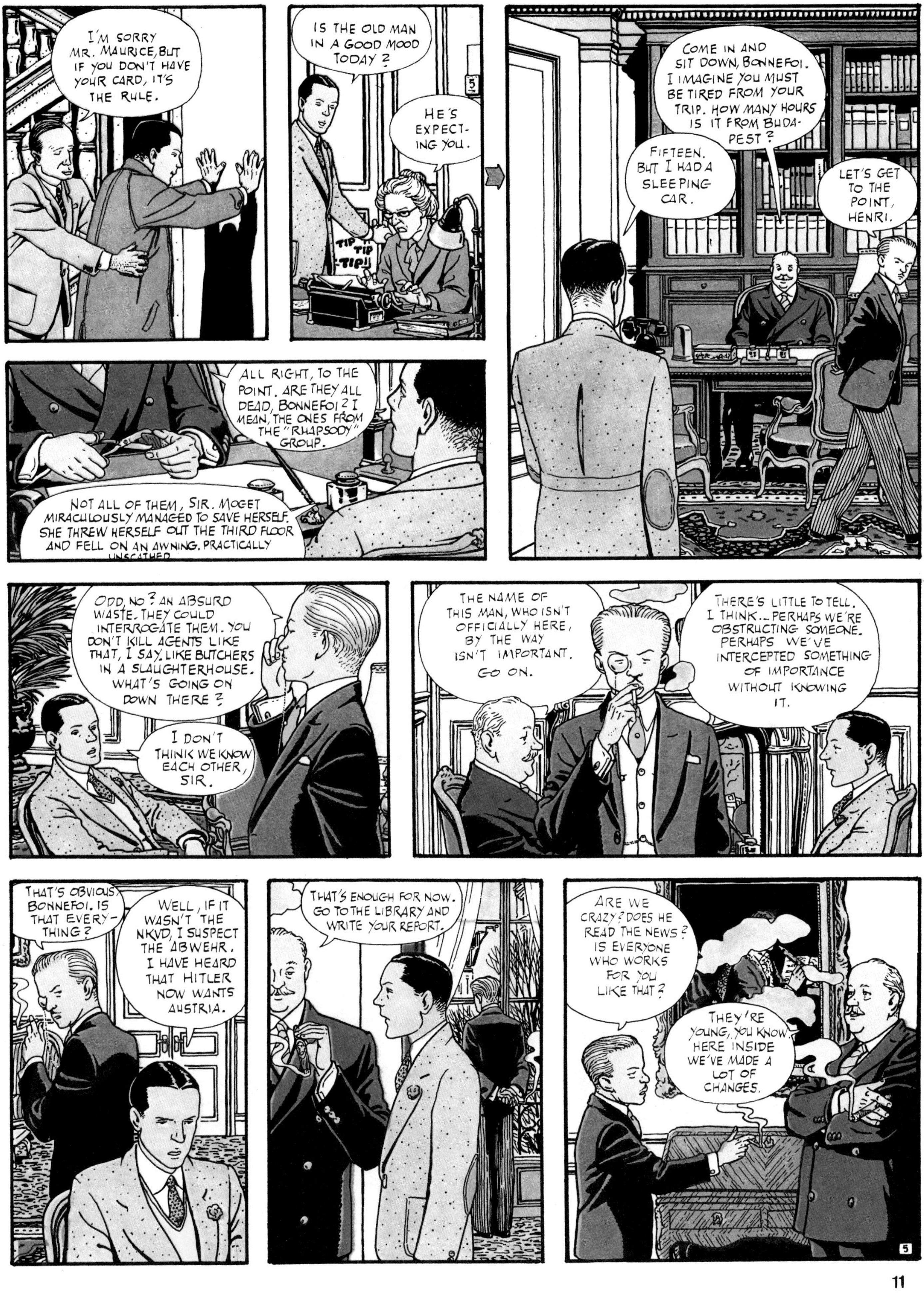
I'M SORRY MR. MAURICE, BUT IF YOU DON'T HAVE YOUR CARD, IT'S THE RULE.
IS THE OLD MAN IN A GOOD MOOD TODAY ?
HE'S EXPECTING YOU.
TIP TIP TIP!!
COME IN AND SIT DOWN, BONNEFOI. I IMAGINE YOU MUST BE TIRED FROM YOUR TRIP. HOW MANY HOURS IS IT FROM BUDAPEST ?
FIFTEEN. BUT I HAD A SLEEPING CAR.
LET'S GET TO THE POINT, HENRI.
ALL RIGHT, TO THE POINT. ARE THEY ALL DEAD, BONNEFOI ? I MEAN, THE ONES FROM THE "RHAPSODY" GROUP.
NOT ALL OF THEM, SIR. MOGET MIRACULOUSLY MANAGED TO SAVE HERSELF. SHE THREW HERSELF OUT THE THIRD FLOOR AND FELL ON AN AWNING. PRACTICALLY UNSCATHED.
ODD, NO ? AN ABSURD WASTE. THEY COULD INTERROGATE THEM. YOU DON'T KILL AGENTS LIKE THAT, I SAY. LIKE BUTCHERS IN A SLAUGHTERHOUSE. WHAT'S GOING ON DOWN THERE ?
I DON'T THINK WE KNOW EACH OTHER, SIR.
THE NAME OF THIS MAN, WHO ISN'T OFFICIALLY HERE, BY THE WAY ISN'T IMPORTANT. GO ON.
THERE'S LITTLE TO TELL. I THINK... PERHAPS WE'RE OBSTRUCTING SOMEONE. PERHAPS WE'VE INTERCEPTED SOMETHING OF IMPORTANCE WITHOUT KNOWING IT.
THAT'S OBVIOUS, BONNEFOI. IS THAT EVERYTHING ?
WELL, IF IT WASN'T THE NKVD, I SUSPECT THE ABWEHR. I HAVE HEARD THAT HITLER NOW WANTS AUSTRIA.
THAT'S ENOUGH FOR NOW. GO TO THE LIBRARY AND WRITE YOUR REPORT.
ARE WE CRAZY ? DOES HE READ THE NEWS ? IS EVERYONE WHO WORKS FOR YOU LIKE THAT ?
THEY'RE YOUNG, YOU KNOW. HERE INSIDE WE'VE MADE A LOT OF CHANGES.
5

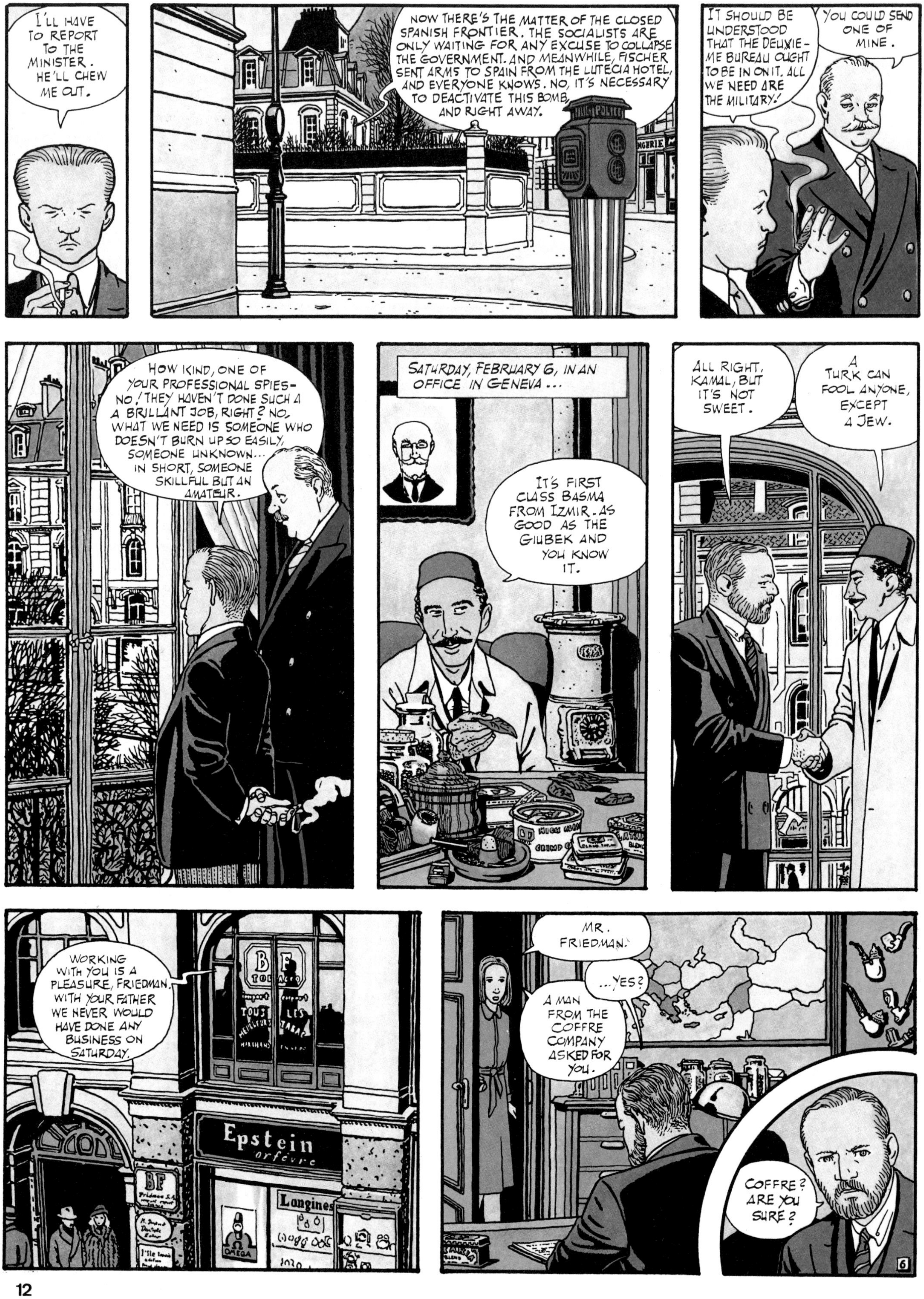
I'LL HAVE TO REPORT TO THE MINISTER. HE'LL CHEW ME OUT.
NOW THERE'S THE MATTER OF THE CLOSED SPANISH FRONTIER. THE SOCIALISTS ARE ONLY WAITING FOR ANY EXCUSE TO COLLAPSE THE GOVERNMENT. AND MEANWHILE, FISCHER SENT ARMS TO SPAIN FROM THE LUTECIA HOTEL, AND EVERYONE KNOWS. NO, IT'S NECESSARY TO DEACTIVATE THIS BOMB, AND RIGHT AWAY.
POLICE
IT SHOULD BE UNDERSTOOD THAT THE DEUXIEME BUREAU OUGHT TO BE IN ON IT. ALL WE NEED ARE THE MILITARY!
YOU COULD SEND ONE OF MINE.
HOW KIND, ONE OF YOUR PROFESSIONAL SPIES-NO! THEY HAVEN'T DONE SUCH A BRILLANT JOB, RIGHT? NO, WHAT WE NEED IS SOMEONE WHO DOESN'T BURN UP SO EASILY, SOMEONE UNKNOWN... IN SHORT, SOMEONE SKILLFUL BUT AN AMATEUR.
SATURDAY, FEBRUARY 6, IN AN OFFICE IN GENEVA...
IT'S FIRST CLASS BASMA FROM IZMIR. AS GOOD AS THE GIUBEK AND YOU KNOW IT.
ALL RIGHT, KAMAL, BUT IT'S NOT SWEET.
A TURK CAN FOOL ANYONE, EXCEPT A JEW.
WORKING WITH YOU IS A PLEASURE, FRIEDMAN. WITH YOUR FATHER WE NEVER WOULD HAVE DONE ANY BUSINESS ON SATURDAY.
BF
TOBACCO
TOUS LES MEILLEURS TABACS
Epstein
orfèvre
Longines
OMEGA
MR. FRIEDMAN.
...YES?
A MAN FROM THE COFFRE COMPANY ASKED FOR YOU.
COFFRE? ARE YOU SURE?
6

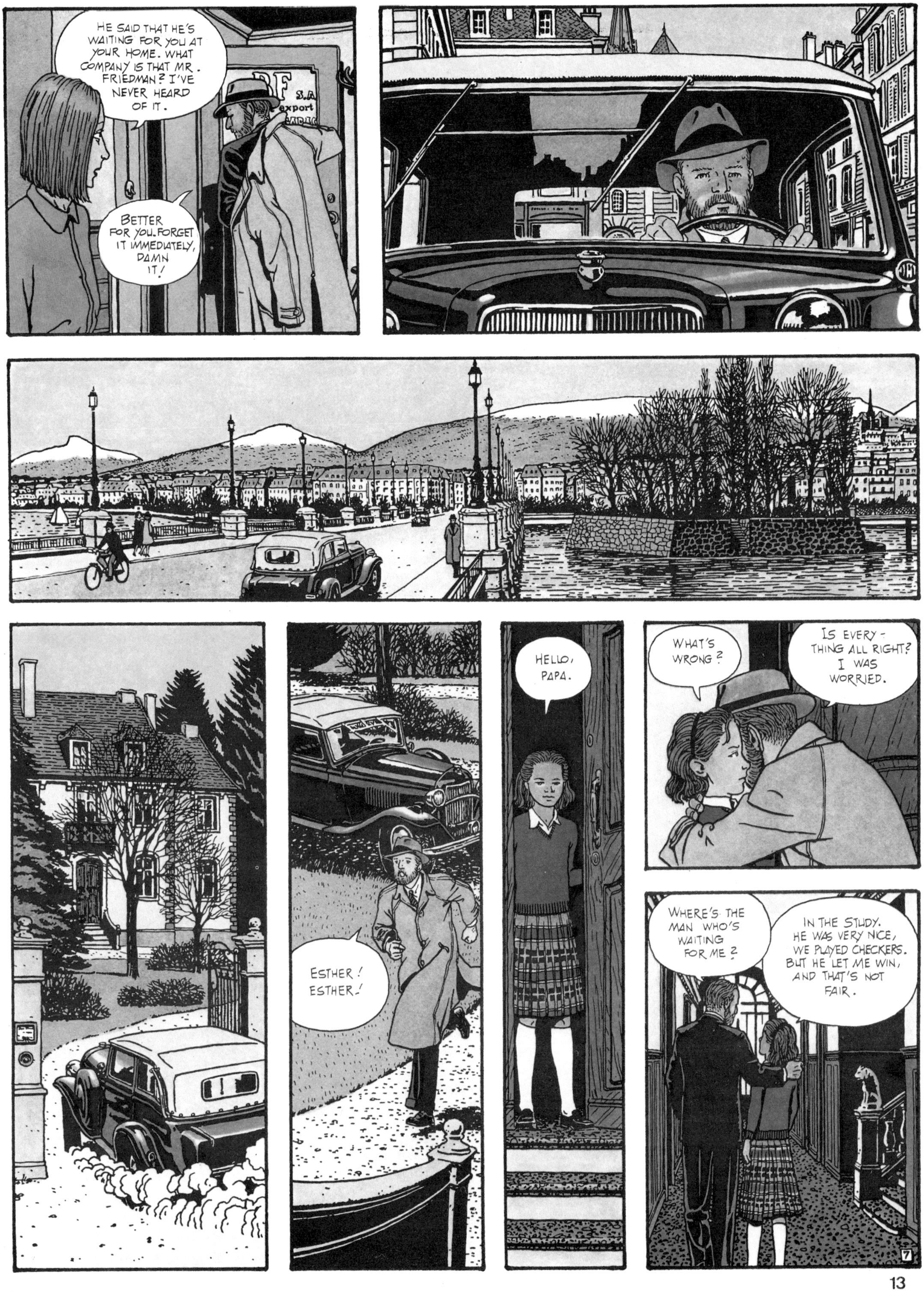

HE SAID THAT HE'S WAITING FOR YOU AT YOUR HOME. WHAT COMPANY IS THAT MR. FRIEDMAN? I'VE NEVER HEARD OF IT.
BETTER FOR YOU. FORGET IT IMMEDIATELY, DAMN IT!
HELLO, PAPA.
ESTHER! ESTHER!
WHAT'S WRONG?
IS EVERY-THING ALL RIGHT? I WAS WORRIED.
WHERE'S THE MAN WHO'S WAITING FOR ME?
IN THE STUDY. HE WAS VERY NICE, WE PLAYED CHECKERS. BUT HE LET ME WIN, AND THAT'S NOT FAIR.
7

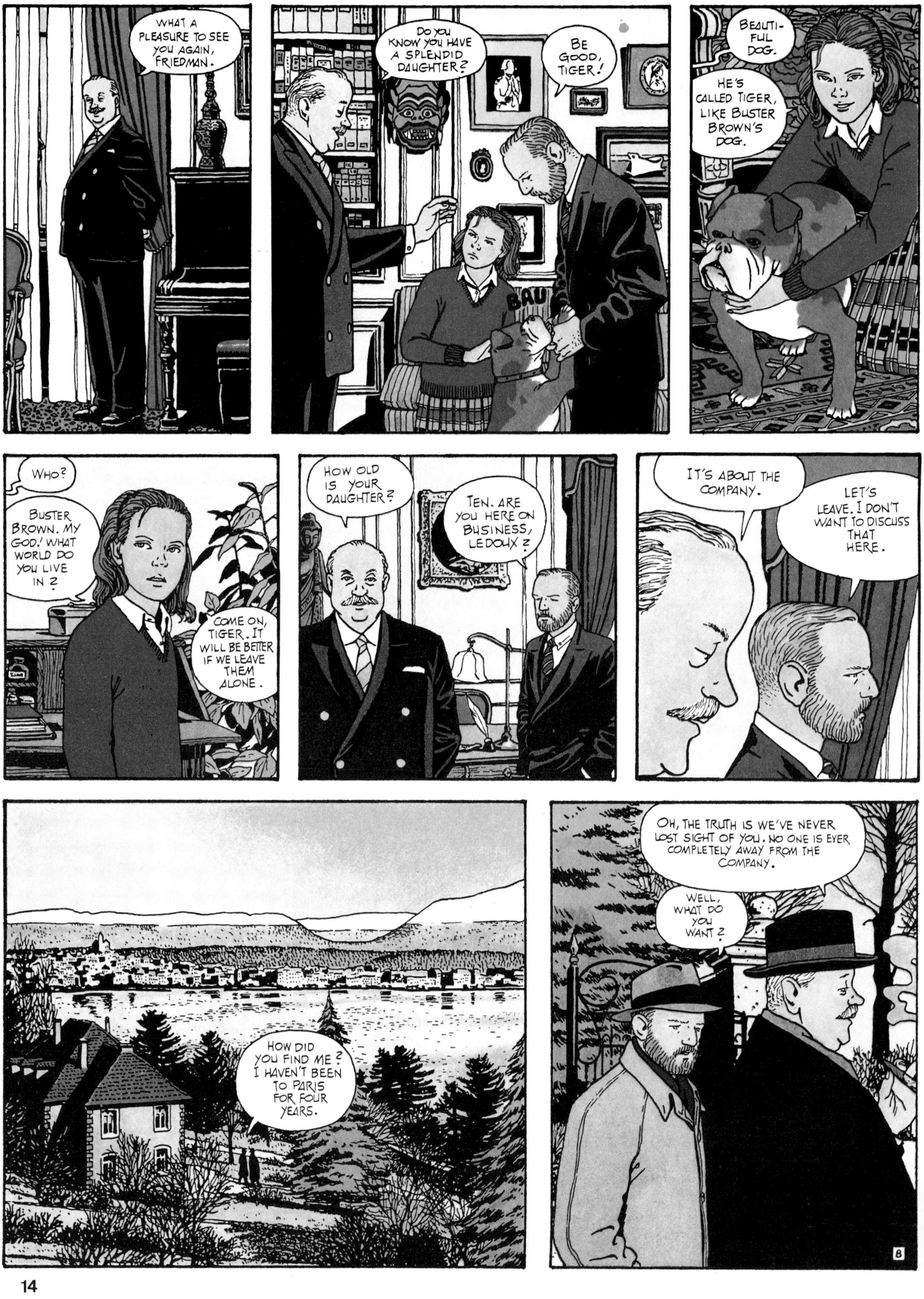
WHAT A PLEASURE TO SEE YOU AGAIN, FRIEDMAN.
Do you KNOW you HAVE A SPLENDID DAUGHTER?
BE GOOD, TIGER!
BAU
BEAUTI-FUL DOG.
HE'S CALLED TIGER, LIKE BUSTER BROWN'S DOG.
WHO?
BUSTER BROWN. MY GOD! WHAT WORLD DO YOU LIVE IN?
COME ON, TIGER. IT WILL BE BETTER IF WE LEAVE THEM ALONE.
HOW OLD IS YOUR DAUGHTER?
TEN. ARE YOU HERE ON BUSINESS, LEDOUX?
IT'S ABOUT THE COMPANY.
LET'S LEAVE. I DON'T WANT TO DISCUSS THAT HERE.
HOW DID YOU FIND ME? I HAVEN'T BEEN TO PARIS FOR FOUR YEARS.
OH, THE TRUTH IS WE'VE NEVER LOST SIGHT OF YOU. NO ONE IS EVER COMPLETELY AWAY FROM THE COMPANY.
WELL, WHAT DO YOU WANT?
8

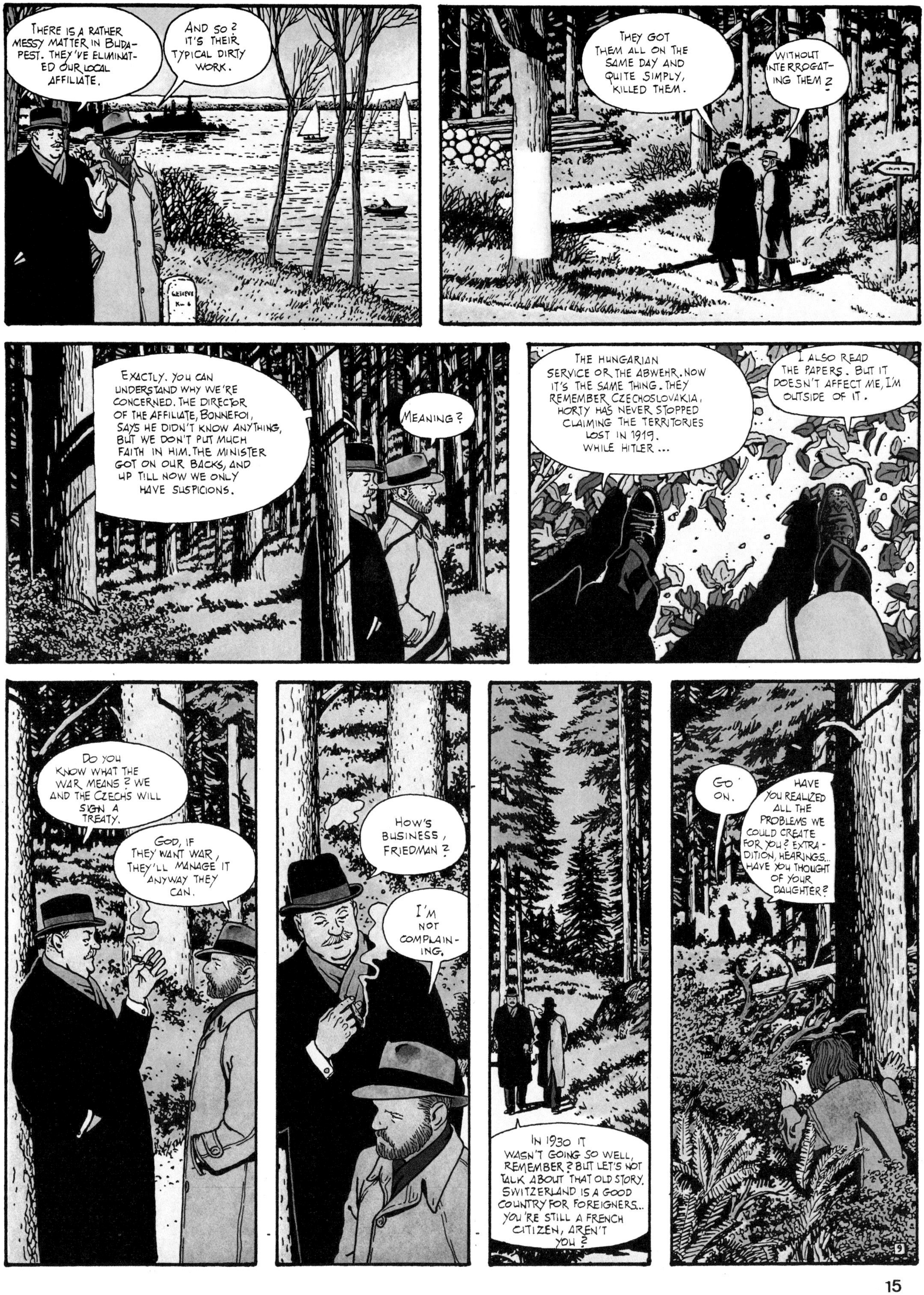
THERE IS A RATHER MESSY MATTER IN BUDAPEST. THEY'VE ELIMINATED OUR LOCAL AFFILIATE.
AND SO? IT'S THEIR TYPICAL DIRTY WORK.
THEY GOT THEM ALL ON THE SAME DAY AND QUITE SIMPLY, KILLED THEM.
WITHOUT INTERROGATING THEM?
EXACTLY. YOU CAN UNDERSTAND WHY WE'RE CONCERNED. THE DIRECTOR OF THE AFFILIATE, BONNEFOI, SAYS HE DIDN'T KNOW ANYTHING, BUT WE DON'T PUT MUCH FAITH IN HIM. THE MINISTER GOT ON OUR BACKS, AND UP TILL NOW WE ONLY HAVE SUSPICIONS.
MEANING?
THE HUNGARIAN SERVICE OR THE ABWEHR. NOW IT'S THE SAME THING. THEY REMEMBER CZECHOSLOVAKIA. HORTY HAS NEVER STOPPED CLAIMING THE TERRITORIES LOST IN 1919. WHILE HITLER ...
I ALSO READ THE PAPERS. BUT IT DOESN'T AFFECT ME, I'M OUTSIDE OF IT.
DO YOU KNOW WHAT THE WAR MEANS? WE AND THE CZECHS WILL SIGN A TREATY.
GOD, IF THEY WANT WAR, THEY'LL MANAGE IT ANYWAY THEY CAN.
HOW'S BUSINESS, FRIEDMAN?
I'M NOT COMPLAINING.
IN 1930 IT WASN'T GOING SO WELL, REMEMBER? BUT LET'S NOT TALK ABOUT THAT OLD STORY. SWITZERLAND IS A GOOD COUNTRY FOR FOREIGNERS.. YOU'RE STILL A FRENCH CITIZEN, AREN'T YOU?
GO ON.
HAVE YOU REALIZED ALL THE PROBLEMS WE COULD CREATE FOR YOU? EXTRADITION, HEARINGS... HAVE YOU THOUGHT OF YOUR DAUGHTER?
9

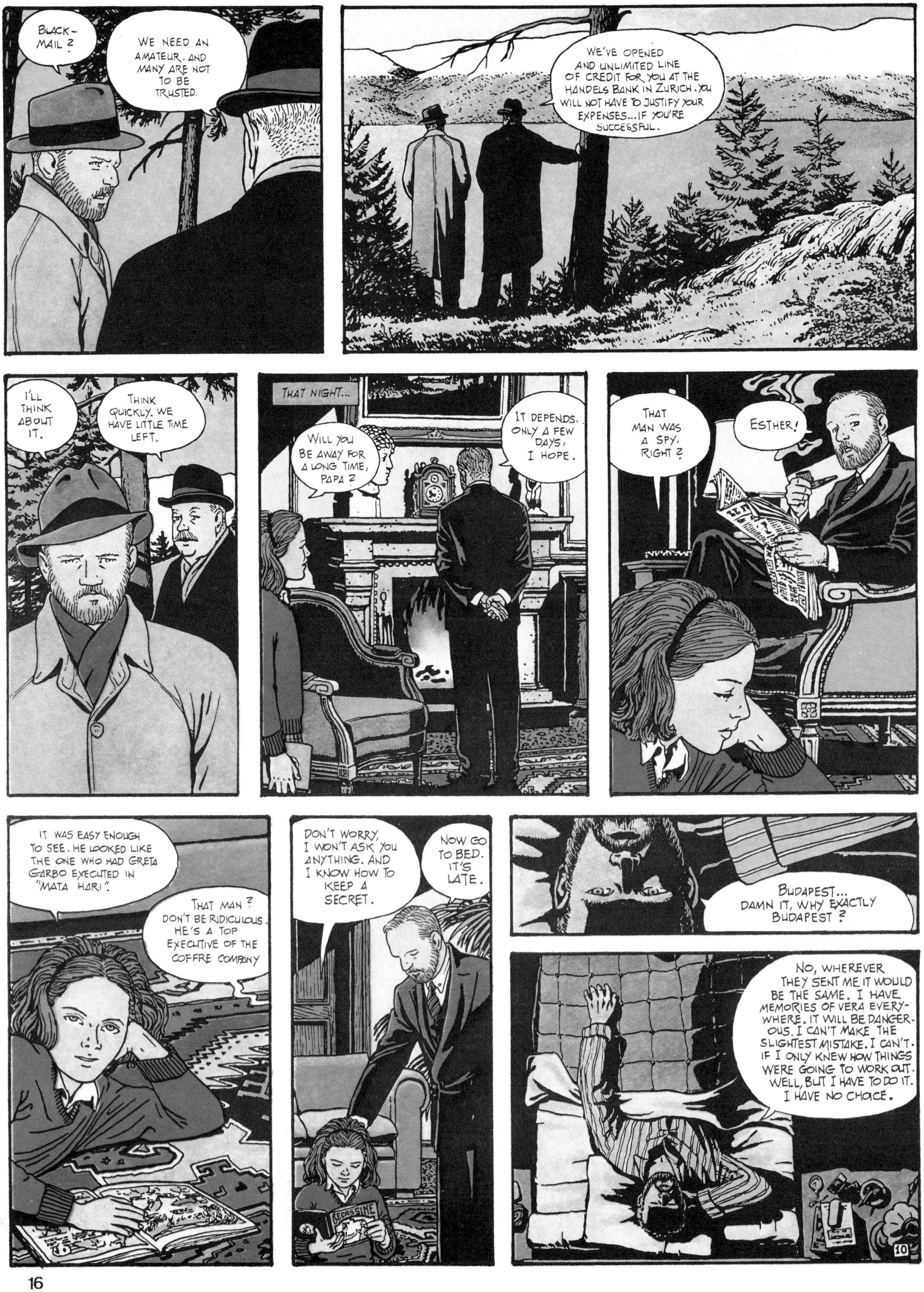
BLACK-MAIL ?
WE NEED AN AMATEUR. AND MANY ARE NOT TO BE TRUSTED.
WE'VE OPENED AND UNLIMITED LINE OF CREDIT FOR YOU AT THE HANDELS BANK IN ZURICH. YOU WILL NOT HAVE TO JUSTIFY YOUR EXPENSES...IF YOU'RE SUCCESSFUL.
I'LL THINK ABOUT IT.
THINK QUICKLY. WE HAVE LITTLE TIME LEFT.
THAT NIGHT...
WILL YOU BE AWAY FOR A LONG TIME, PAPA ?
IT DEPENDS. ONLY A FEW DAYS, I HOPE.
THAT MAN WAS A SPY, RIGHT ?
ESTHER!
IT WAS EASY ENOUGH TO SEE. HE LOOKED LIKE THE ONE WHO HAD GRETA GARBO EXECUTED IN "MATA HARI".
THAT MAN ? DON'T BE RIDICULOUS. HE'S A TOP EXECUTIVE OF THE COFFRE COMPANY
DON'T WORRY, I WON'T ASK YOU ANYTHING. AND I KNOW HOW TO KEEP A SECRET.
NOW GO TO BED. IT'S LATE.
BECASSINE
BUDAPEST... DAMN IT, WHY EXACTLY BUDAPEST ?
NO, WHEREVER THEY SENT ME IT WOULD BE THE SAME. I HAVE MEMORIES OF VERA EVERYWHERE. IT WILL BE DANGEROUS. I CAN'T MAKE THE SLIGHTEST MISTAKE. I CAN'T. IF I ONLY KNEW HOW THINGS WERE GOING TO WORK OUT. WELL, BUT I HAVE TO DO IT. I HAVE NO CHOICE.
10

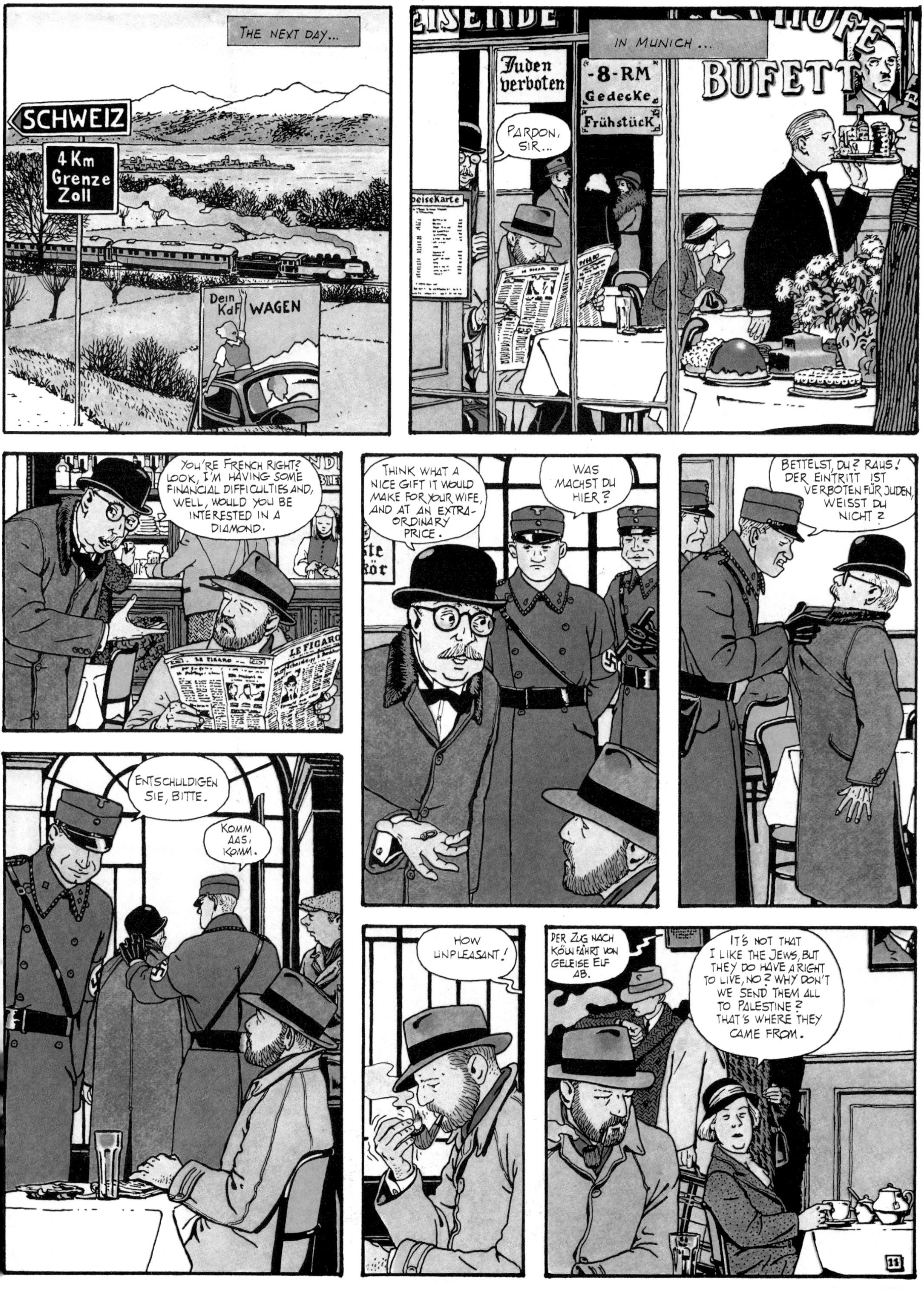
THE NEXT DAY...
SCHWEIZ
4 Km
Grenze
Zoll
Dein KdF WAGEN
IN MUNICH...
Juden verboten
-8-RM
Gedecke
Frühstück
BÜFETT
PARDON, SIR...
YOU'RE FRENCH RIGHT? LOOK, I'M HAVING SOME FINANCIAL DIFFICULTIES AND, WELL, WOULD YOU BE INTERESTED IN A DIAMOND.
LE FIGARO
THINK WHAT A NICE GIFT IT WOULD MAKE FOR YOUR WIFE, AND AT AN EXTRA-ORDINARY PRICE.
WAS MACHST DU HIER?
BETTELST, DU? RAUS! DER EINTRITT IST VERBOTEN FÜR JUDEN, WEISST DU NICHT?
ENTSCHULDIGEN SIE, BITTE.
KOMM AAS, KOMM.
HOW UNPLEASANT!
DER ZUG NACH KÖLN FÄHRT VON GELEISE ELF AB.
IT'S NOT THAT I LIKE THE JEWS, BUT THEY DO HAVE A RIGHT TO LIVE, NO? WHY DON'T WE SEND THEM ALL TO PALESTINE? THAT'S WHERE THEY CAME FROM.
11

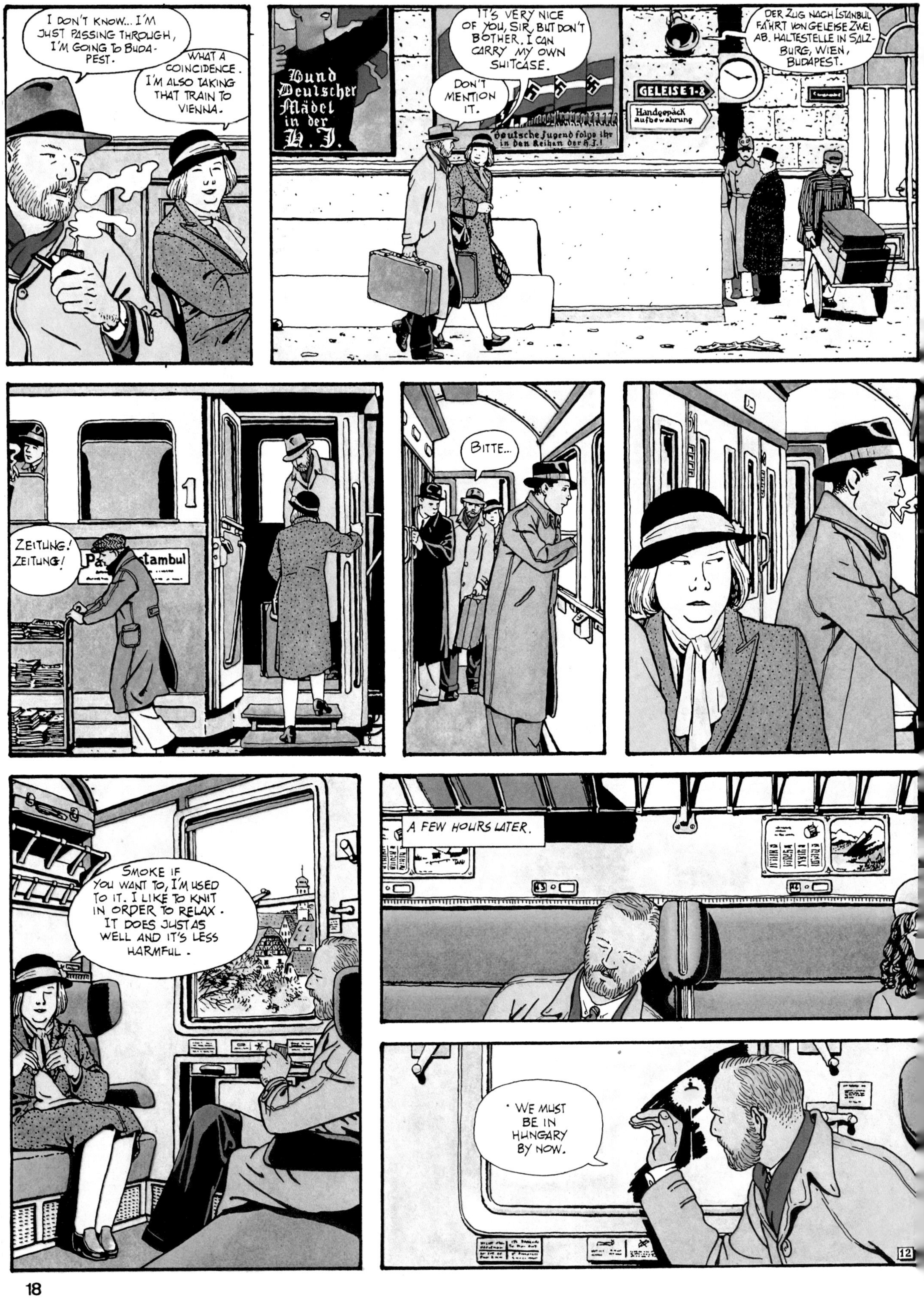
I DON'T KNOW... I'M JUST PASSING THROUGH, I'M GOING TO BUDA-PEST.
WHAT A COINCIDENCE. I'M ALSO TAKING THAT TRAIN TO VIENNA.
Bund Deutscher Mädel in der H. J.
IT'S VERY NICE OF YOU, SIR, BUT DON'T BOTHER. I CAN CARRY MY OWN SHITCASE.
DON'T MENTION IT.
Deutsche Jugend folge ihr in den Reihen der H.J.!
GELEISE 1-8
Handgepäck aufbewahrung
DER ZUG NACH ISTANBUL FÄHRT VON GELEISE ZWEI AB. HALTESTELLE IN SALZBURG, WIEN, BUDAPEST.
1
ZEITUNG! ZEITUNG!
BITTE...
SMOKE IF YOU WANT TO, I'M USED TO IT. I LIKE TO KNIT IN ORDER TO RELAX. IT DOES JUST AS WELL AND IT'S LESS HARMFUL.
A FEW HOURS LATER.
WE MUST BE IN HUNGARY BY NOW.
12

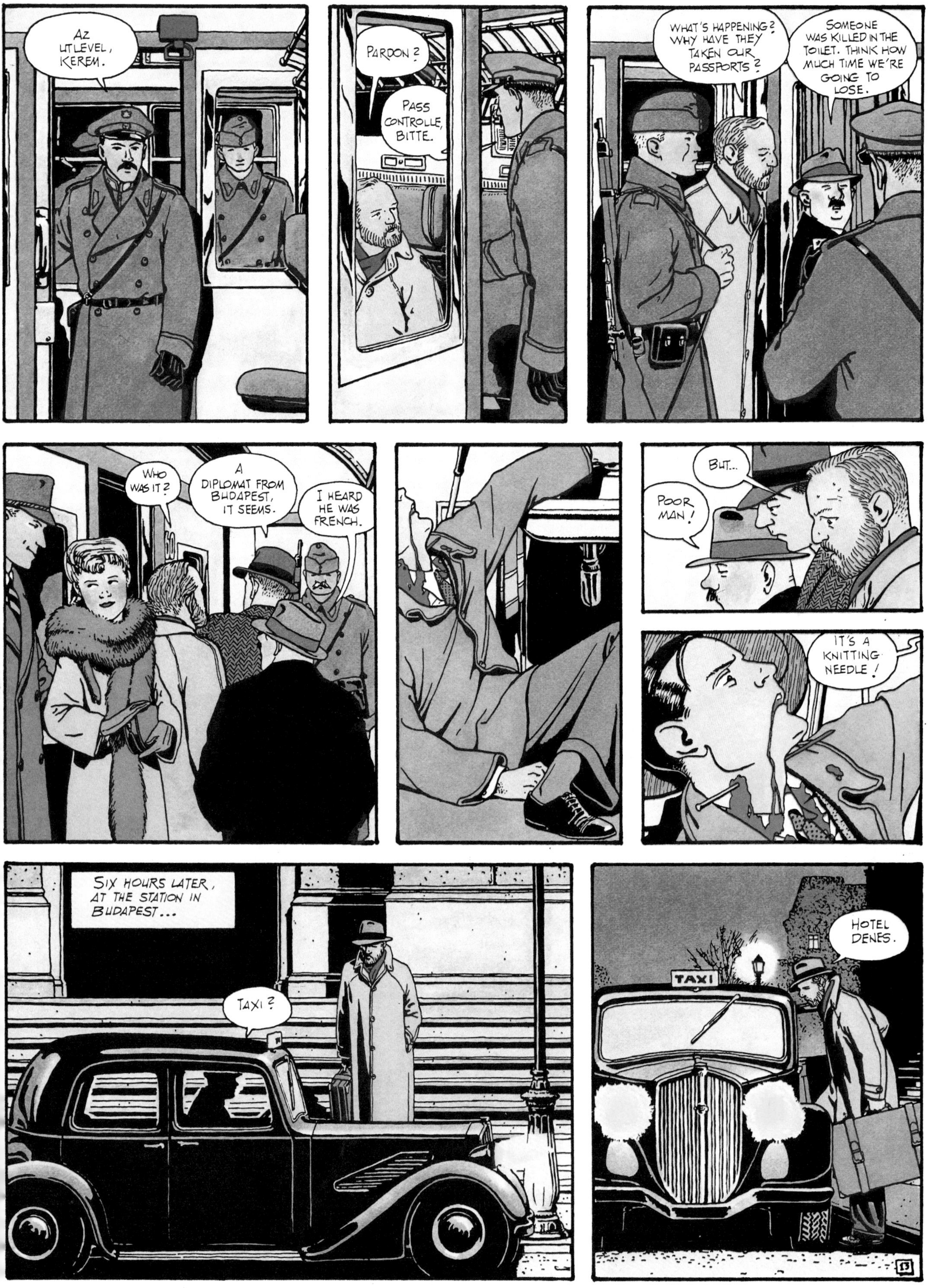
AZ UTLEVEL, KEREM.
PARDON ?
PASS CONTROLLE, BITTE.
WHAT'S HAPPENING ? WHY HAVE THEY TAKEN OUR PASSPORTS ?
SOMEONE WAS KILLED IN THE TOILET. THINK HOW MUCH TIME WE'RE GOING TO LOSE.
WHO WAS IT ?
A DIPLOMAT FROM BUDAPEST, IT SEEMS.
I HEARD HE WAS FRENCH.
BUT...
POOR MAN !
IT'S A KNITTING NEEDLE !
SIX HOURS LATER, AT THE STATION IN BUDAPEST...
TAXI ?
HOTEL DENES.
TAXI

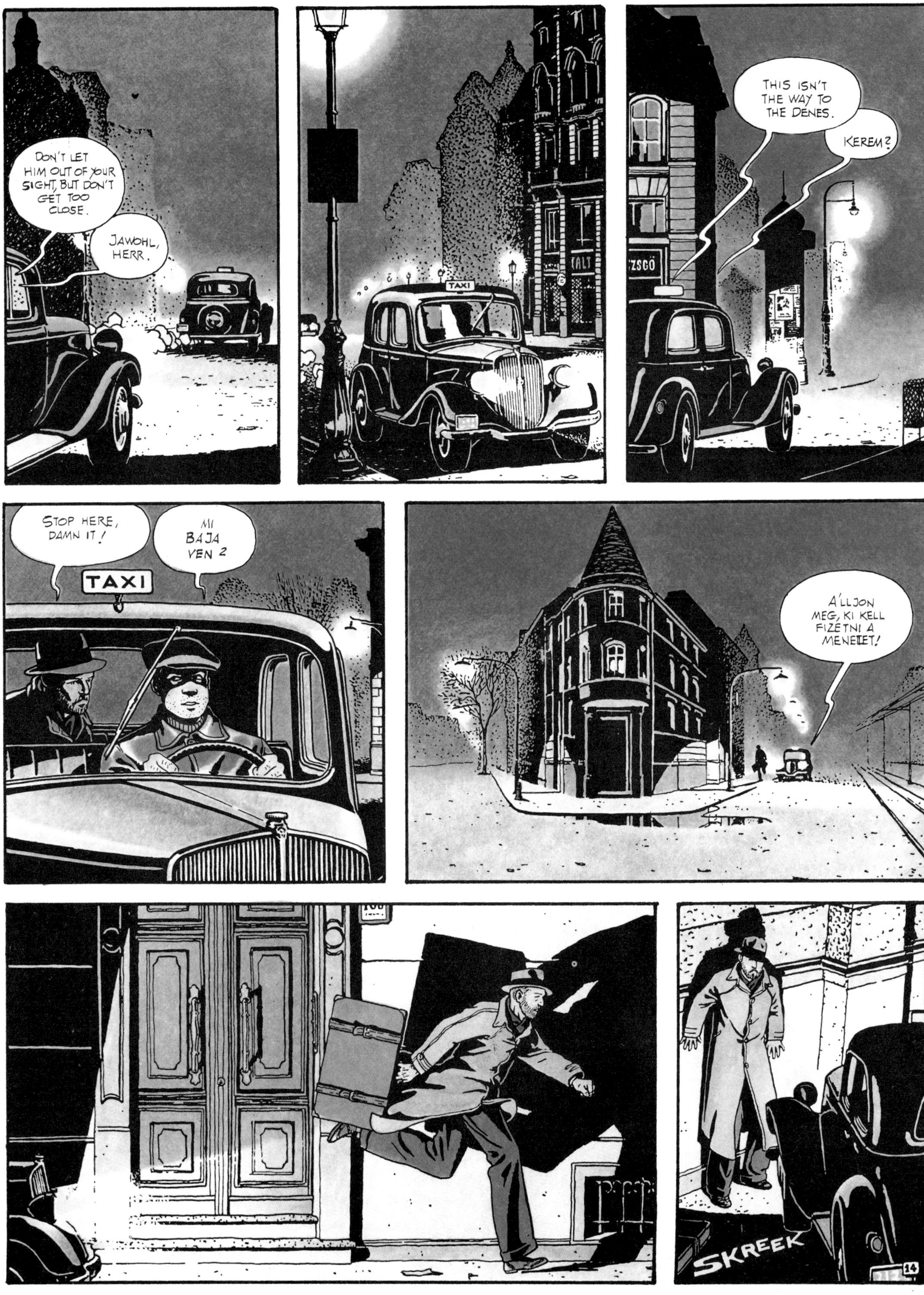

DON'T LET HIM OUT OF YOUR SIGHT, BUT DON'T GET TOO CLOSE.
JAWOHL, HERR.
TAXI
THIS ISN'T THE WAY TO THE DENES.
KEREM?
STOP HERE, DAMN IT!
MI BAJA VEN?
TAXI
ÁLLJON MEG, KI KELL FIZÉTNI A MENETET!
SKREEK

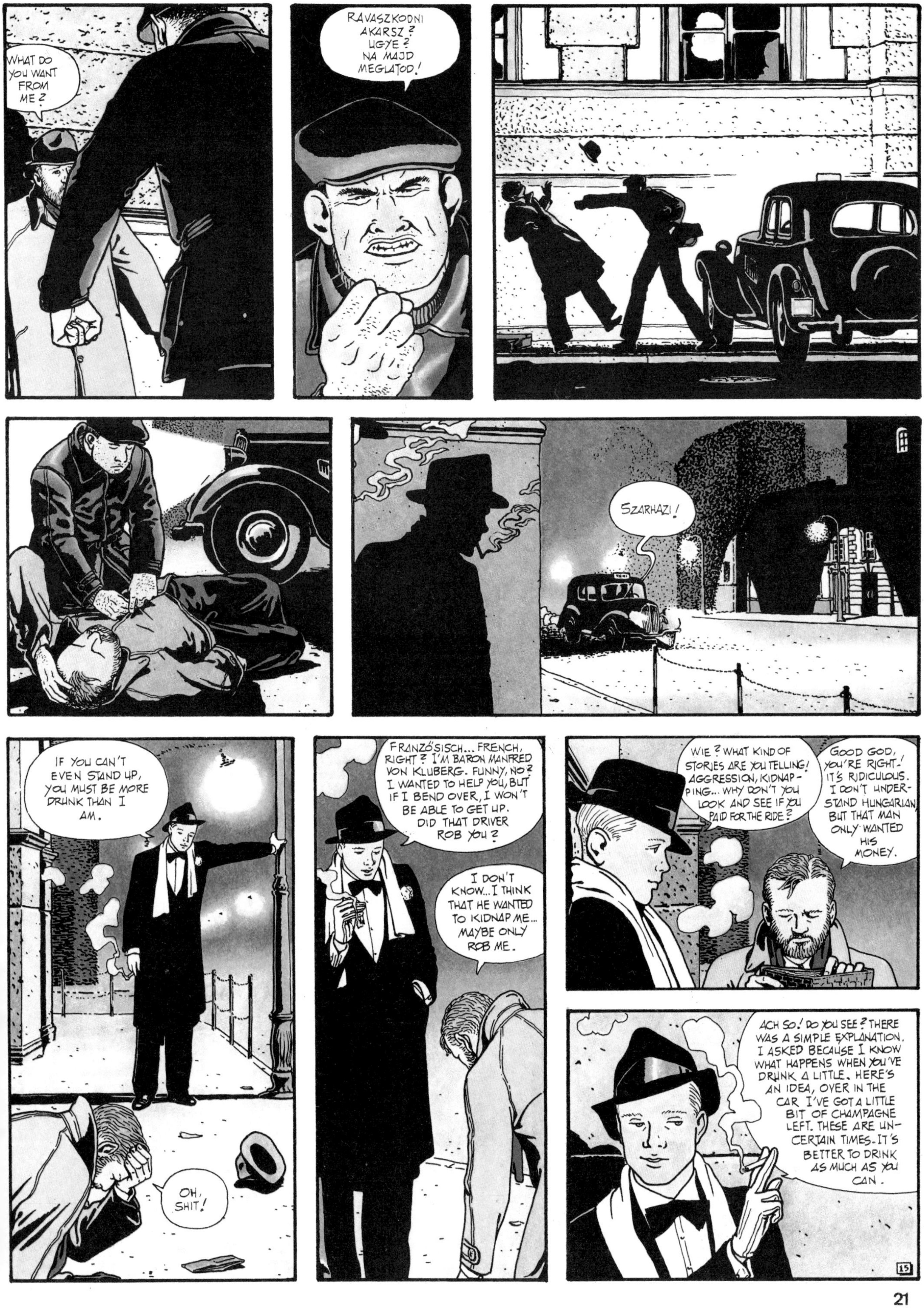
WHAT DO YOU WANT FROM ME?
RAVASZKODNI AKARSZ? UGYE? NA MAJD MEGLATOD!
SZARHAZI!
IF YOU CAN'T EVEN STAND UP, YOU MUST BE MORE DRUNK THAN I AM.
OH, SHIT!
FRANZÖSISCH... FRENCH, RIGHT? I'M BARON MANFRED VON KLUBERG. FUNNY, NO? I WANTED TO HELP YOU, BUT IF I BEND OVER, I WON'T BE ABLE TO GET UP. DID THAT DRIVER ROB YOU?
I DON'T KNOW... I THINK THAT HE WANTED TO KIDNAP ME... MAYBE ONLY ROB ME.
WIE? WHAT KIND OF STORIES ARE YOU TELLING! AGGRESSION, KIDNAPPING... WHY DON'T YOU LOOK AND SEE IF YOU PAID FOR THE RIDE?
GOOD GOD, YOU'RE RIGHT! IT'S RIDICULOUS. I DON'T UNDERSTAND HUNGARIAN, BUT THAT MAN ONLY WANTED HIS MONEY.
ACH SO! DO YOU SEE? THERE WAS A SIMPLE EXPLANATION. I ASKED BECAUSE I KNOW WHAT HAPPENS WHEN YOU'VE DRUNK A LITTLE. HERE'S AN IDEA, OVER IN THE CAR I'VE GOT A LITTLE BIT OF CHAMPAGNE LEFT. THESE ARE UNCERTAIN TIMES. IT'S BETTER TO DRINK AS MUCH AS YOU CAN.
15

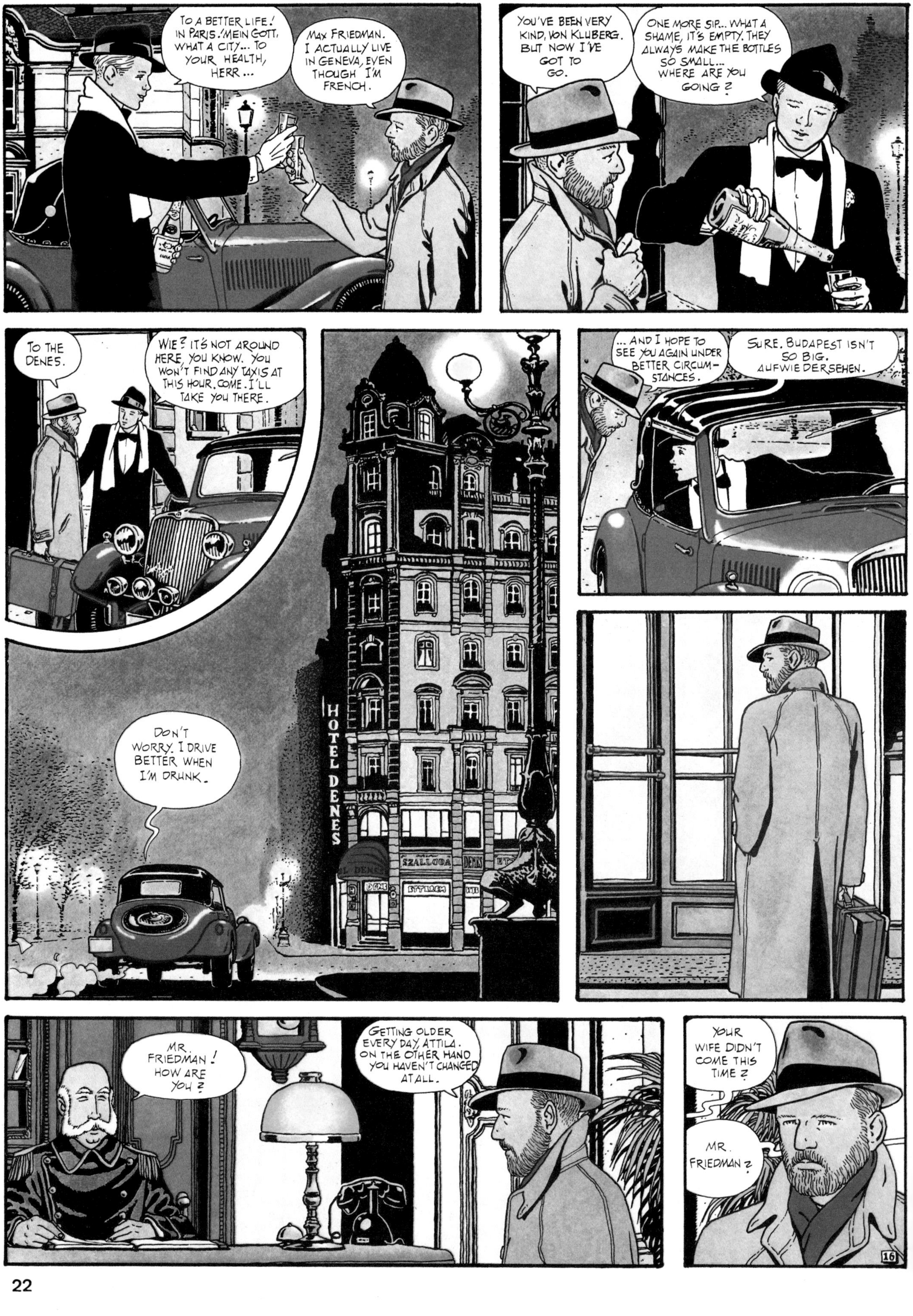
TO A BETTER LIFE! IN PARIS! MEIN GOTT, WHAT A CITY... TO YOUR HEALTH, HERR...
MAX FRIEDMAN. I ACTUALLY LIVE IN GENEVA, EVEN THOUGH I'M FRENCH.
YOU'VE BEEN VERY KIND, VON KLUBERG. BUT NOW I'VE GOT TO GO.
ONE MORE SIP... WHAT A SHAME, IT'S EMPTY. THEY ALWAYS MAKE THE BOTTLES SO SMALL... WHERE ARE YOU GOING?
TO THE DENES.
WIE? IT'S NOT AROUND HERE, YOU KNOW. YOU WON'T FIND ANY TAXIS AT THIS HOUR. COME. I'LL TAKE YOU THERE.
HOTEL DENES
SZALLODA
DENES
ETTEREM
DON'T WORRY. I DRIVE BETTER WHEN I'M DRUNK.
... AND I HOPE TO SEE YOU AGAIN UNDER BETTER CIRCUMSTANCES.
SURE. BUDAPEST ISN'T SO BIG. AUFWIEDERSEHEN.
MR. FRIEDMAN! HOW ARE YOU?
GETTING OLDER EVERY DAY, ATTILA. ON THE OTHER HAND YOU HAVEN'T CHANGED AT ALL.
YOUR WIFE DIDN'T COME THIS TIME?
MR. FRIEDMAN?
16

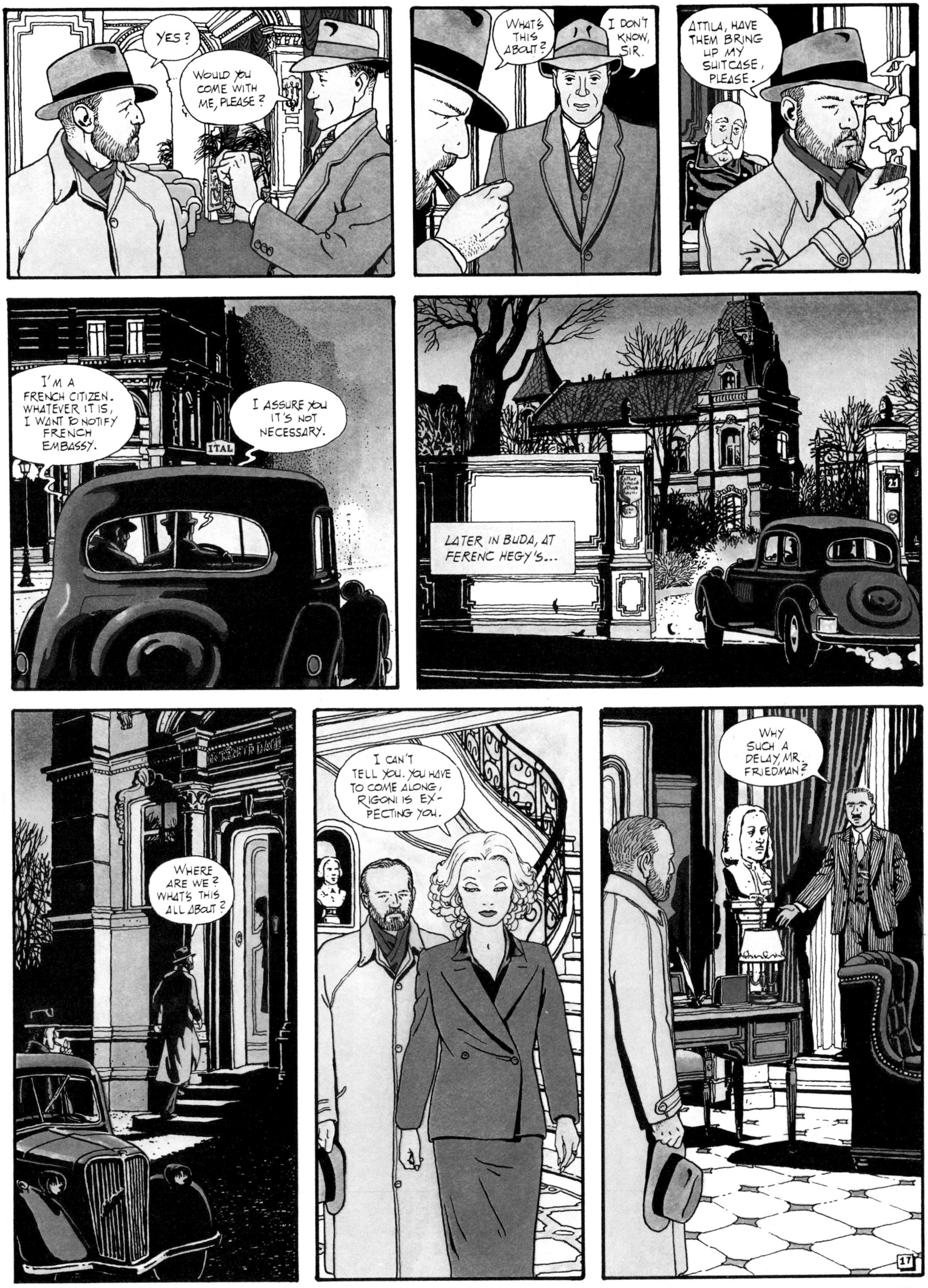
YES?
WOULD YOU COME WITH ME, PLEASE?
WHAT'S THIS ABOUT?
I DON'T KNOW, SIR.
ATTILA, HAVE THEM BRING UP MY SUITCASE, PLEASE.
I'M A FRENCH CITIZEN. WHATEVER IT IS, I WANT TO NOTIFY FRENCH EMBASSY.
I ASSURE YOU IT'S NOT NECESSARY.
ITAL
LATER IN BUDA, AT FERENC HEGY'S...
21
WHERE ARE WE? WHAT'S THIS ALL ABOUT?
I CAN'T TELL YOU. YOU HAVE TO COME ALONG, RIGONI IS EXPECTING YOU.
WHY SUCH A DELAY, MR. FRIEDMAN?
17

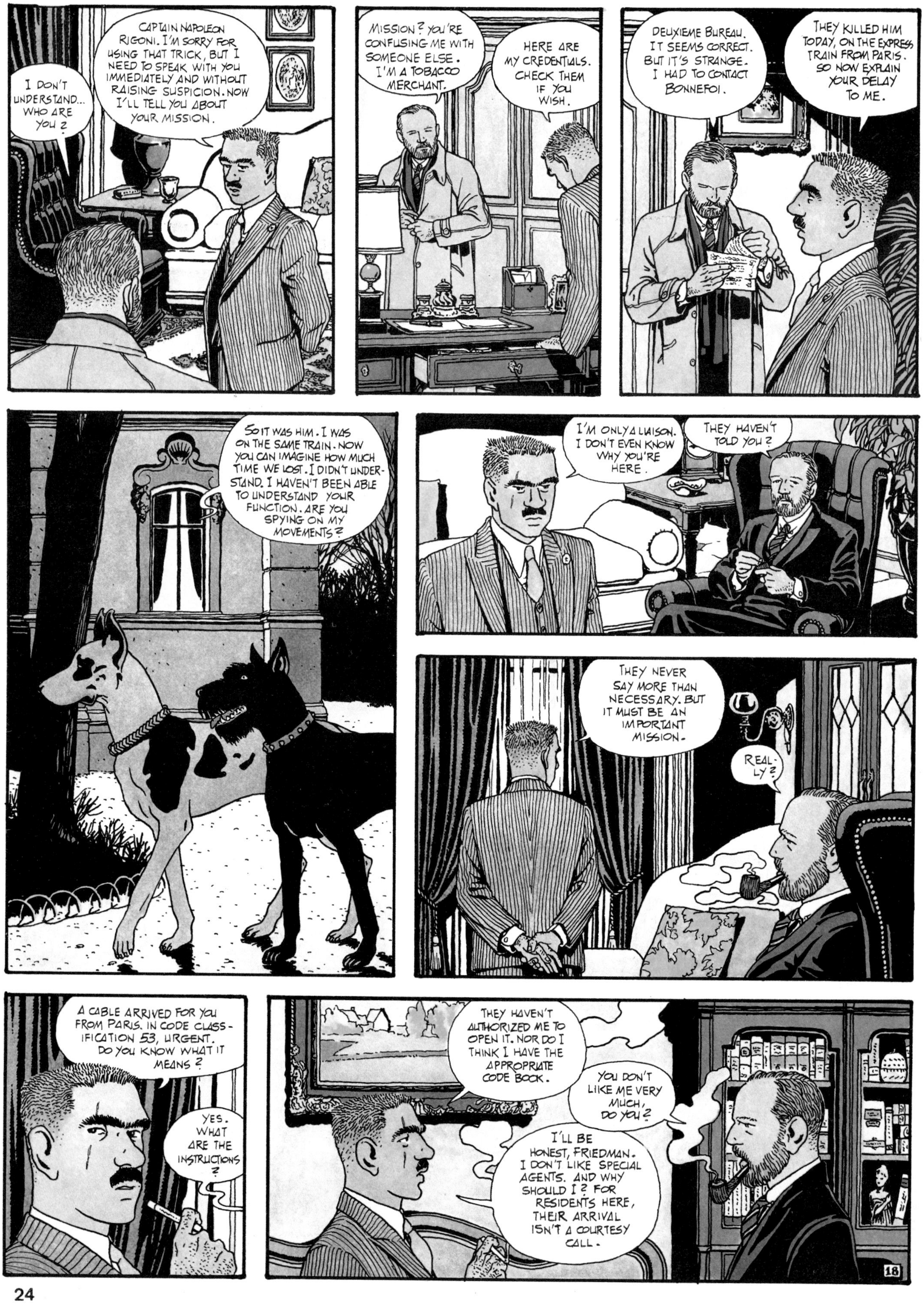
I DON'T UNDERSTAND... WHO ARE YOU ?
CAPTAIN NAPOLEON RIGONI. I'M SORRY FOR USING THAT TRICK, BUT I NEED TO SPEAK WITH YOU IMMEDIATELY AND WITHOUT RAISING SUSPICION. NOW I'LL TELL YOU ABOUT YOUR MISSION.
MISSION? YOU'RE CONFUSING ME WITH SOMEONE ELSE. I'M A TOBACCO MERCHANT.
HERE ARE MY CREDENTIALS. CHECK THEM IF YOU WISH.
DEUXIEME BUREAU. IT SEEMS CORRECT. BUT IT'S STRANGE. I HAD TO CONTACT BONNEFOI.
THEY KILLED HIM TODAY, ON THE EXPRESS TRAIN FROM PARIS. SO NOW EXPLAIN YOUR DELAY TO ME.
SO IT WAS HIM. I WAS ON THE SAME TRAIN. NOW YOU CAN IMAGINE HOW MUCH TIME WE LOST. I DIDN'T UNDERSTAND. I HAVEN'T BEEN ABLE TO UNDERSTAND YOUR FUNCTION. ARE YOU SPYING ON MY MOVEMENTS?
I'M ONLY A LIAISON. I DON'T EVEN KNOW WHY YOU'RE HERE.
THEY HAVEN'T TOLD YOU ?
THEY NEVER SAY MORE THAN NECESSARY. BUT IT MUST BE AN IMPORTANT MISSION.
REALLY ?
A CABLE ARRIVED FOR YOU FROM PARIS. IN CODE CLASSIFICATION 53, URGENT. DO YOU KNOW WHAT IT MEANS ?
YES. WHAT ARE THE INSTRUCTIONS ?
THEY HAVEN'T AUTHORIZED ME TO OPEN IT. NOR DO I THINK I HAVE THE APPROPRIATE CODE BOOK.
YOU DON'T LIKE ME VERY MUCH, DO YOU ?
I'LL BE HONEST, FRIEDMAN. I DON'T LIKE SPECIAL AGENTS. AND WHY SHOULD I ? FOR RESIDENTS HERE, THEIR ARRIVAL ISN'T A COURTESY CALL.
18

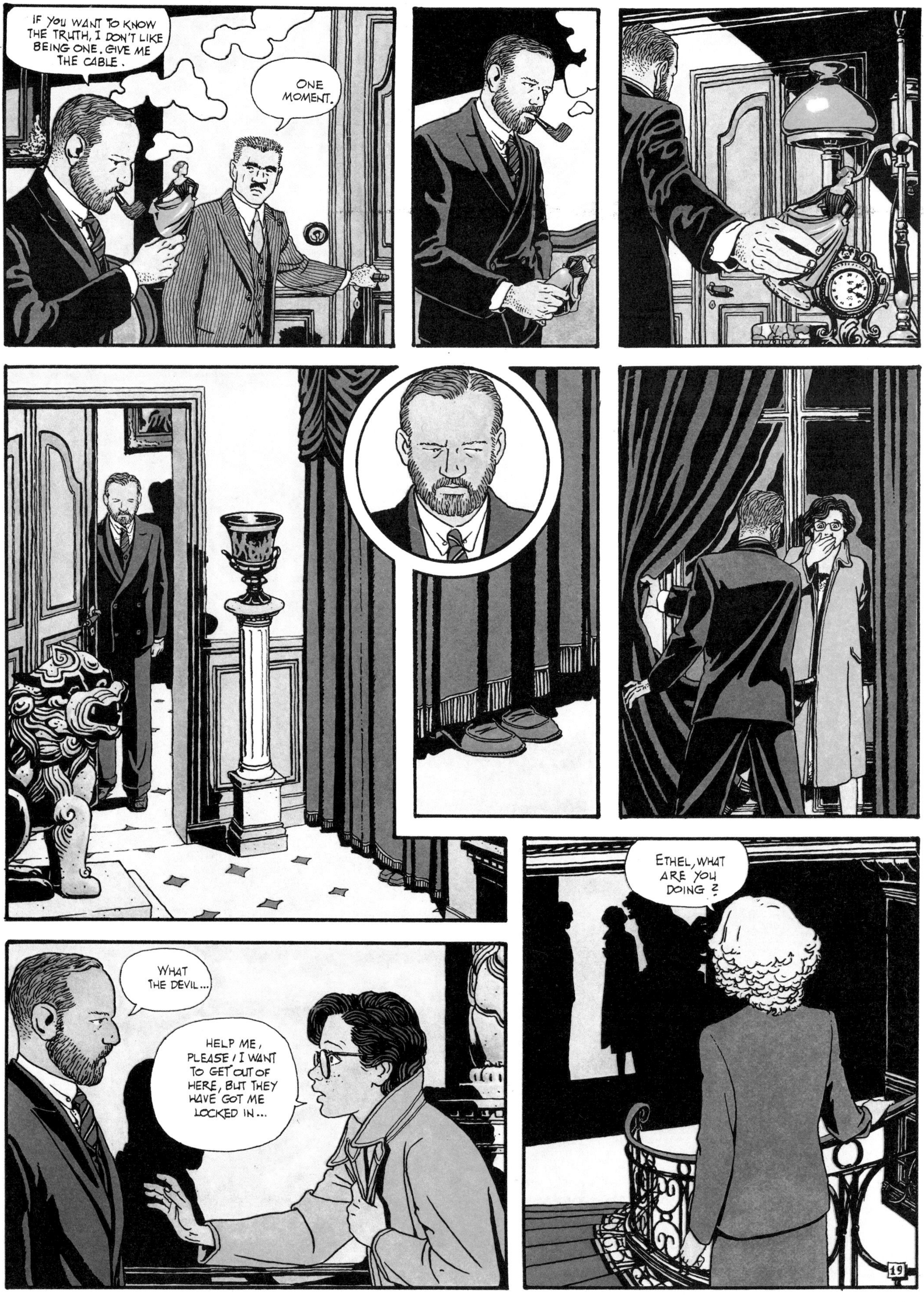
IF YOU WANT TO KNOW THE TRUTH, I DON'T LIKE BEING ONE. GIVE ME THE CABLE.
ONE MOMENT.
ETHEL, WHAT ARE YOU DOING ?
WHAT THE DEVIL...
HELP ME, PLEASE! I WANT TO GET OUT OF HERE, BUT THEY HAVE GOT ME LOCKED IN...
19

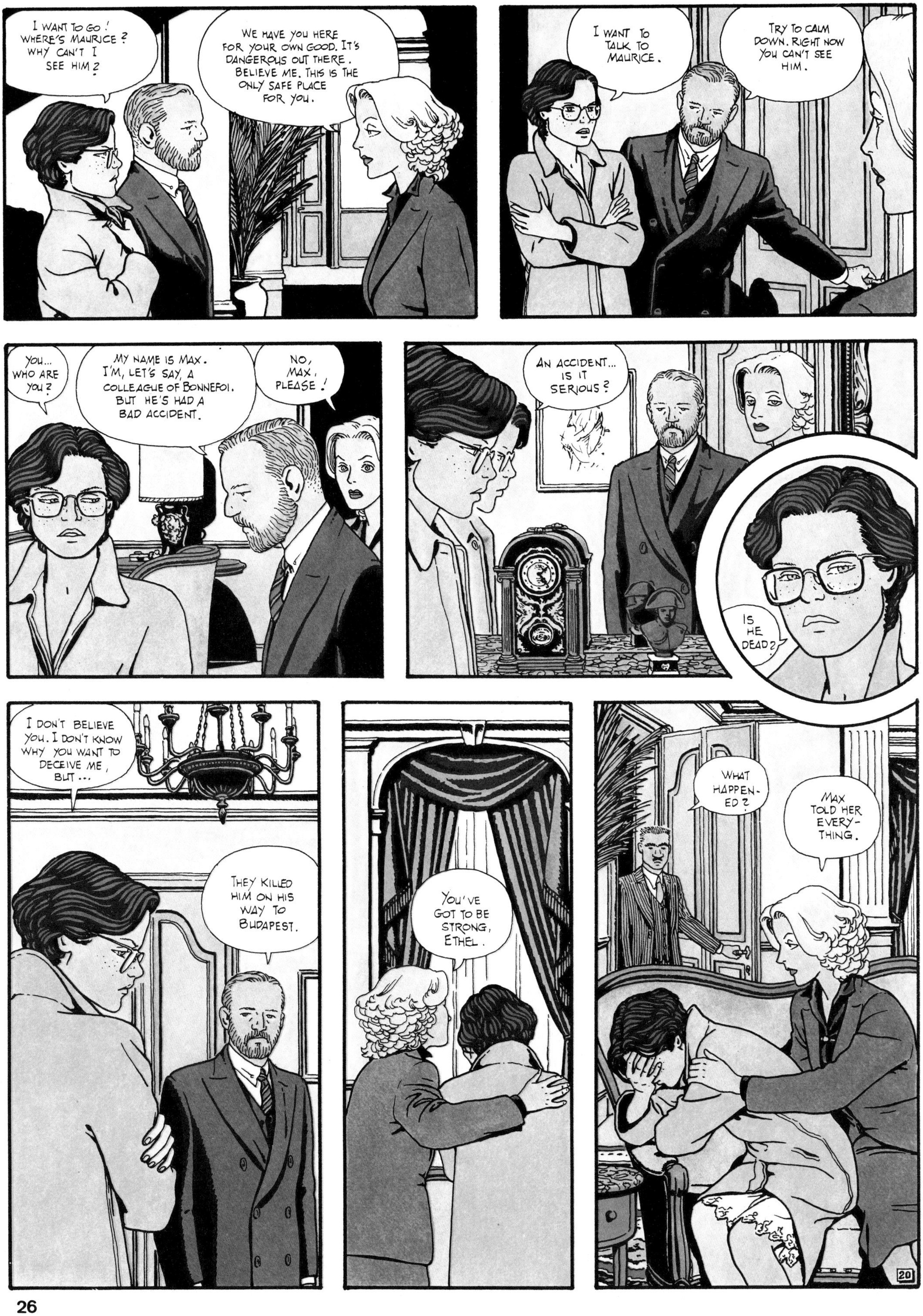

I WANT TO GO! WHERE'S MAURICE? WHY CAN'T I SEE HIM?
WE HAVE YOU HERE FOR YOUR OWN GOOD. IT'S DANGEROUS OUT THERE. BELIEVE ME. THIS IS THE ONLY SAFE PLACE FOR YOU.
I WANT TO TALK TO MAURICE.
TRY TO CALM DOWN. RIGHT NOW YOU CAN'T SEE HIM.
YOU... WHO ARE YOU?
MY NAME IS MAX. I'M, LET'S SAY, A COLLEAGUE OF BONNEFOI. BUT HE'S HAD A BAD ACCIDENT.
NO, MAX, PLEASE!
AN ACCIDENT... IS IT SERIOUS?
IS HE DEAD?
I DON'T BELIEVE YOU. I DON'T KNOW WHY YOU WANT TO DECEIVE ME, BUT...
THEY KILLED HIM ON HIS WAY TO BUDAPEST.
YOU'VE GOT TO BE STRONG, ETHEL.
WHAT HAPPEN-ED?
MAX TOLD HER EVERY-THING.
20

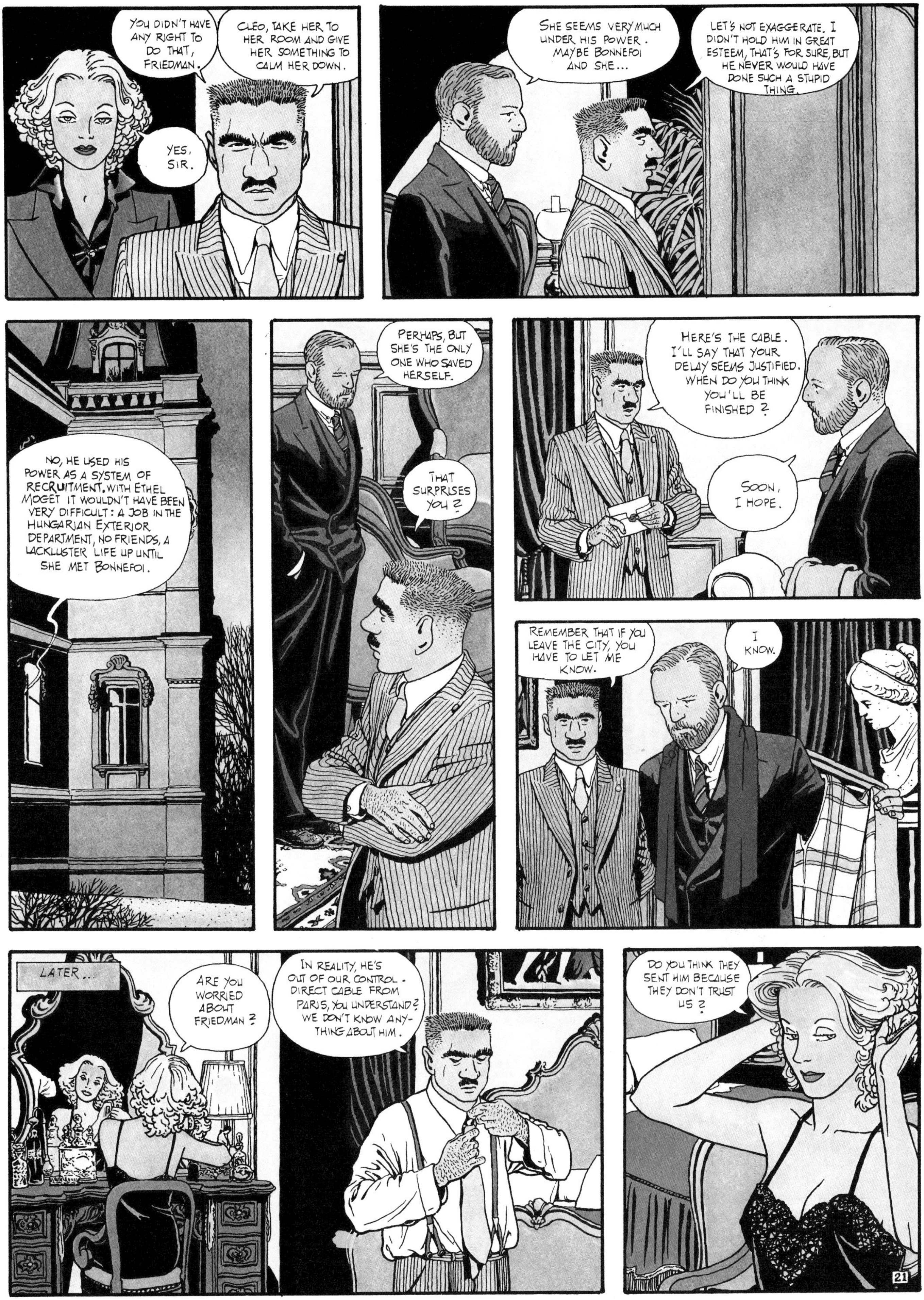

YOU DIDN'T HAVE ANY RIGHT TO DO THAT, FRIEDMAN.
CLEO, TAKE HER TO HER ROOM AND GIVE HER SOMETHING TO CALM HER DOWN.
YES, SIR.
SHE SEEMS VERY MUCH UNDER HIS POWER. MAYBE BONNEFOI AND SHE...
LET'S NOT EXAGGERATE. I DIDN'T HOLD HIM IN GREAT ESTEEM, THAT'S FOR SURE, BUT HE NEVER WOULD HAVE DONE SUCH A STUPID THING.
NO, HE USED HIS POWER AS A SYSTEM OF RECRUITMENT. WITH ETHEL MOGET IT WOULDN'T HAVE BEEN VERY DIFFICULT: A JOB IN THE HUNGARIAN EXTERIOR DEPARTMENT, NO FRIENDS, A LACKLUSTER LIFE UP UNTIL SHE MET BONNEFOI.
PERHAPS, BUT SHE'S THE ONLY ONE WHO SAVED HERSELF.
THAT SURPRISES YOU?
HERE'S THE CABLE. I'LL SAY THAT YOUR DELAY SEEMS JUSTIFIED. WHEN DO YOU THINK YOU'LL BE FINISHED?
SOON, I HOPE.
REMEMBER THAT IF YOU LEAVE THE CITY, YOU HAVE TO LET ME KNOW.
I KNOW.
LATER...
ARE YOU WORRIED ABOUT FRIEDMAN?
IN REALITY, HE'S OUT OF OUR CONTROL - DIRECT CABLE FROM PARIS, YOU UNDERSTAND? WE DON'T KNOW ANYTHING ABOUT HIM.
DO YOU THINK THEY SENT HIM BECAUSE THEY DON'T TRUST US?
21

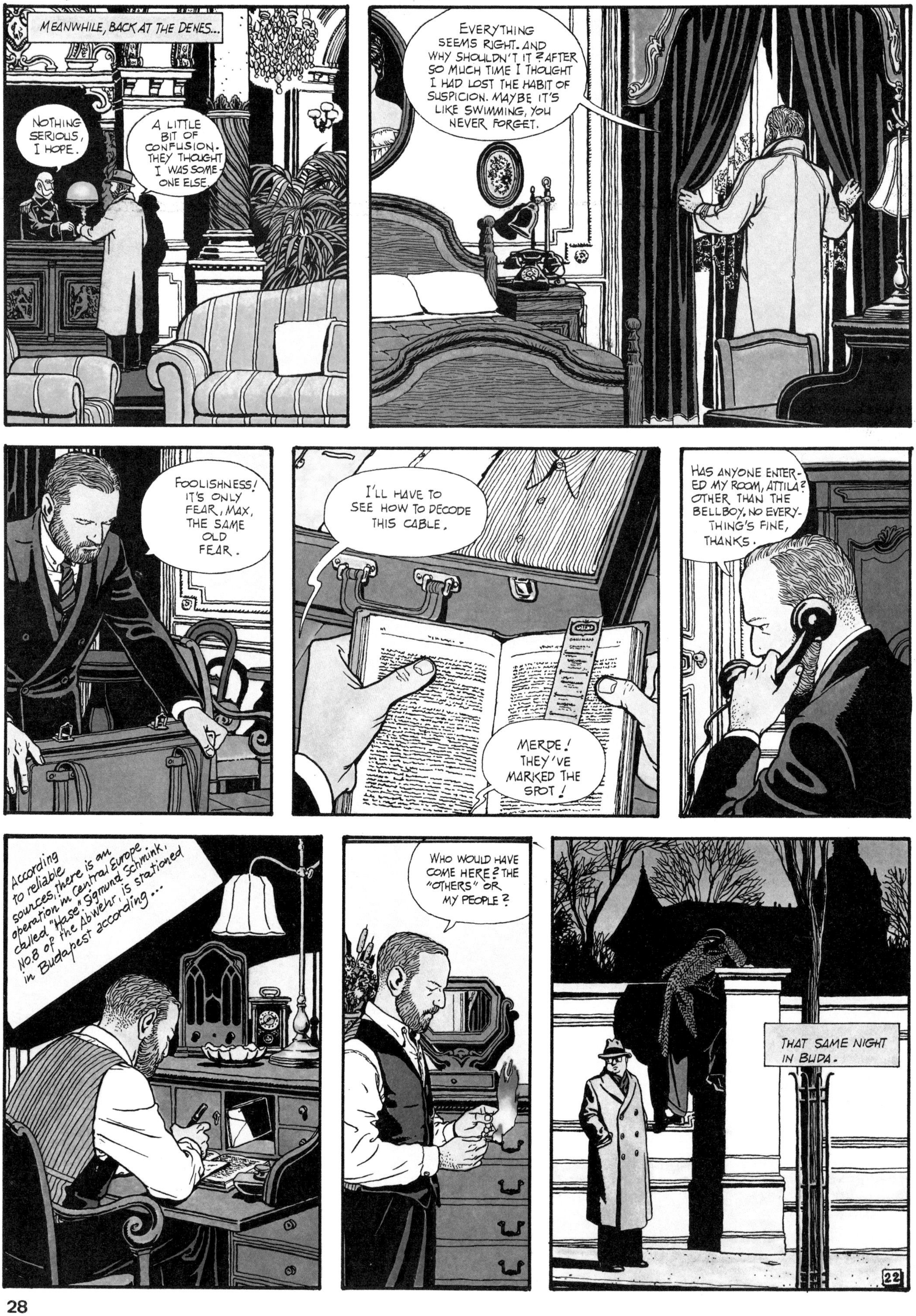
MEANWHILE, BACK AT THE DENES...
NOTHING SERIOUS, I HOPE.
A LITTLE BIT OF CONFUSION. THEY THOUGHT I WAS SOMEONE ELSE.
EVERYTHING SEEMS RIGHT. AND WHY SHOULDN'T IT? AFTER SO MUCH TIME I THOUGHT I HAD LOST THE HABIT OF SUSPICION. MAYBE IT'S LIKE SWIMMING, YOU NEVER FORGET.
FOOLISHNESS! IT'S ONLY FEAR, MAX, THE SAME OLD FEAR.
I'LL HAVE TO SEE HOW TO DECODE THIS CABLE.
MERDE! THEY'VE MARKED THE SPOT!
HAS ANYONE ENTERED MY ROOM, ATTILA? OTHER THAN THE BELLBOY. NO EVERYTHING'S FINE, THANKS.
According to reliable sources, there is an operation in Central Europe called "Hase." Sigmund Schmink, No.8 of the Abwehr, is stationed in Budapest according...
WHO WOULD HAVE COME HERE? THE "OTHERS" OR MY PEOPLE?
THAT SAME NIGHT IN BUDA.
22

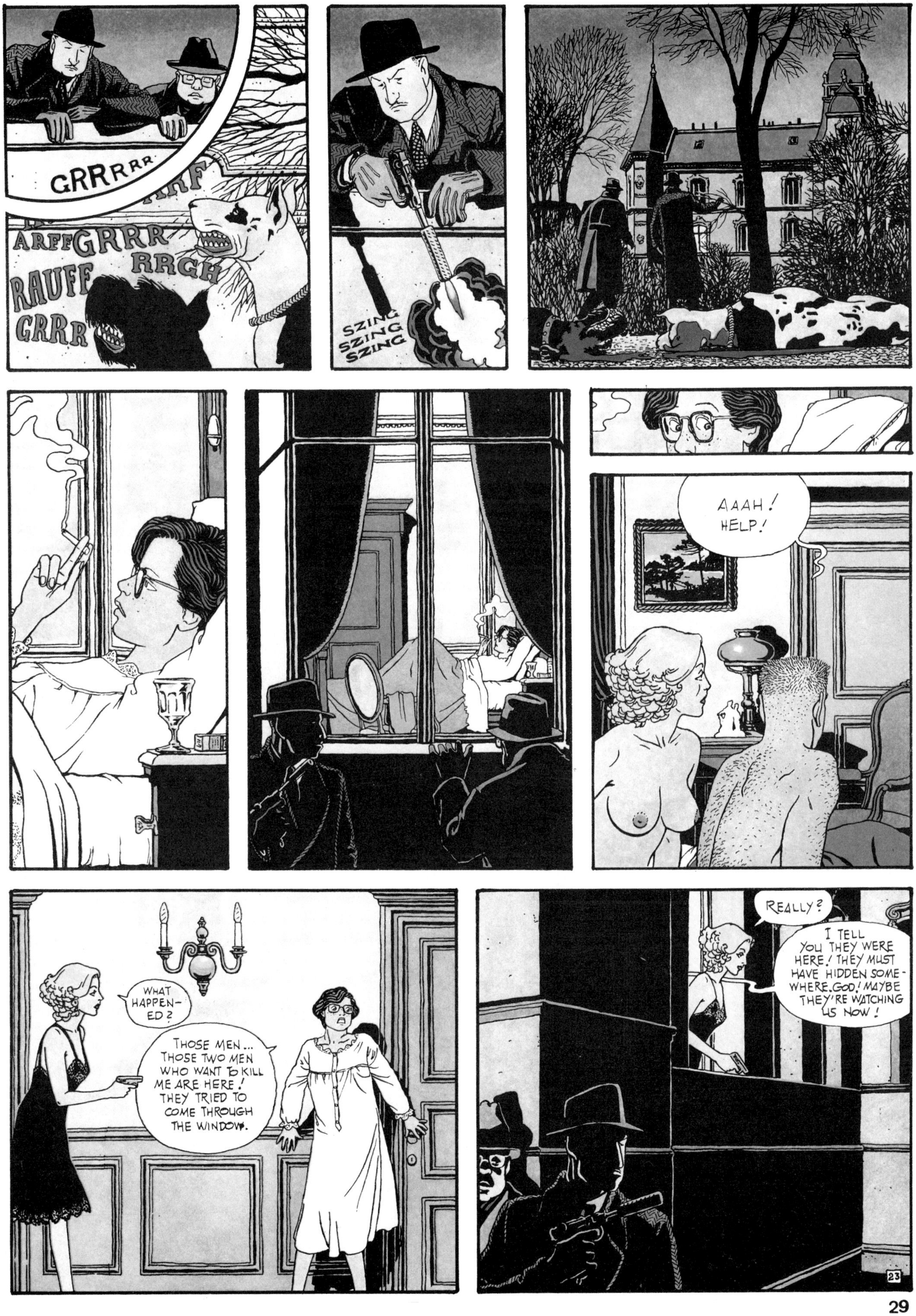

GRRrrr
ARF
ARFF GRRR
RRGH
RAUFF
GRRR
SZING
SZING
SZING
AAAH! HELP!
WHAT HAPPEN-ED?
THOSE MEN... THOSE TWO MEN WHO WANT TO KILL ME ARE HERE! THEY TRIED TO COME THROUGH THE WINDOW.
REALLY?
I TELL YOU THEY WERE HERE! THEY MUST HAVE HIDDEN SOME-WHERE. GOD! MAYBE THEY'RE WATCHING US NOW!
23

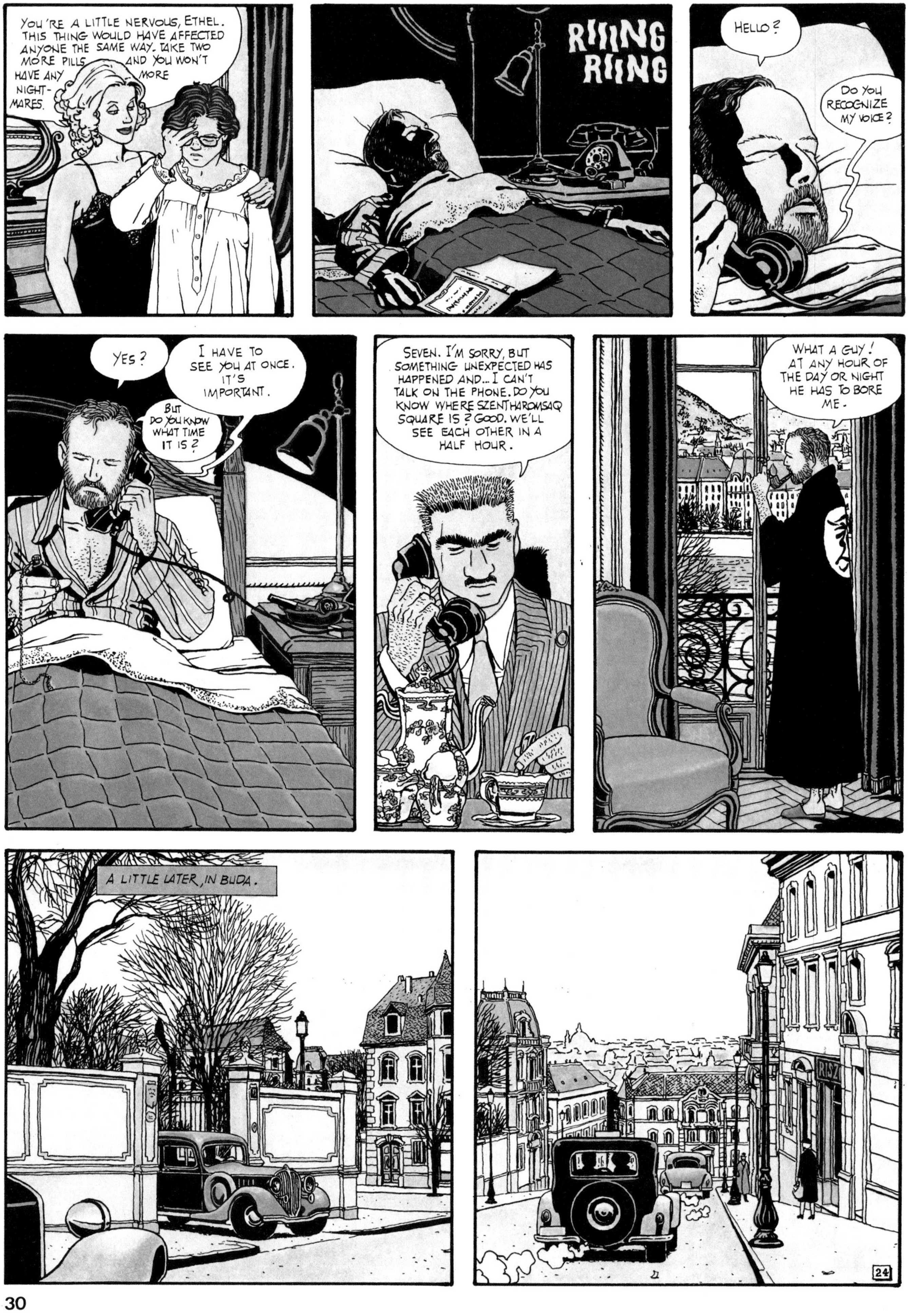
YOU'RE A LITTLE NERVOUS, ETHEL. THIS THING WOULD HAVE AFFECTED ANYONE THE SAME WAY. TAKE TWO MORE PILLS AND YOU WON'T HAVE ANY MORE NIGHT-MARES.
RIIING RIIING
HELLO ?
DO YOU RECOGNIZE MY VOICE ?
YES ?
I HAVE TO SEE YOU AT ONCE. IT'S IMPORTANT.
BUT DO YOU KNOW WHAT TIME IT IS ?
SEVEN. I'M SORRY, BUT SOMETHING UNEXPECTED HAS HAPPENED AND... I CAN'T TALK ON THE PHONE. DO YOU KNOW WHERE SZENTHAROMSAQ SQUARE IS ? GOOD. WE'LL SEE EACH OTHER IN A HALF HOUR.
WHAT A GUY ! AT ANY HOUR OF THE DAY OR NIGHT HE HAS TO BORE ME.
A LITTLE LATER, IN BUDA.
24

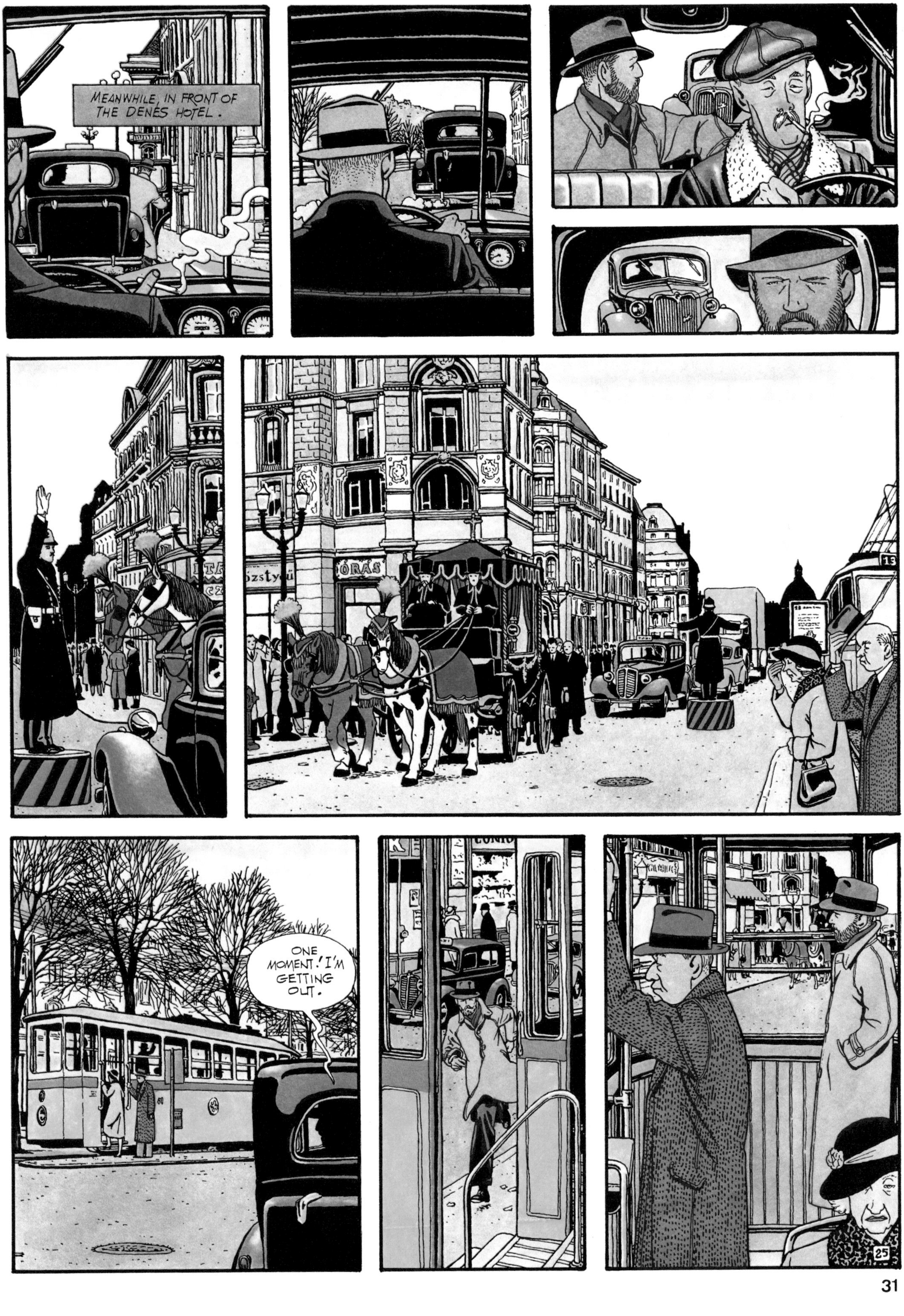
MEANWHILE, IN FRONT OF THE DENÉS HOTEL.
ÓRÁS
ONE MOMENT! I'M GETTING OUT.
25

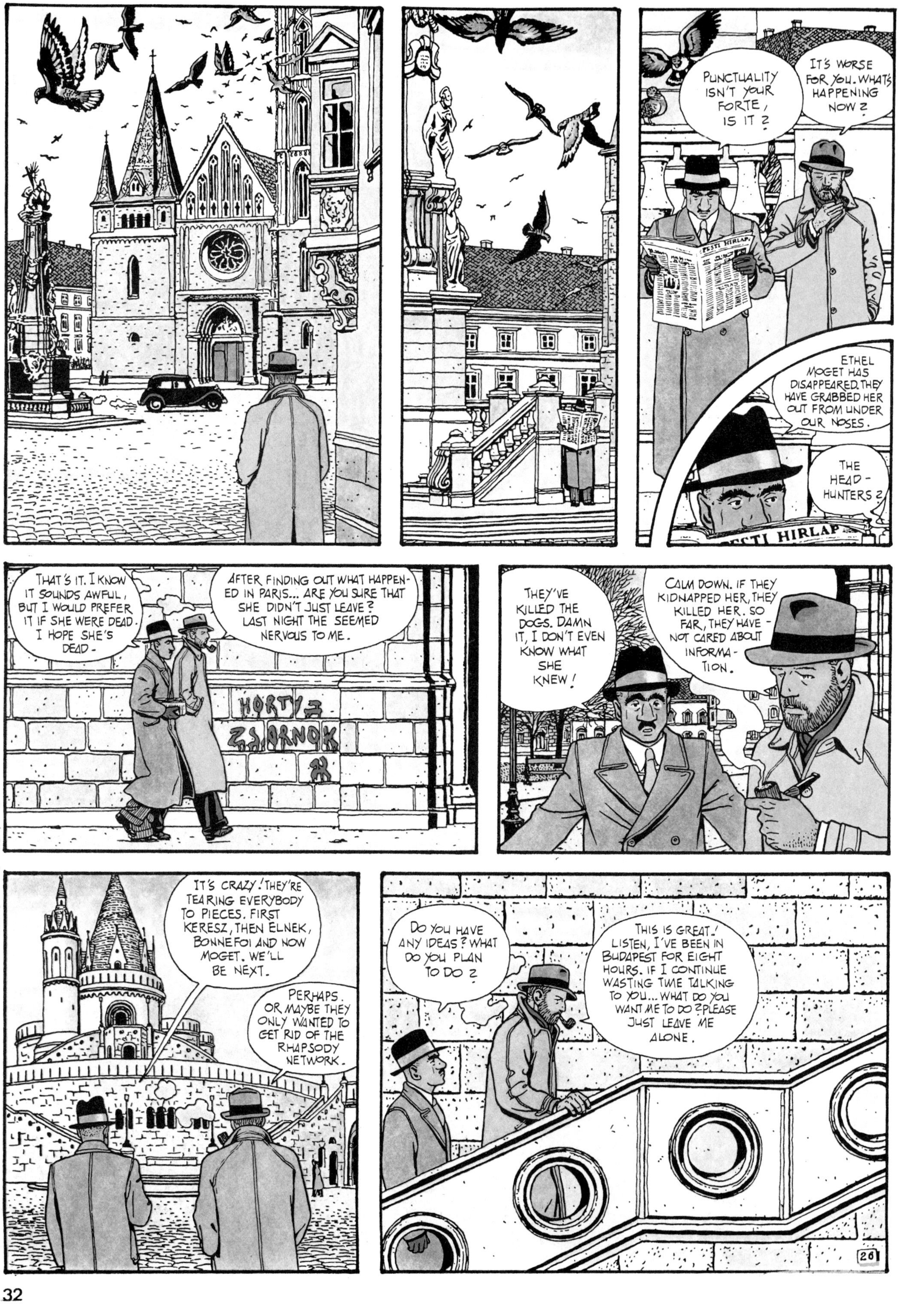
PUNCTUALITY ISN'T YOUR FORTE, IS IT?
IT'S WORSE FOR YOU. WHAT'S HAPPENING NOW?
PESTI HIRLAP
ETHEL MOGET HAS DISAPPEARED. THEY HAVE GRABBED HER OUT FROM UNDER OUR NOSES.
THE HEAD-HUNTERS?
PESTI HIRLAP
THAT'S IT. I KNOW IT SOUNDS AWFUL, BUT I WOULD PREFER IT IF SHE WERE DEAD. I HOPE SHE'S DEAD-
AFTER FINDING OUT WHAT HAPPENED IN PARIS... ARE YOU SURE THAT SHE DIDN'T JUST LEAVE? LAST NIGHT THE SEEMED NERVOUS TO ME.
HORTY
ZSARNOK
THEY'VE KILLED THE DOGS. DAMN IT, I DON'T EVEN KNOW WHAT SHE KNEW!
CALM DOWN. IF THEY KIDNAPPED HER, THEY KILLED HER. SO FAR, THEY HAVE NOT CARED ABOUT INFORMATION.
IT'S CRAZY! THEY'RE TEARING EVERYBODY TO PIECES. FIRST KERESZ, THEN ELNEK, BONNEFOI AND NOW MOGET. WE'LL BE NEXT.
PERHAPS. OR MAYBE THEY ONLY WANTED TO GET RID OF THE RHAPSODY NETWORK.
DO YOU HAVE ANY IDEAS? WHAT DO YOU PLAN TO DO?
THIS IS GREAT! LISTEN, I'VE BEEN IN BUDAPEST FOR EIGHT HOURS. IF I CONTINUE WASTING TIME TALKING TO YOU... WHAT DO YOU WANT ME TO DO? PLEASE JUST LEAVE ME ALONE.
26

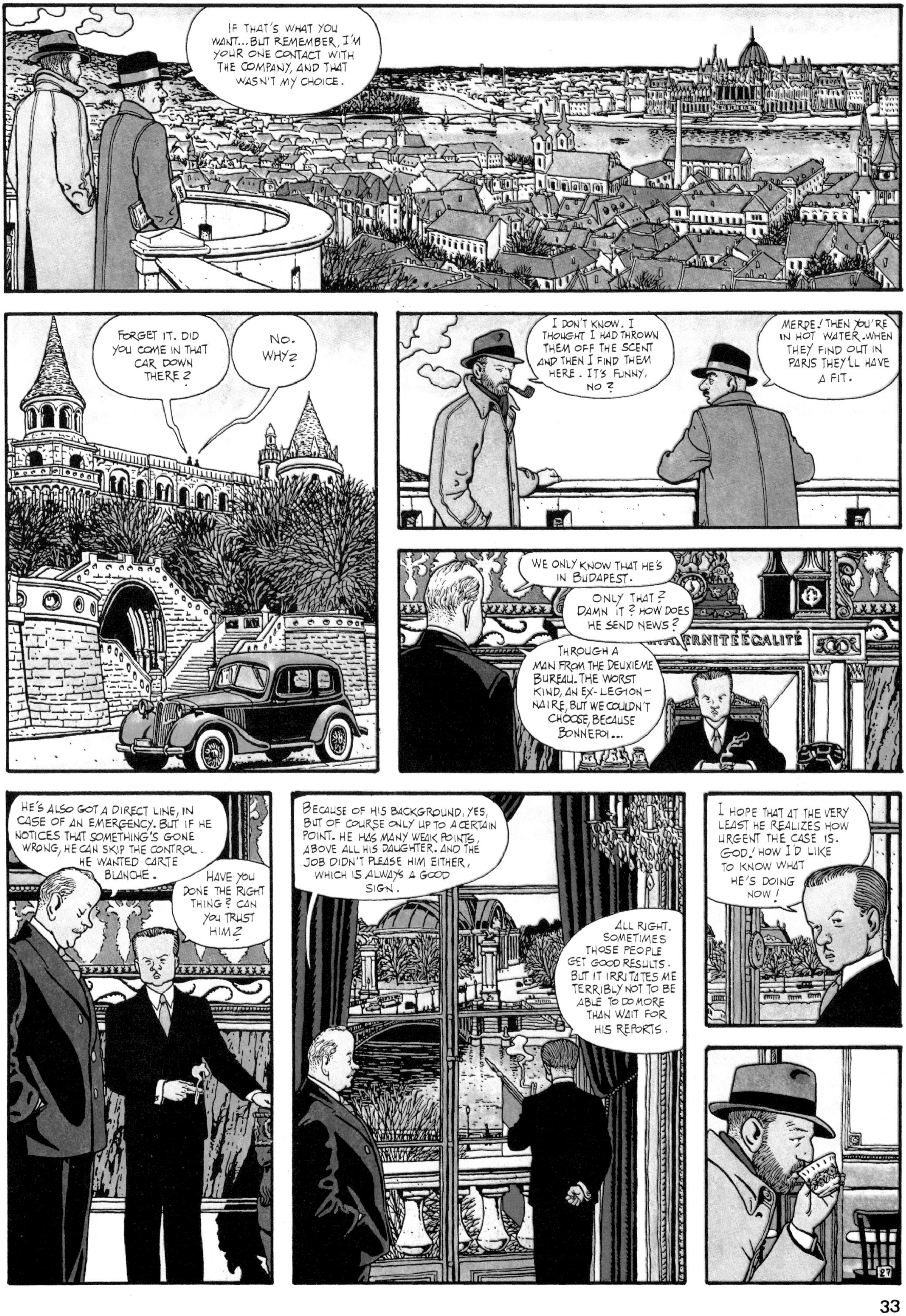
IF THAT'S WHAT YOU WANT... BUT REMEMBER, I'M YOUR ONE CONTACT WITH THE COMPANY, AND THAT WASN'T MY CHOICE.
FORGET IT. DID YOU COME IN THAT CAR DOWN THERE?
NO. WHY?
I DON'T KNOW. I THOUGHT I HAD THROWN THEM OFF THE SCENT AND THEN I FIND THEM HERE. IT'S FUNNY, NO?
MERDE! THEN YOU'RE IN HOT WATER. WHEN THEY FIND OUT IN PARIS THEY'LL HAVE A FIT.
WE ONLY KNOW THAT HE'S IN BUDAPEST.
ONLY THAT? DAMN IT? HOW DOES HE SEND NEWS?
THROUGH A MAN FROM THE DEUXIEME BUREAU. THE WORST KIND, AN EX-LEGIONNAIRE, BUT WE COULDN'T CHOOSE, BECAUSE BONNEFOI...
HE'S ALSO GOT A DIRECT LINE, IN CASE OF AN EMERGENCY. BUT IF HE NOTICES THAT SOMETHING'S GONE WRONG, HE CAN SKIP THE CONTROL. HE WANTED CARTE BLANCHE.
HAVE YOU DONE THE RIGHT THING? CAN YOU TRUST HIM?
BECAUSE OF HIS BACKGROUND, YES, BUT OF COURSE ONLY UP TO A CERTAIN POINT. HE HAS MANY WEAK POINTS, ABOVE ALL HIS DAUGHTER. AND THE JOB DIDN'T PLEASE HIM EITHER, WHICH IS ALWAYS A GOOD SIGN.
ALL RIGHT. SOMETIMES THOSE PEOPLE GET GOOD RESULTS. BUT IT IRRITATES ME TERRIBLY NOT TO BE ABLE TO DO MORE THAN WAIT FOR HIS REPORTS.
I HOPE THAT AT THE VERY LEAST HE REALIZES HOW URGENT THE CASE IS. GOD! HOW I'D LIKE TO KNOW WHAT HE'S DOING NOW!
27

MR. MAX...

YOU?

RIGONI IS CONVINCED THAT THEY'VE KIDNAPPED YOU.

HE CAN THINK WHATEVER HE WANTS, I'M NOT GOING BACK THERE. LAST NIGHT THEY TRIED TO KILL ME AND NO ONE BELIEVED ME. GOD! IT WAS A NIGHTMARE! SO I ESCAPED. YOU CAME TO REPLACE MAURICE, RIGHT?

IN A WAY. HOW IN THE DEVIL DID YOU FIND ME?

I THOUGHT THAT RIGONI WOULD CONTACT YOU AND I FOLLOWED HIM. IT COST ME A FORTUNE IN TAXIS, BUT THEY BROUGHT ME HERE.

MR. MAX, I CAN'T TAKE IT ANYMORE. I DIDN'T THINK THAT GIVING SOME INFORMATION TO MAURICE WOULD LEAD TO THIS.

YOU DIDN'T EXPECT IT? AND WHAT GAME DID YOU THINK YOU WERE PLAYING? WHETHER YOU LIKE IT OR NOT, YOU'RE INVOLVED IN THIS UP TO YOUR NECK.

BUT I'M NOT A SPY! IT WAS ONLY LIBRARY RESEARCH. HOLY HEAVEN, WHAT SHOULD I DO?

GET AS FAR AWAY FROM HERE AS POSSIBLE, CHANGE YOUR NAME, YOUR LIFE, EVERYTHING. PERHAPS THAT WAY YOU'LL SAVE YOURSELF. YOU DON'T HAVE ANYONE WHO CAN HIDE YOU FOR A WHILE?

I'D ALREADY THOUGHT OF THAT, BUT I'VE ONLY GOT SOME RELATIVES THAT I NEVER SEE. NOBODY IS READY NO TROUBLE HIMSELF FOR ME.

BY ALL MEANS, WE HAVE TO GET OUT OF HERE. DO YOU SEE THAT PARKED CAR? DO YOU KNOW THE MAN AT THE WHEEL?

REDY CUKRA

NO SHOULD I RECOGNIZE HIM?

I DON'T KNOW. DAMN IT. I DON'T SPEAK HUNGARIAN. ASK IF WE CAN LEAVE THROUGH THE BACK DOOR.

RÉTES PALACSINTA

HAB FAGYLALT

28

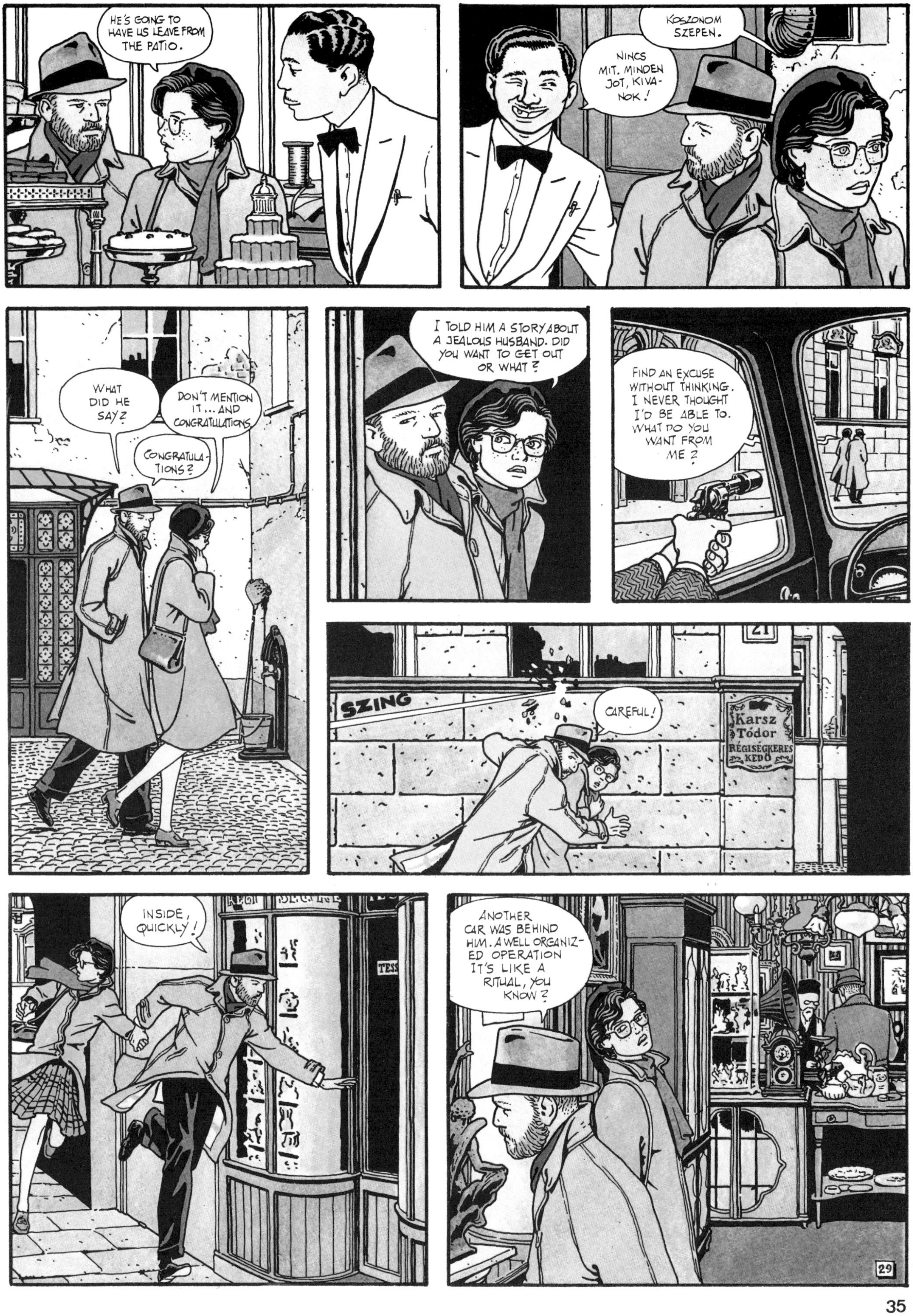

HE'S GOING TO HAVE US LEAVE FROM THE PATIO.
NINCS MIT. MINDEN JOT, KIVA-NOK!
KOSZONOM SZEPEN.
WHAT DID HE SAY?
DON'T MENTION IT... AND CONGRATULATIONS.
CONGRATULA-TIONS?
I TOLD HIM A STORY ABOUT A JEALOUS HUSBAND. DID YOU WANT TO GET OUT OR WHAT?
FIND AN EXCUSE WITHOUT THINKING. I NEVER THOUGHT I'D BE ABLE TO. WHAT DO YOU WANT FROM ME?
21
SZING
CAREFUL!
Karsz Tódor RÉGISÉGKERES KEDŐ
INSIDE, QUICKLY!
ANOTHER CAR WAS BEHIND HIM. A WELL ORGANIZ-ED OPERATION IT'S LIKE A RITUAL, YOU KNOW?
29

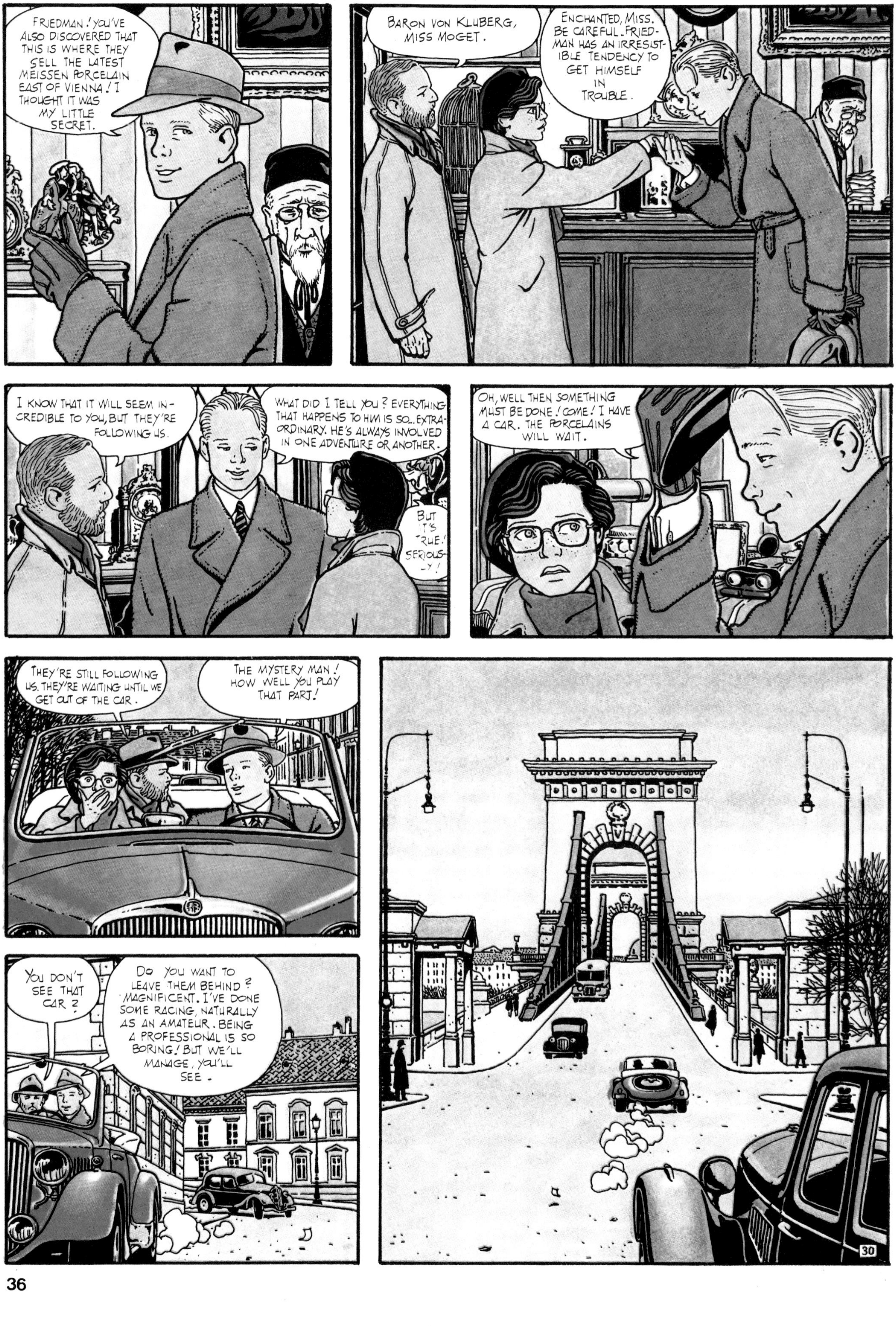
FRIEDMAN! YOU'VE ALSO DISCOVERED THAT THIS IS WHERE THEY SELL THE LATEST MEISSEN PORCELAIN EAST OF VIENNA! I THOUGHT IT WAS MY LITTLE SECRET.
BARON VON KLUBERG, MISS MOGET.
ENCHANTED, MISS. BE CAREFUL. FRIEDMAN HAS AN IRRESISTIBLE TENDENCY TO GET HIMSELF IN TROUBLE.
I KNOW THAT IT WILL SEEM INCREDIBLE TO YOU, BUT THEY'RE FOLLOWING US.
WHAT DID I TELL YOU? EVERYTHING THAT HAPPENS TO HIM IS SO...EXTRAORDINARY. HE'S ALWAYS INVOLVED IN ONE ADVENTURE OR ANOTHER.
BUT IT'S TRUE! SERIOUSLY!
OH, WELL THEN SOMETHING MUST BE DONE! COME! I HAVE A CAR. THE PORCELAINS WILL WAIT.
THEY'RE STILL FOLLOWING US. THEY'RE WAITING UNTIL WE GET OUT OF THE CAR.
THE MYSTERY MAN! HOW WELL YOU PLAY THAT PART!
YOU DON'T SEE THAT CAR?
DO YOU WANT TO LEAVE THEM BEHIND? MAGNIFICENT. I'VE DONE SOME RACING, NATURALLY AS AN AMATEUR. BEING A PROFESSIONAL IS SO BORING! BUT WE'LL MANAGE, YOU'LL SEE.
30

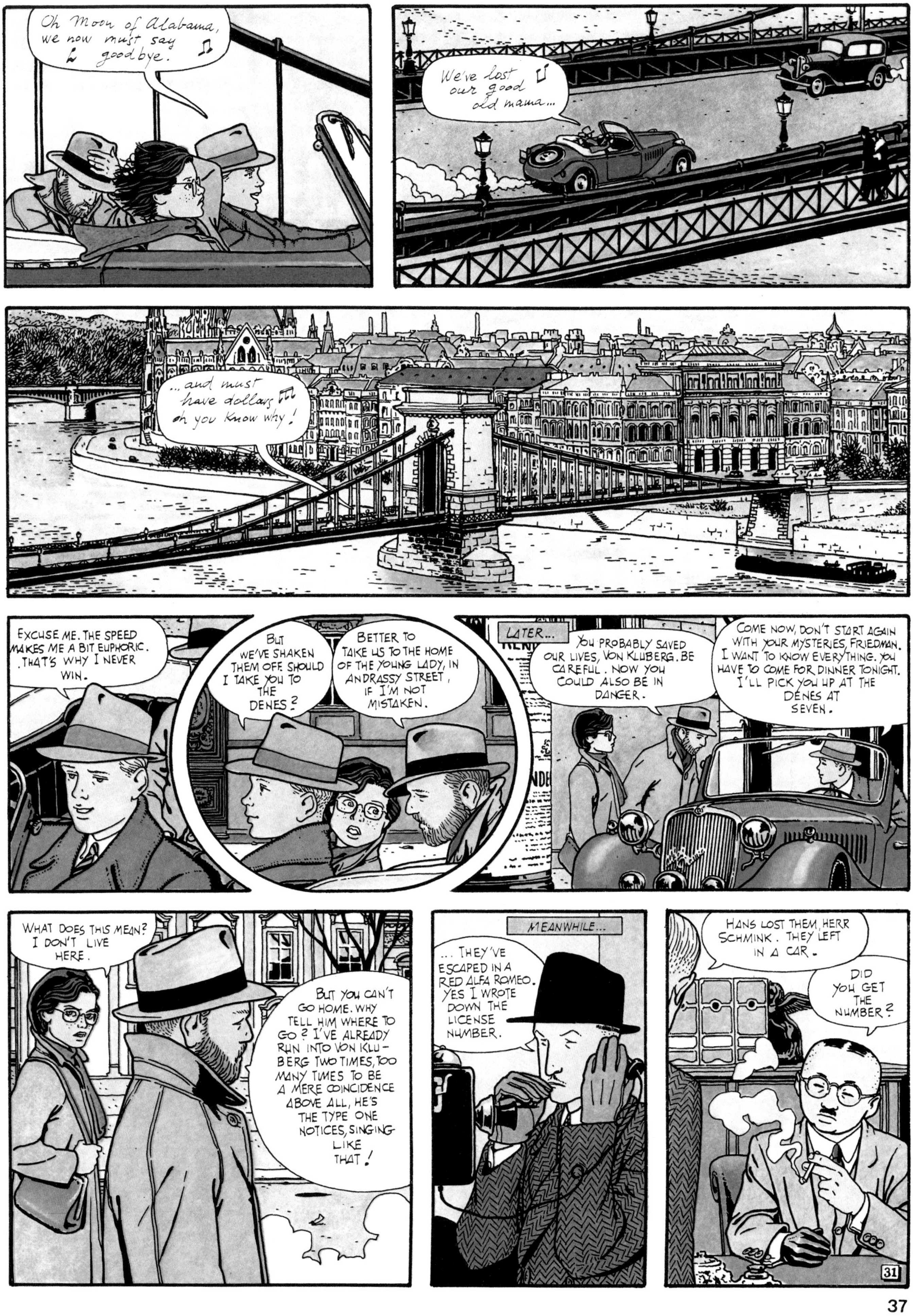
Oh Moon of Alabama, we now must say goodbye.
We've lost our good old mama...
...and must have dollars oh you know why!
EXCUSE ME. THE SPEED MAKES ME A BIT EUPHORIC. THAT'S WHY I NEVER WIN.
BUT WE'VE SHAKEN THEM OFF. SHOULD I TAKE YOU TO THE DENES?
BETTER TO TAKE US TO THE HOME OF THE YOUNG LADY, IN ANDRASSY STREET, IF I'M NOT MISTAKEN.
LATER...
YOU PROBABLY SAVED OUR LIVES, VON KLUBERG. BE CAREFUL. NOW YOU COULD ALSO BE IN DANGER.
COME NOW, DON'T START AGAIN WITH YOUR MYSTERIES, FRIEDMAN. I WANT TO KNOW EVERYTHING. YOU HAVE TO COME FOR DINNER TONIGHT. I'LL PICK YOU UP AT THE DENES AT SEVEN.
WHAT DOES THIS MEAN? I DON'T LIVE HERE.
BUT YOU CAN'T GO HOME. WHY TELL HIM WHERE TO GO? I'VE ALREADY RUN INTO VON KLU-BERG TWO TIMES, TOO MANY TIMES TO BE A MERE COINCIDENCE ABOVE ALL, HE'S THE TYPE ONE NOTICES, SINGING LIKE THAT!
MEANWHILE...
...THEY'VE ESCAPED IN A RED ALFA ROMEO. YES I WROTE DOWN THE LICENSE NUMBER.
HANS LOST THEM, HERR SCHMINK. THEY LEFT IN A CAR.
DID YOU GET THE NUMBER?
31

IT BELONGS TO VON KLUBERG, SIR.

HIM AGAIN? WHAT'S THE STORY NOW?

IT'S NOT SUCH A GREAT PLACE.

IF YOU'RE LOOKING FOR LUXURY, YOU'RE RIGHT. BUT IF YOU'RE LOOKING FOR QUIET, IN PEST THERE ISN'T ANYTHING BETTER. BESIDES, LOOK! WHAT A VIEW!

THE LADY'S NAME WILL BE ENOUGH. A FORMALITY, YOU KNOW. ANY NAME WILL DO. WELL, I'LL LEAVE YOU ALONE.

I'M AFRAID YOU'LL HAVE TO DO THE CLEANING.

OH, I'M ALREADY ACCUSTOMED TO THAT, BUT... THAT LADY TOOK US FOR TWO... WELL, A SECRET LOVE AFFAIR.

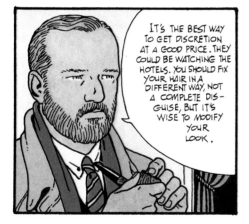

IT'S THE BEST WAY TO GET DISCRETION AT A GOOD PRICE. THEY COULD BE WATCHING THE HOTELS. YOU SHOULD FIX YOUR HAIR IN A DIFFERENT WAY, NOT A COMPLETE DISGUISE, BUT IT'S WISE TO MODIFY YOUR LOOK.

WHY ARE YOU DOING ALL THIS FOR ME?

WHY?! BECAUSE YOU'RE THE SOLE SURVIVOR OF RHAPSODY. BECAUSE WITHOUT MY HELP YOU WOULDN'T BE ALIVE MUCH LONGER, AND BESIDES I NEED YOU TO GET OUT OF THIS DAMNED MESS. AS SOON AS I ARRIVED, SOMETHING DAWNED ON ME. THEY ALREADY KNEW WHO I WAS. THEY'VE ALWAYS KNOWN EVERYTHING, EXCEPT THAT WE'RE HERE NOW. DO YOU UNDERSTAND WHAT THAT MEANS?

LISTEN, MAYBE THERE'S NOT MUCH TIME LEFT. YOU SHOULD TALK.

MY REPORT IS IN MAURICE'S FILES.

IF THERE WAS ANYTHING INTERESTING THERE, THEY WOULD HAVE ALREADY FOUND IT. I WANT SOMETHING THAT ISN'T IN THE REPORT. WHAT MAURICE TOLD YOU TO KEEP SECRET, ISN'T THAT RIGHT?

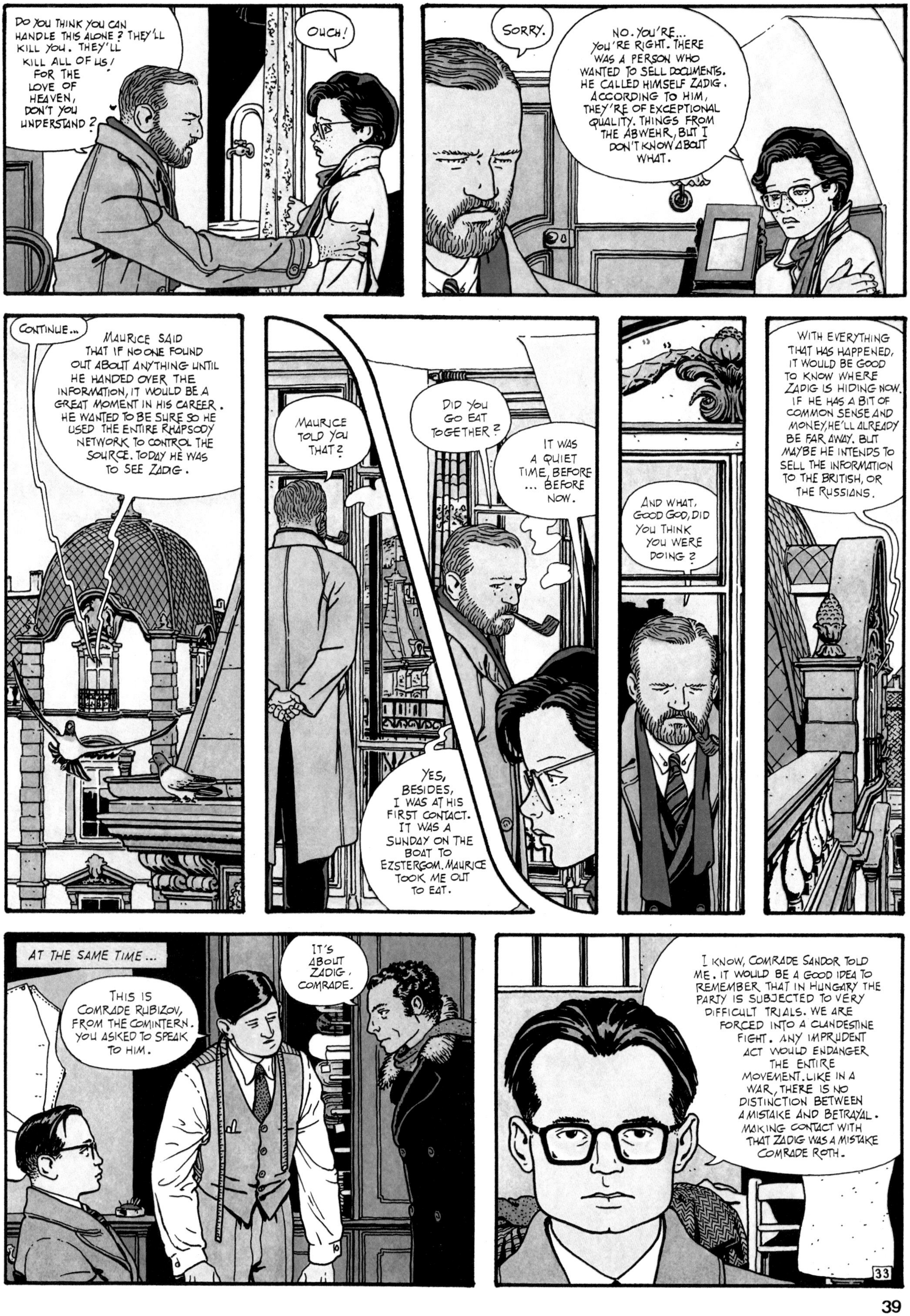

Do you think you can handle this alone? They'll kill you. They'll kill all of us! For the love of heaven, don't you understand?
Ouch!
Sorry.
No. You're... you're right. There was a person who wanted to sell documents. He called himself Zadig. According to him, they're of exceptional quality. Things from the Abwehr, but I don't know about what.
Continue...
Maurice said that if no one found out about anything until he handed over the information, it would be a great moment in his career. He wanted to be sure so he used the entire Rhapsody network to control the source. Today he was to see Zadig.
Maurice told you that?
Yes, besides, I was at his first contact. It was a Sunday on the boat to Ezstergom. Maurice took me out to eat.
Did you go eat together?
It was a quiet time, before ... before now.
And what, good God, did you think you were doing?
With everything that has happened, it would be good to know where Zadig is hiding now. If he has a bit of common sense and money, he'll already be far away. But maybe he intends to sell the information to the British, or the Russians.
At the same time...
This is Comrade Rubizov, from the Comintern. You asked to speak to him.
It's about Zadig, comrade.
I know, Comrade Sandor told me. It would be a good idea to remember that in Hungary the party is subjected to very difficult trials. We are forced into a clandestine fight. Any imprudent act would endanger the entire movement. Like in a war, there is no distinction between a mistake and betrayal. Making contact with that Zadig was a mistake Comrade Roth.
33

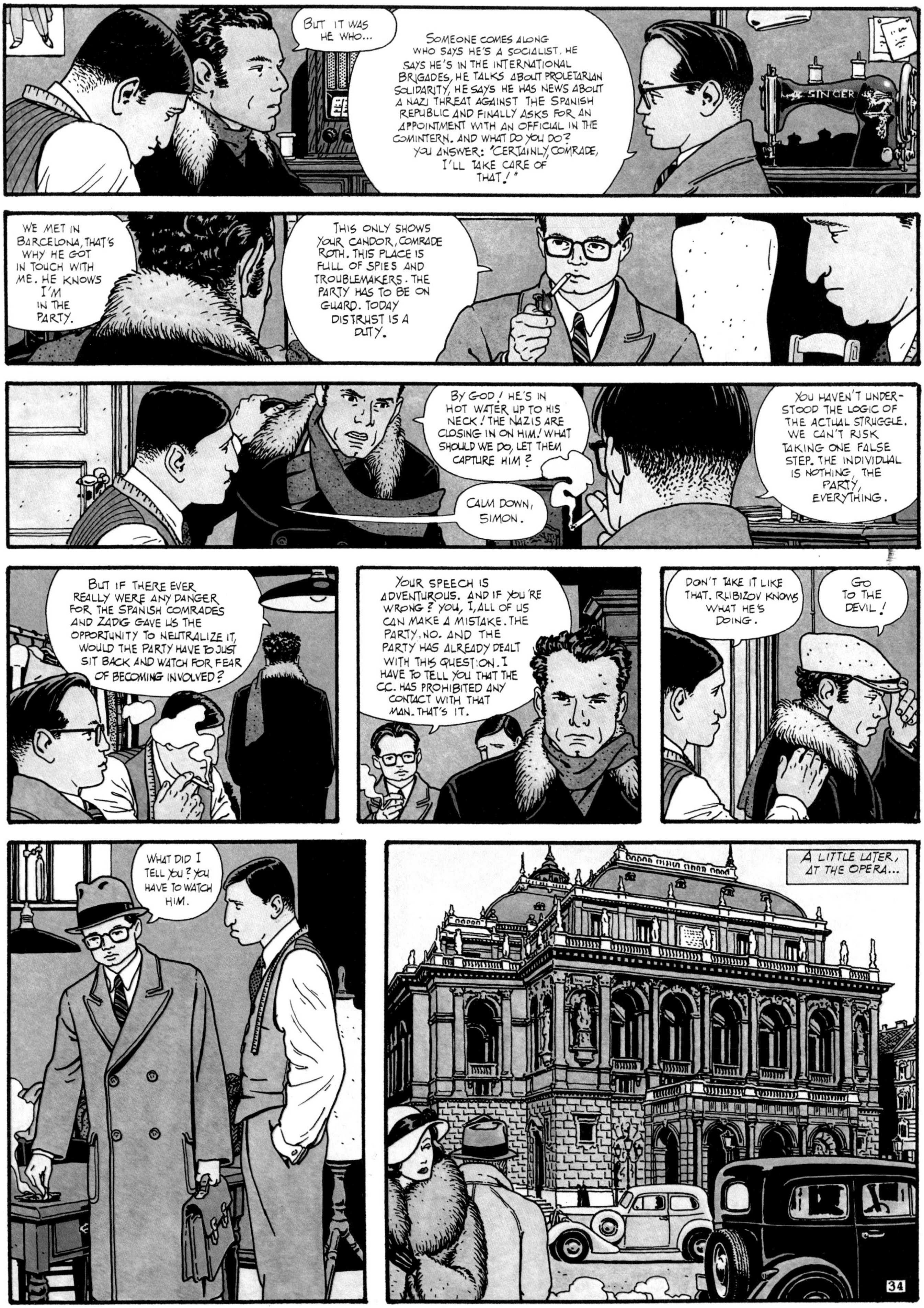

BUT IT WAS HE WHO...
SOMEONE COMES ALONG WHO SAYS HE'S A SOCIALIST, HE SAYS HE'S IN THE INTERNATIONAL BRIGADES, HE TALKS ABOUT PROLETARIAN SOLIDARITY, HE SAYS HE HAS NEWS ABOUT A NAZI THREAT AGAINST THE SPANISH REPUBLIC AND FINALLY ASKS FOR AN APPOINTMENT WITH AN OFFICIAL IN THE COMINTERN. AND WHAT DO YOU DO? YOU ANSWER: "CERTAINLY, COMRADE, I'LL TAKE CARE OF THAT!"
SINGER
WE MET IN BARCELONA, THAT'S WHY HE GOT IN TOUCH WITH ME. HE KNOWS I'M IN THE PARTY.
THIS ONLY SHOWS YOUR CANDOR, COMRADE ROTH. THIS PLACE IS FULL OF SPIES AND TROUBLEMAKERS. THE PARTY HAS TO BE ON GUARD. TODAY DISTRUST IS A DUTY.
BY GOD! HE'S IN HOT WATER UP TO HIS NECK! THE NAZIS ARE CLOSING IN ON HIM! WHAT SHOULD WE DO, LET THEM CAPTURE HIM?
CALM DOWN, SIMON.
YOU HAVEN'T UNDERSTOOD THE LOGIC OF THE ACTUAL STRUGGLE. WE CAN'T RISK TAKING ONE FALSE STEP. THE INDIVIDUAL IS NOTHING, THE PARTY, EVERYTHING.
BUT IF THERE EVER REALLY WERE ANY DANGER FOR THE SPANISH COMRADES AND ZADIG GAVE US THE OPPORTUNITY TO NEUTRALIZE IT, WOULD THE PARTY HAVE TO JUST SIT BACK AND WATCH FOR FEAR OF BECOMING INVOLVED?
YOUR SPEECH IS ADVENTUROUS. AND IF YOU'RE WRONG? YOU, I, ALL OF US CAN MAKE A MISTAKE. THE PARTY, NO. AND THE PARTY HAS ALREADY DEALT WITH THIS QUESTION. I HAVE TO TELL YOU THAT THE CC. HAS PROHIBITED ANY CONTACT WITH THAT MAN. THAT'S IT.
DON'T TAKE IT LIKE THAT. RUBIZOV KNOWS WHAT HE'S DOING.
GO TO THE DEVIL!
WHAT DID I TELL YOU? YOU HAVE TO WATCH HIM.
A LITTLE LATER, AT THE OPERA...
34

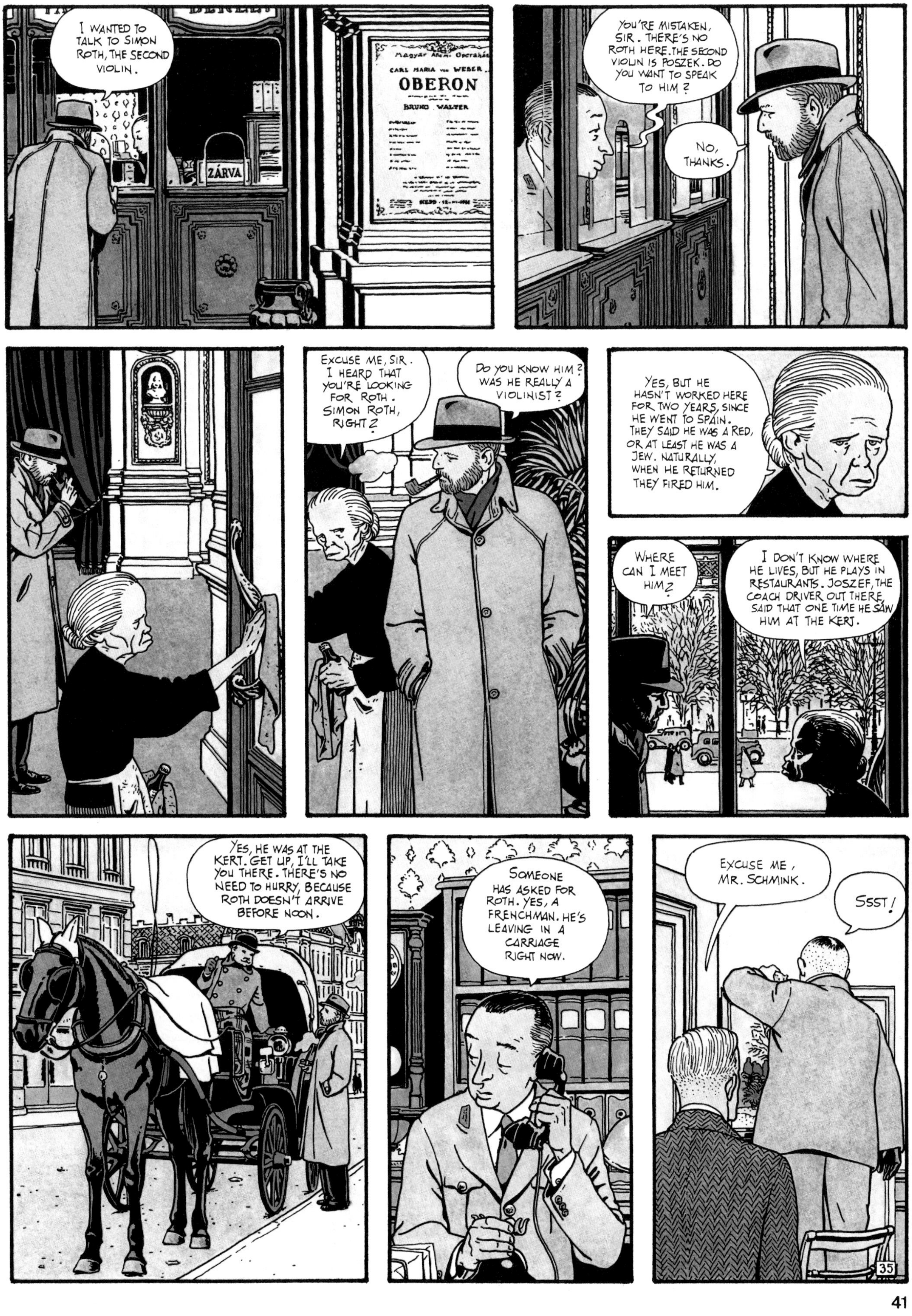

I WANTED TO TALK TO SIMON ROTH, THE SECOND VIOLIN.
CARL MARIA von WEBER
OBERON
BRUNO WALTER
ZÁRVA
YOU'RE MISTAKEN, SIR. THERE'S NO ROTH HERE. THE SECOND VIOLIN IS POSZEK. DO YOU WANT TO SPEAK TO HIM?
NO, THANKS.
EXCUSE ME, SIR. I HEARD THAT YOU'RE LOOKING FOR ROTH. SIMON ROTH, RIGHT?
DO YOU KNOW HIM? WAS HE REALLY A VIOLINIST?
YES, BUT HE HASN'T WORKED HERE FOR TWO YEARS, SINCE HE WENT TO SPAIN. THEY SAID HE WAS A RED, OR AT LEAST HE WAS A JEW. NATURALLY, WHEN HE RETURNED THEY FIRED HIM.
WHERE CAN I MEET HIM?
I DON'T KNOW WHERE HE LIVES, BUT HE PLAYS IN RESTAURANTS. JOSZEF, THE COACH DRIVER OUT THERE, SAID THAT ONE TIME HE SAW HIM AT THE KERT.
YES, HE WAS AT THE KERT. GET UP, I'LL TAKE YOU THERE. THERE'S NO NEED TO HURRY, BECAUSE ROTH DOESN'T ARRIVE BEFORE NOON.
SOMEONE HAS ASKED FOR ROTH. YES, A FRENCHMAN. HE'S LEAVING IN A CARRIAGE RIGHT NOW.
EXCUSE ME, MR. SCHMINK.
SSST!
35

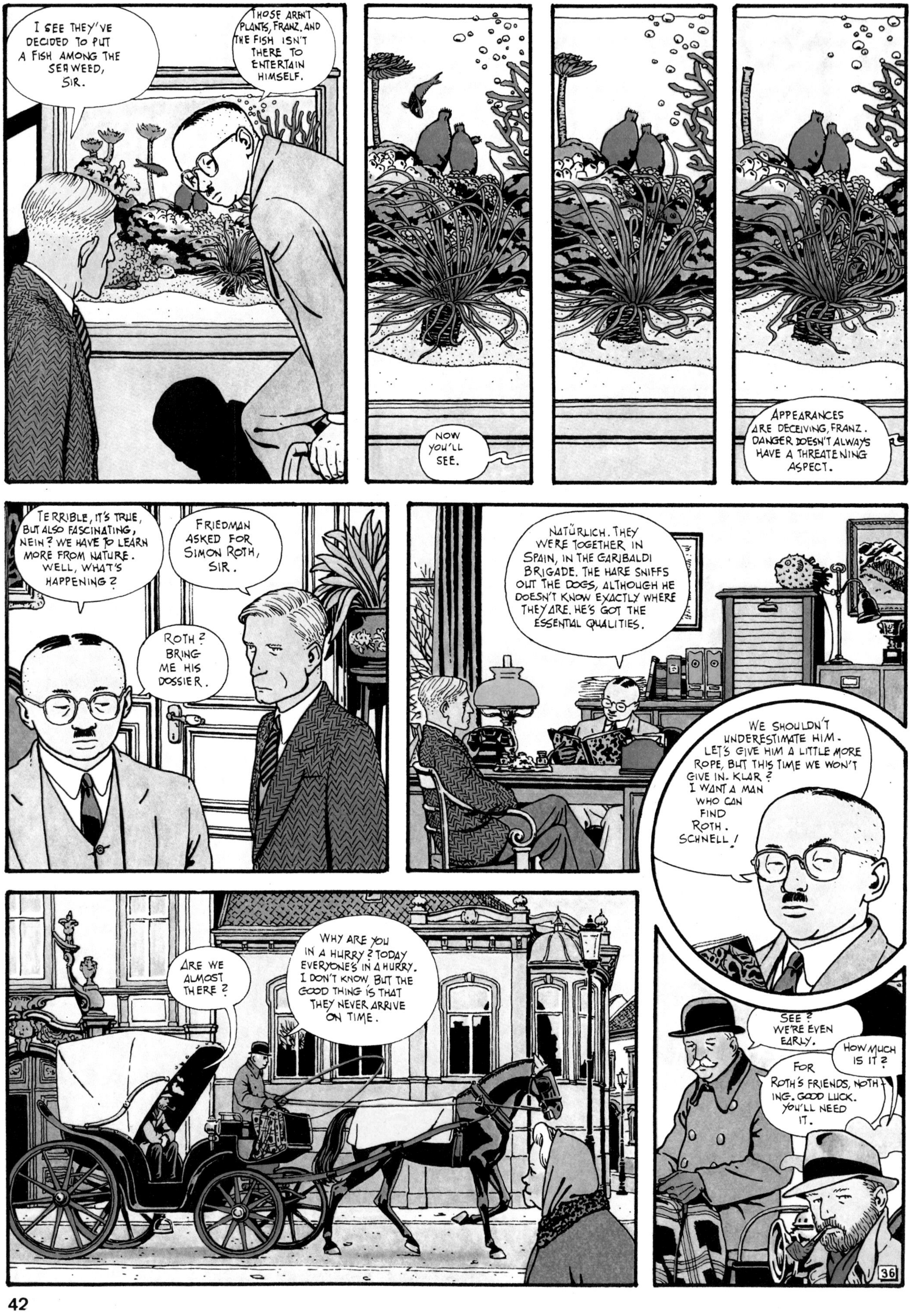
I SEE THEY'VE DECIDED TO PUT A FISH AMONG THE SEAWEED, SIR.
THOSE AREN'T PLANTS, FRANZ. AND THE FISH ISN'T THERE TO ENTERTAIN HIMSELF.
NOW YOU'LL SEE.
APPEARANCES ARE DECEIVING, FRANZ. DANGER DOESN'T ALWAYS HAVE A THREATENING ASPECT.
TERRIBLE, IT'S TRUE, BUT ALSO FASCINATING, NEIN? WE HAVE TO LEARN MORE FROM NATURE. WELL, WHAT'S HAPPENING?
FRIEDMAN ASKED FOR SIMON ROTH, SIR.
ROTH? BRING ME HIS DOSSIER.
NATÜRLICH. THEY WERE TOGETHER IN SPAIN, IN THE GARIBALDI BRIGADE. THE HARE SNIFFS OUT THE DOGS, ALTHOUGH HE DOESN'T KNOW EXACTLY WHERE THEY ARE. HE'S GOT THE ESSENTIAL QUALITIES.
WE SHOULDN'T UNDERESTIMATE HIM. LET'S GIVE HIM A LITTLE MORE ROPE, BUT THIS TIME WE WON'T GIVE IN. KLAR? I WANT A MAN WHO CAN FIND ROTH. SCHNELL!
ARE WE ALMOST THERE?
WHY ARE YOU IN A HURRY? TODAY EVERYONE'S IN A HURRY. I DON'T KNOW, BUT THE GOOD THING IS THAT THEY NEVER ARRIVE ON TIME.
SEE? WE'RE EVEN EARLY.
HOW MUCH IS IT?
FOR ROTH'S FRIENDS, NOTHING. GOOD LUCK. YOU'LL NEED IT.
36

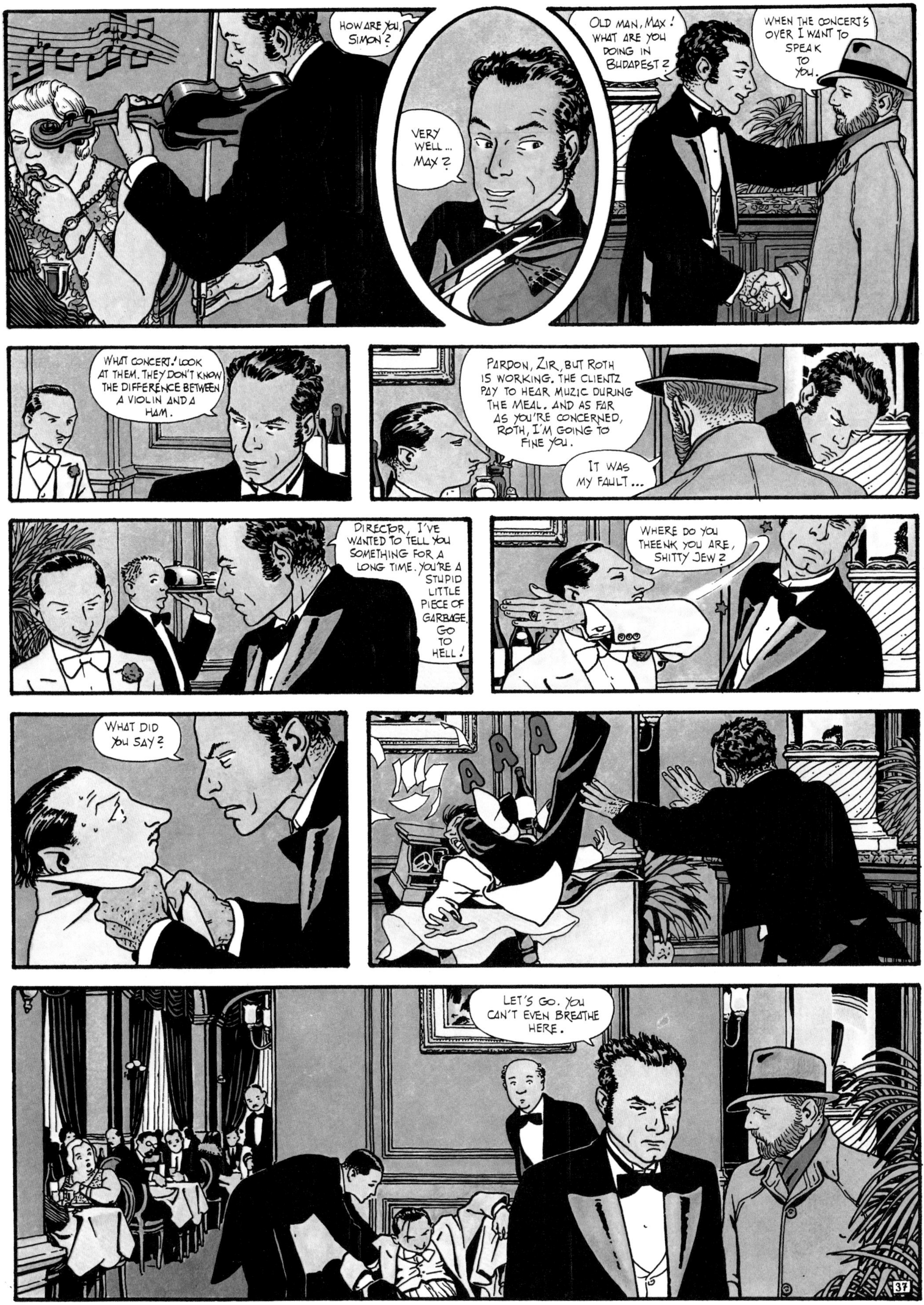
HOW ARE YOU, SIMON?
VERY WELL... MAX?
OLD MAN, MAX! WHAT ARE YOU DOING IN BUDAPEST?
WHEN THE CONCERT'S OVER I WANT TO SPEAK TO YOU.
WHAT CONCERT! LOOK AT THEM. THEY DON'T KNOW THE DIFFERENCE BETWEEN A VIOLIN AND A HAM.
PARDON, ZIR, BUT ROTH IS WORKING. THE CLIENTZ PAY TO HEAR MUZIC DURING THE MEAL. AND AS FAR AS YOU'RE CONCERNED, ROTH, I'M GOING TO FINE YOU.
IT WAS MY FAULT...
DIRECTOR, I'VE WANTED TO TELL YOU SOMETHING FOR A LONG TIME. YOU'RE A STUPID LITTLE PIECE OF GARBAGE. GO TO HELL!
WHERE DO YOU THEENK YOU ARE, SHITTY JEW?
WHAT DID YOU SAY?
A A A
LET'S GO. YOU CAN'T EVEN BREATHE HERE.
37

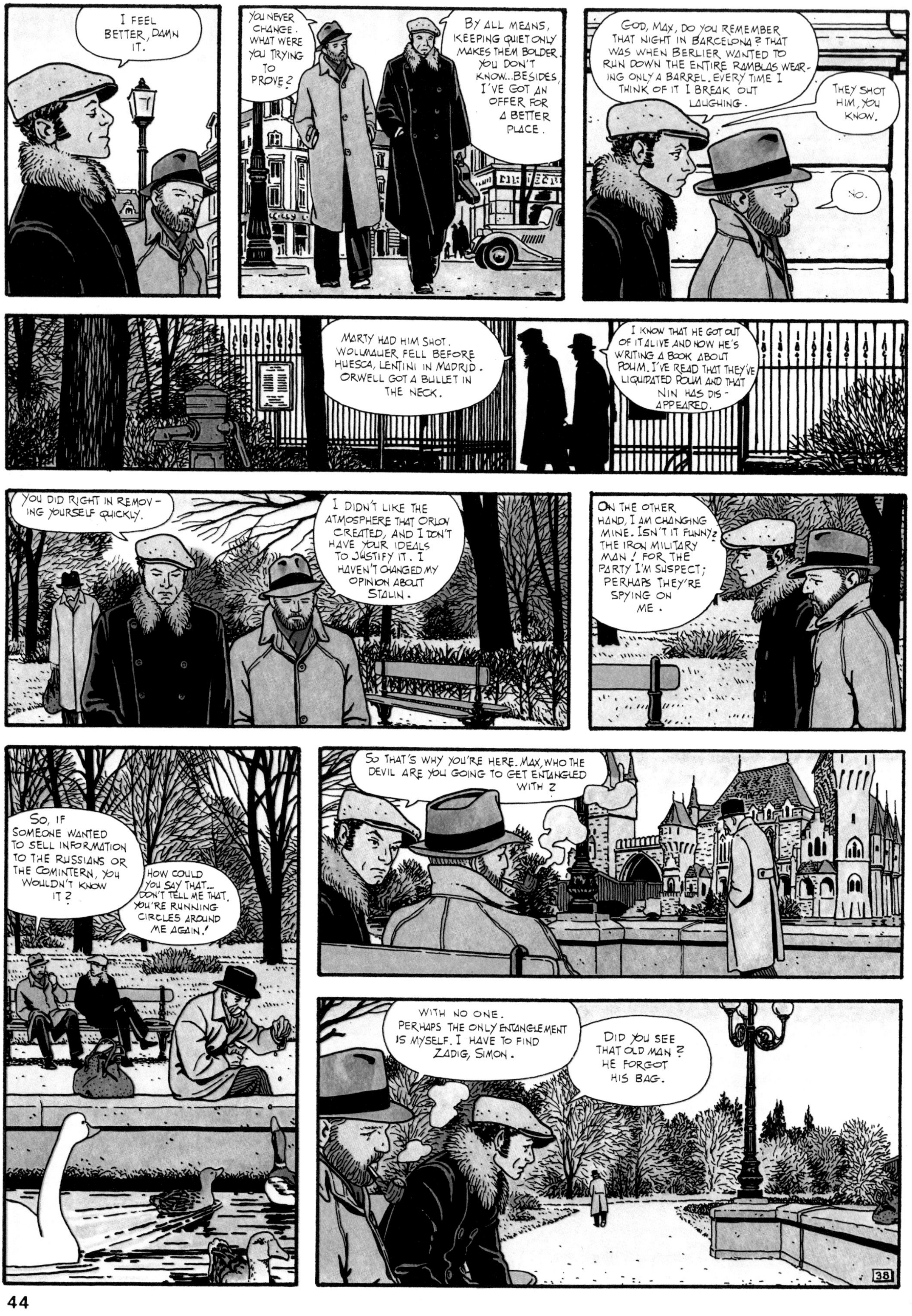
I FEEL BETTER, DAMN IT.
YOU NEVER CHANGE. WHAT WERE YOU TRYING TO PROVE?
BY ALL MEANS, KEEPING QUIET ONLY MAKES THEM BOLDER. YOU DON'T KNOW...BESIDES, I'VE GOT AN OFFER FOR A BETTER PLACE.
GOD, MAX, DO YOU REMEMBER THAT NIGHT IN BARCELONA? THAT WAS WHEN BERLIER WANTED TO RUN DOWN THE ENTIRE RAMBLAS WEARING ONLY A BARREL. EVERY TIME I THINK OF IT I BREAK OUT LAUGHING.
THEY SHOT HIM, YOU KNOW.
NO.
MARTY HAD HIM SHOT. WOLLMAUER FELL BEFORE HUESCA, LENTINI IN MADRID. ORWELL GOT A BULLET IN THE NECK.
I KNOW THAT HE GOT OUT OF IT ALIVE AND NOW HE'S WRITING A BOOK ABOUT POUM. I'VE READ THAT THEY'VE LIQUIDATED POUM AND THAT NIN HAS DISAPPEARED.
YOU DID RIGHT IN REMOVING YOURSELF QUICKLY.
I DIDN'T LIKE THE ATMOSPHERE THAT ORLOV CREATED, AND I DON'T HAVE YOUR IDEALS TO JUSTIFY IT. I HAVEN'T CHANGED MY OPINION ABOUT STALIN.
ON THE OTHER HAND, I AM CHANGING MINE. ISN'T IT FUNNY? THE IRON MILITARY MAN! FOR THE PARTY I'M SUSPECT; PERHAPS THEY'RE SPYING ON ME.
SO, IF SOMEONE WANTED TO SELL INFORMATION TO THE RUSSIANS OR THE COMINTERN, YOU WOULDN'T KNOW IT?
HOW COULD YOU SAY THAT... DON'T TELL ME THAT. YOU'RE RUNNING CIRCLES AROUND ME AGAIN!
SO THAT'S WHY YOU'RE HERE. MAX, WHO THE DEVIL ARE YOU GOING TO GET ENTANGLED WITH?
WITH NO ONE. PERHAPS THE ONLY ENTANGLEMENT IS MYSELF. I HAVE TO FIND ZADIG, SIMON.
DID YOU SEE THAT OLD MAN? HE FORGOT HIS BAG.
38

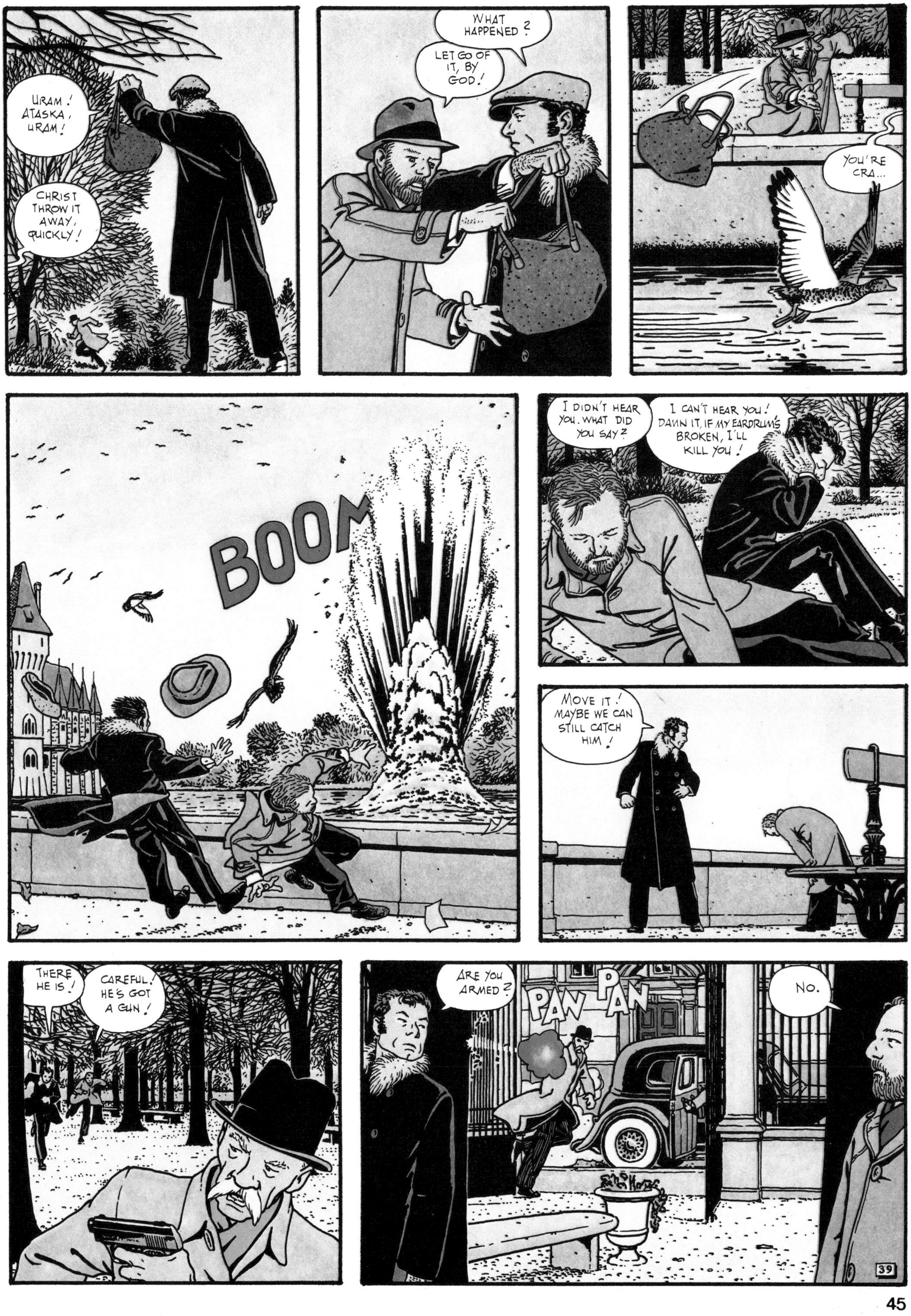
URAM! ATASKA, URAM!
CHRIST THROW IT AWAY, QUICKLY!
WHAT HAPPENED?
LET GO OF IT, BY GOD!
YOU'RE CRA...
BOOM
I DIDN'T HEAR YOU. WHAT DID YOU SAY?
I CAN'T HEAR YOU! DAMN IT, IF MY EARDRUM'S BROKEN, I'LL KILL YOU!
MOVE IT! MAYBE WE CAN STILL CATCH HIM!
THERE HE IS!
CAREFUL! HE'S GOT A GUN!
ARE YOU ARMED?
PAN PAN
NO.
39

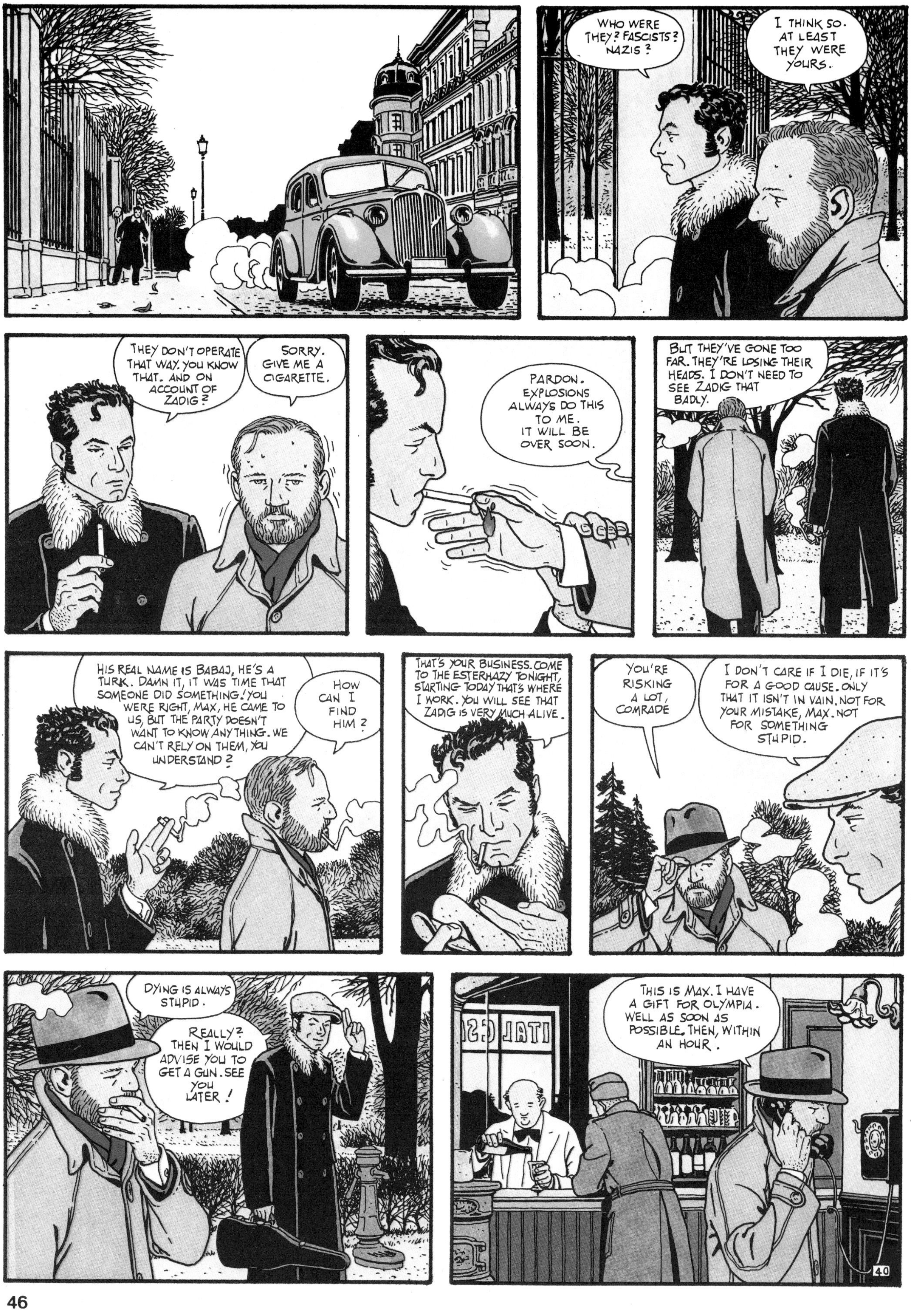
WHO WERE THEY? FASCISTS? NAZIS?
I THINK SO. AT LEAST THEY WERE YOURS.
THEY DON'T OPERATE THAT WAY. YOU KNOW THAT. AND ON ACCOUNT OF ZADIG?
SORRY. GIVE ME A CIGARETTE.
PARDON. EXPLOSIONS ALWAYS DO THIS TO ME. IT WILL BE OVER SOON.
BUT THEY'VE GONE TOO FAR. THEY'RE LOSING THEIR HEADS. I DON'T NEED TO SEE ZADIG THAT BADLY.
HIS REAL NAME IS BABAJ, HE'S A TURK. DAMN IT, IT WAS TIME THAT SOMEONE DID SOMETHING! YOU WERE RIGHT, MAX, HE CAME TO US, BUT THE PARTY DOESN'T WANT TO KNOW ANYTHING. WE CAN'T RELY ON THEM, YOU UNDERSTAND?
HOW CAN I FIND HIM?
THAT'S YOUR BUSINESS. COME TO THE ESTERHAZY TONIGHT, STARTING TODAY THAT'S WHERE I WORK. YOU WILL SEE THAT ZADIG IS VERY MUCH ALIVE.
YOU'RE RISKING A LOT, COMRADE
I DON'T CARE IF I DIE, IF IT'S FOR A GOOD CAUSE. ONLY THAT IT ISN'T IN VAIN. NOT FOR YOUR MISTAKE, MAX. NOT FOR SOMETHING STUPID.
DYING IS ALWAYS STUPID.
REALLY? THEN I WOULD ADVISE YOU TO GET A GUN. SEE YOU LATER!
THIS IS MAX. I HAVE A GIFT FOR OLYMPIA. WELL AS SOON AS POSSIBLE. THEN, WITHIN AN HOUR.
40

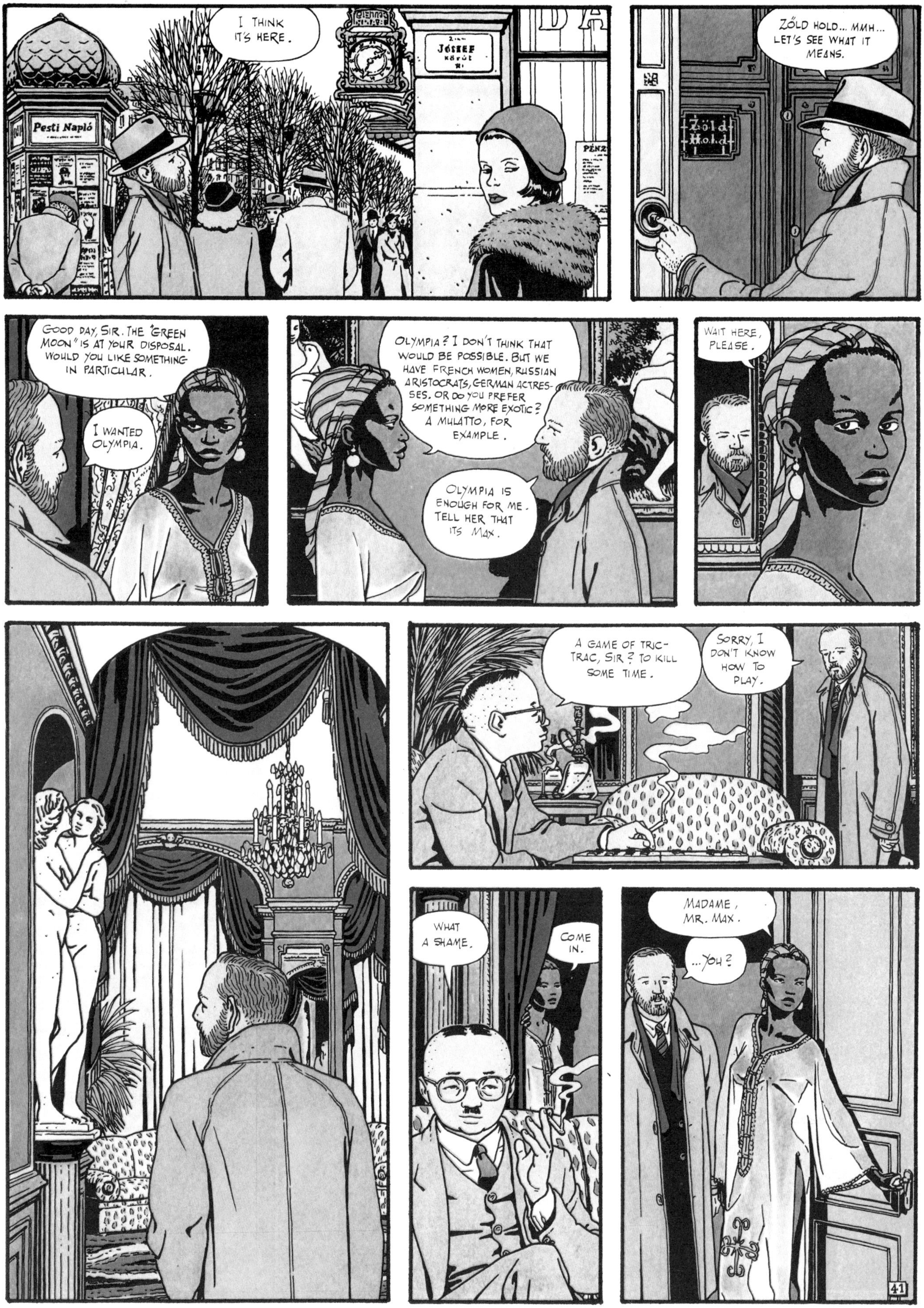
I THINK IT'S HERE.
Pesti Napló
JÓZSEF körút
ZŐLD HOLD... MMH... LET'S SEE WHAT IT MEANS.
Zöld Hold
GOOD DAY, SIR. THE "GREEN MOON" IS AT YOUR DISPOSAL. WOULD YOU LIKE SOMETHING IN PARTICULAR.
I WANTED OLYMPIA.
OLYMPIA? I DON'T THINK THAT WOULD BE POSSIBLE. BUT WE HAVE FRENCH WOMEN, RUSSIAN ARISTOCRATS, GERMAN ACTRESSES. OR DO YOU PREFER SOMETHING MORE EXOTIC? A MULATTO, FOR EXAMPLE.
OLYMPIA IS ENOUGH FOR ME. TELL HER THAT ITS MAX.
WAIT HERE, PLEASE.
A GAME OF TRIC-TRAC, SIR? TO KILL SOME TIME.
SORRY, I DON'T KNOW HOW TO PLAY.
WHAT A SHAME.
COME IN.
MADAME, MR. MAX.
...YOU?
41

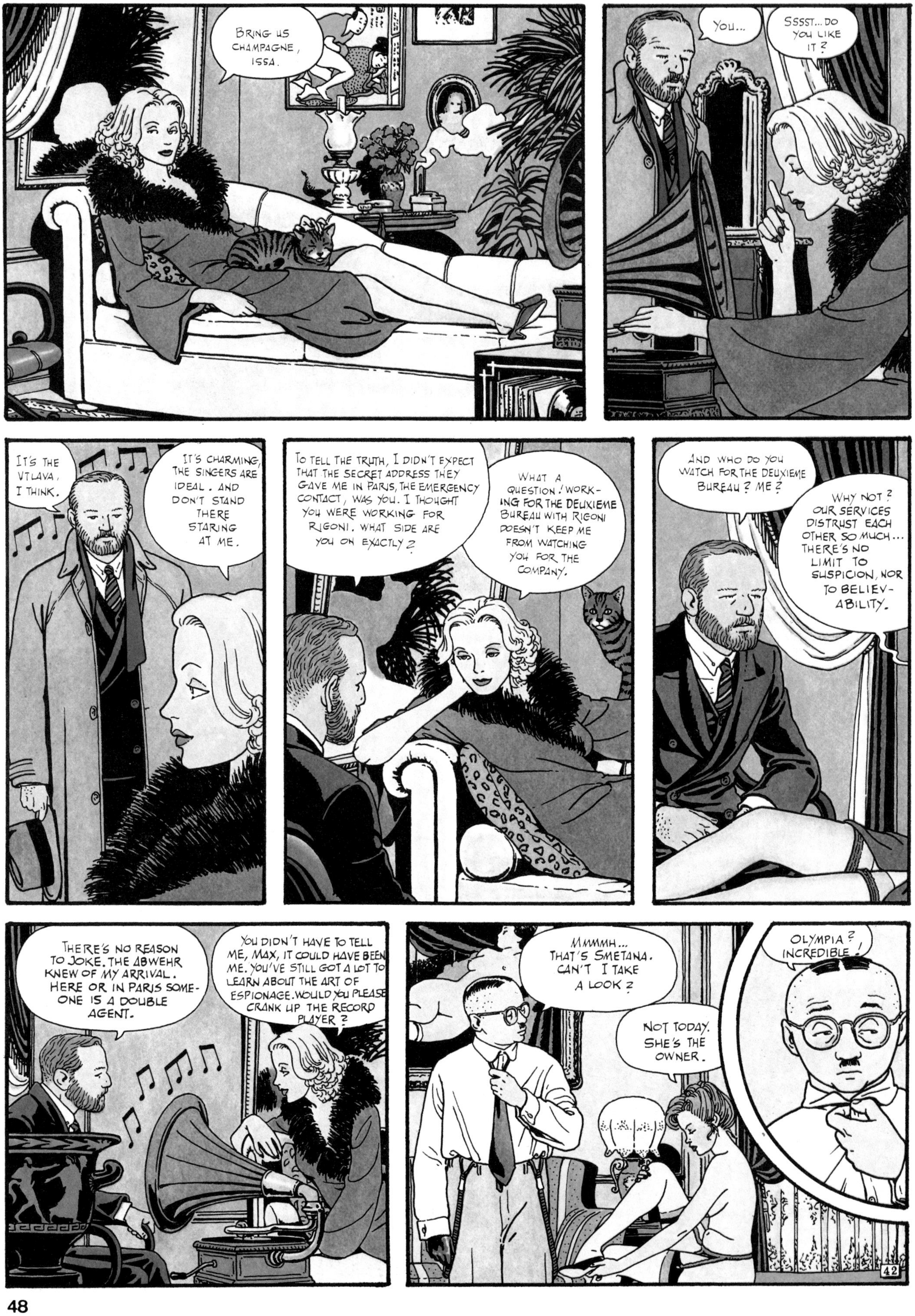
BRING US CHAMPAGNE, ISSA.
YOU...
SSSST... DO YOU LIKE IT?
IT'S THE VTLAVA, I THINK.
IT'S CHARMING, THE SINGERS ARE IDEAL. AND DON'T STAND THERE STARING AT ME.
TO TELL THE TRUTH, I DIDN'T EXPECT THAT THE SECRET ADDRESS THEY GAVE ME IN PARIS, THE EMERGENCY CONTACT, WAS YOU. I THOUGHT YOU WERE WORKING FOR RIGONI. WHAT SIDE ARE YOU ON EXACTLY?
WHAT A QUESTION! WORKING FOR THE DEUXIEME BUREAU WITH RIGONI DOESN'T KEEP ME FROM WATCHING YOU FOR THE COMPANY.
AND WHO DO YOU WATCH FOR THE DEUXIEME BUREAU? ME?
WHY NOT? OUR SERVICES DISTRUST EACH OTHER SO MUCH... THERE'S NO LIMIT TO SUSPICION, NOR TO BELIEVABILITY.
THERE'S NO REASON TO JOKE. THE ABWEHR KNEW OF MY ARRIVAL. HERE OR IN PARIS SOMEONE IS A DOUBLE AGENT.
YOU DIDN'T HAVE TO TELL ME, MAX, IT COULD HAVE BEEN ME. YOU'VE STILL GOT A LOT TO LEARN ABOUT THE ART OF ESPIONAGE. WOULD YOU PLEASE CRANK UP THE RECORD PLAYER?
MMMMH... THAT'S SMETANA. CAN'T I TAKE A LOOK?
NOT TODAY. SHE'S THE OWNER.
OLYMPIA? INCREDIBLE!
42

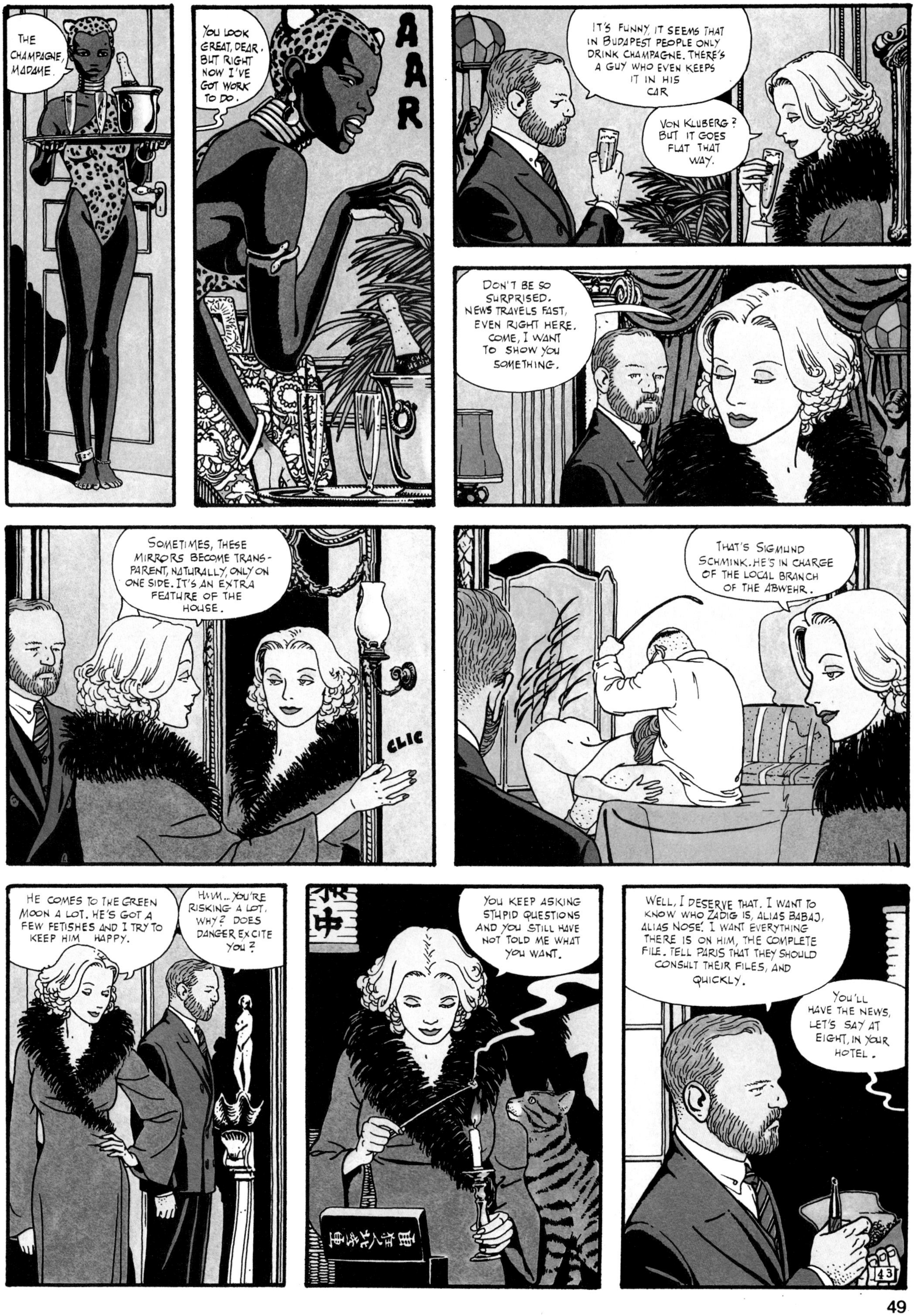
THE CHAMPAGNE, MADAME.
YOU LOOK GREAT, DEAR, BUT RIGHT NOW I'VE GOT WORK TO DO.
AAR
IT'S FUNNY, IT SEEMS THAT IN BUDAPEST PEOPLE ONLY DRINK CHAMPAGNE. THERE'S A GUY WHO EVEN KEEPS IT IN HIS CAR
VON KLUBERG? BUT IT GOES FLAT THAT WAY.
DON'T BE SO SURPRISED. NEWS TRAVELS FAST, EVEN RIGHT HERE. COME, I WANT TO SHOW YOU SOMETHING.
SOMETIMES, THESE MIRRORS BECOME TRANS-PARENT, NATURALLY, ONLY ON ONE SIDE. IT'S AN EXTRA FEATURE OF THE HOUSE.
CLIC
THAT'S SIGMUND SCHMINK. HE'S IN CHARGE OF THE LOCAL BRANCH OF THE ABWEHR.
HE COMES TO THE GREEN MOON A LOT. HE'S GOT A FEW FETISHES AND I TRY TO KEEP HIM HAPPY.
HMM.. YOU'RE RISKING A LOT. WHY? DOES DANGER EXCITE YOU?
YOU KEEP ASKING STUPID QUESTIONS AND YOU STILL HAVE NOT TOLD ME WHAT YOU WANT.
WELL, I DESERVE THAT. I WANT TO KNOW WHO ZADIG IS, ALIAS BABAJ, ALIAS NOSE. I WANT EVERYTHING THERE IS ON HIM, THE COMPLETE FILE. TELL PARIS THAT THEY SHOULD CONSULT THEIR FILES, AND QUICKLY.
YOU'LL HAVE THE NEWS, LET'S SAY AT EIGHT, IN YOUR HOTEL.
43

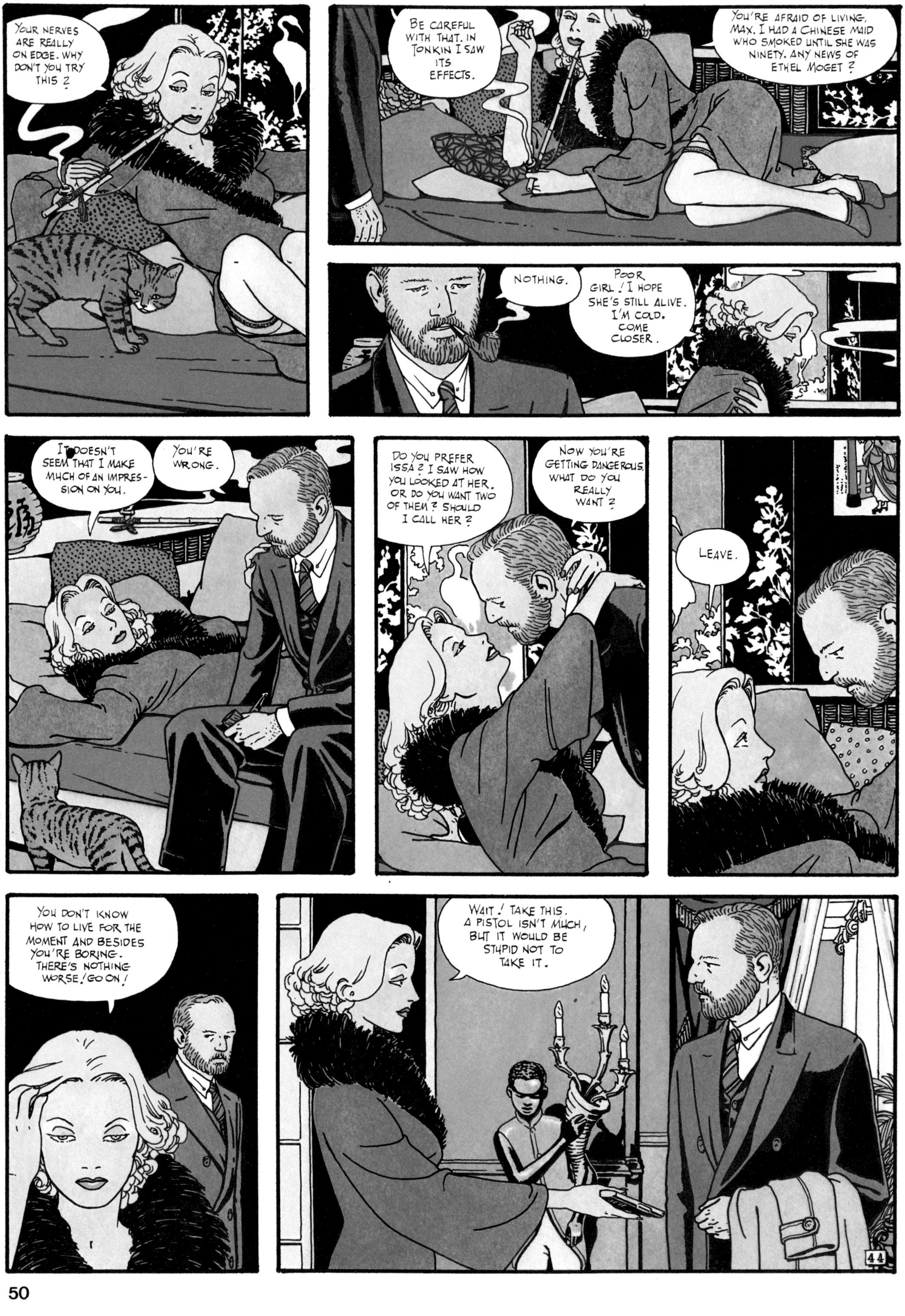
YOUR NERVES ARE REALLY ON EDGE. WHY DON'T YOU TRY THIS?
BE CAREFUL WITH THAT. IN TONKIN I SAW ITS EFFECTS.
YOU'RE AFRAID OF LIVING, MAX. I HAD A CHINESE MAID WHO SMOKED UNTIL SHE WAS NINETY. ANY NEWS OF ETHEL MOGET?
NOTHING.
POOR GIRL! I HOPE SHE'S STILL ALIVE. I'M COLD. COME CLOSER.
IT DOESN'T SEEM THAT I MAKE MUCH OF AN IMPRESSION ON YOU.
YOU'RE WRONG.
DO YOU PREFER ISSA? I SAW HOW YOU LOOKED AT HER. OR DO YOU WANT TWO OF THEM? SHOULD I CALL HER?
NOW YOU'RE GETTING DANGEROUS. WHAT DO YOU REALLY WANT?
LEAVE.
YOU DON'T KNOW HOW TO LIVE FOR THE MOMENT AND BESIDES YOU'RE BORING. THERE'S NOTHING WORSE! GO ON!
WAIT! TAKE THIS. A PISTOL ISN'T MUCH, BUT IT WOULD BE STUPID NOT TO TAKE IT.
44

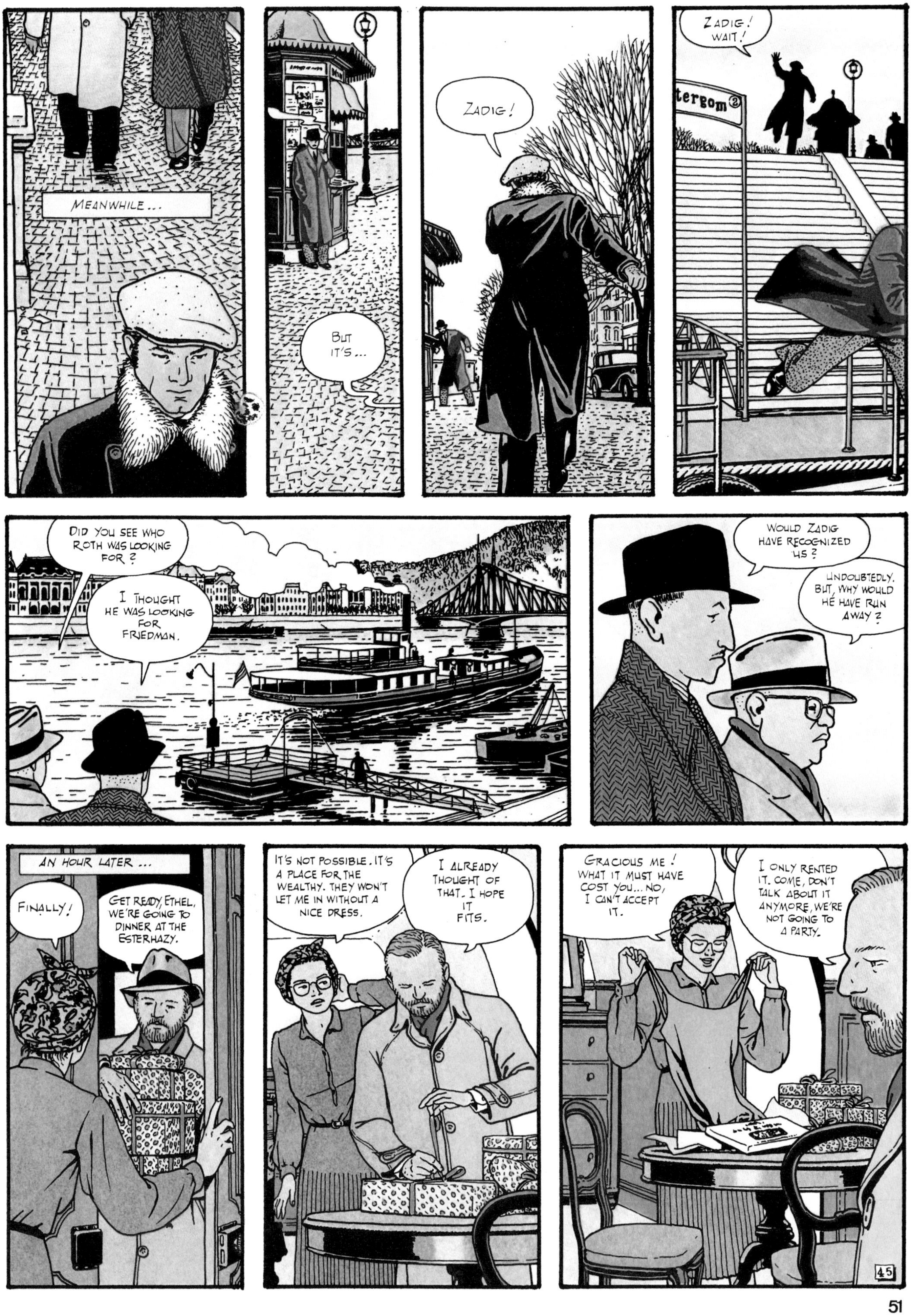
MEANWHILE...
BUT IT'S...
ZADIG!
ZADIG! WAIT!
tergom ②
DID YOU SEE WHO ROTH WAS LOOKING FOR?
I THOUGHT HE WAS LOOKING FOR FRIEDMAN.
WOULD ZADIG HAVE RECOGNIZED US?
UNDOUBTEDLY. BUT, WHY WOULD HE HAVE RUN AWAY?
AN HOUR LATER...
FINALLY!
GET READY, ETHEL, WE'RE GOING TO DINNER AT THE ESTERHAZY.
IT'S NOT POSSIBLE. IT'S A PLACE FOR THE WEALTHY. THEY WON'T LET ME IN WITHOUT A NICE DRESS.
I ALREADY THOUGHT OF THAT. I HOPE IT FITS.
GRACIOUS ME! WHAT IT MUST HAVE COST YOU... NO, I CAN'T ACCEPT IT.
I ONLY RENTED IT. COME, DON'T TALK ABOUT IT ANYMORE, WE'RE NOT GOING TO A PARTY.
45

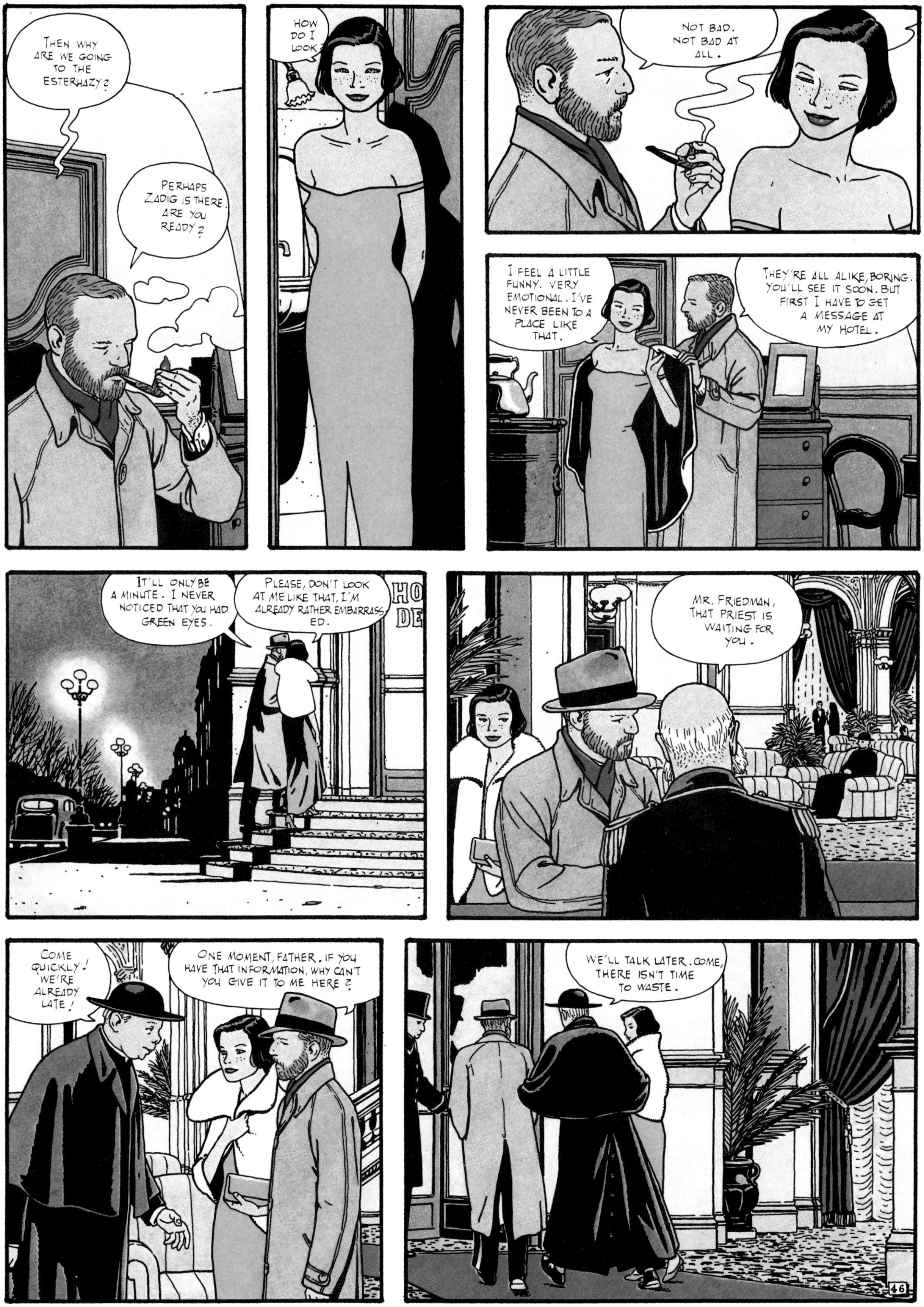
THEN WHY ARE WE GOING TO THE ESTERHAZY ?
PERHAPS ZADIG IS THERE. ARE YOU READY ?
HOW DO I LOOK ?
NOT BAD. NOT BAD AT ALL.
I FEEL A LITTLE FUNNY. VERY EMOTIONAL. I'VE NEVER BEEN TO A PLACE LIKE THAT.
THEY'RE ALL ALIKE, BORING. YOU'LL SEE IT SOON. BUT FIRST I HAVE TO GET A MESSAGE AT MY HOTEL.
IT'LL ONLY BE A MINUTE. I NEVER NOTICED THAT YOU HAD GREEN EYES.
PLEASE, DON'T LOOK AT ME LIKE THAT, I'M ALREADY RATHER EMBARRASS-ED.
MR. FRIEDMAN, THAT PRIEST IS WAITING FOR YOU.
COME QUICKLY ! WE'RE ALREADY LATE !
ONE MOMENT, FATHER. IF YOU HAVE THAT INFORMATION, WHY CAN'T YOU GIVE IT TO ME HERE ?
WE'LL TALK LATER. COME, THERE ISN'T TIME TO WASTE.
46

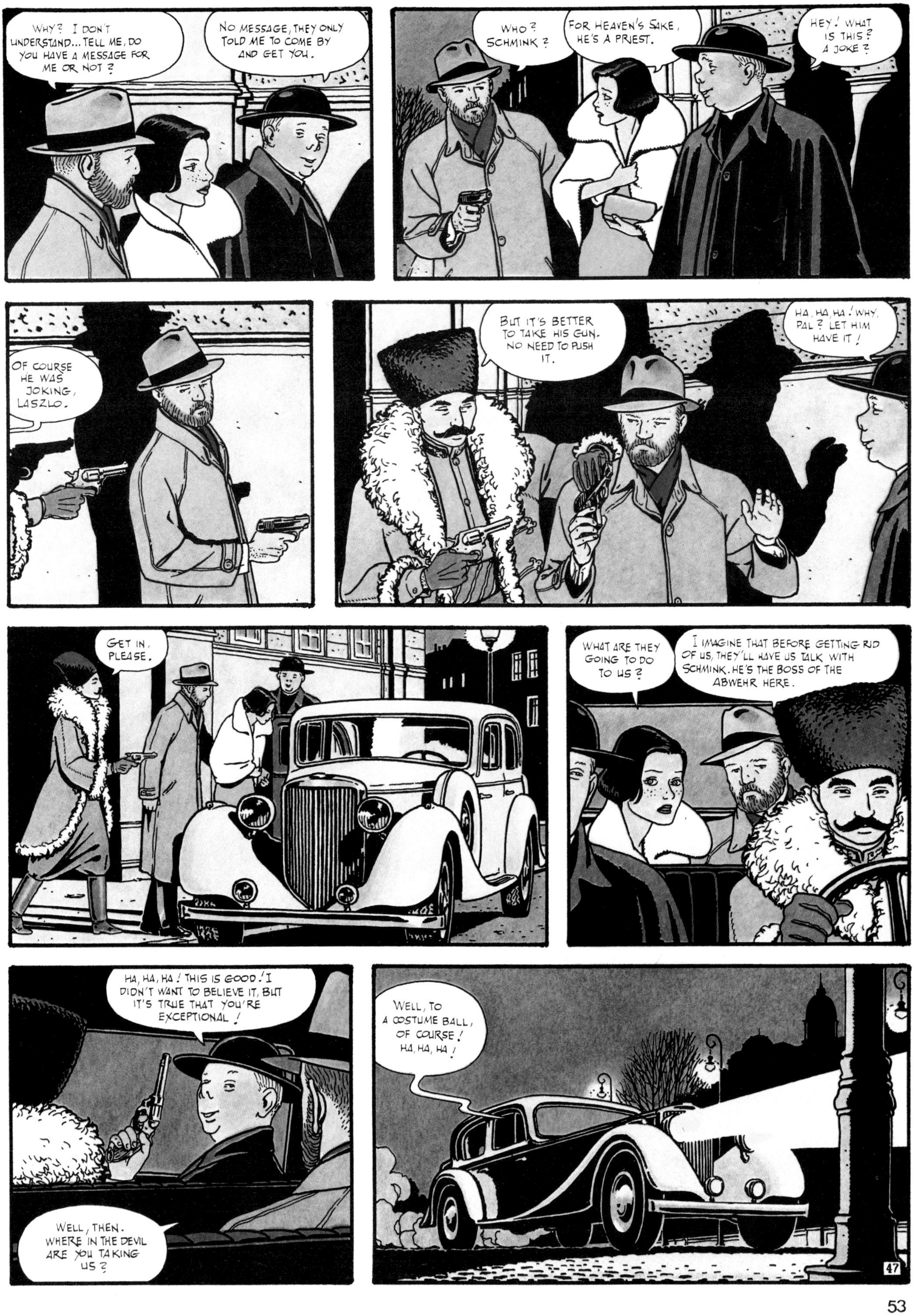
WHY? I DON'T UNDERSTAND... TELL ME, DO YOU HAVE A MESSAGE FOR ME OR NOT?
NO MESSAGE, THEY ONLY TOLD ME TO COME BY AND GET YOU.
WHO? SCHMINK?
FOR HEAVEN'S SAKE, HE'S A PRIEST.
HEY! WHAT IS THIS? A JOKE?
OF COURSE HE WAS JOKING, LASZLO.
BUT IT'S BETTER TO TAKE HIS GUN. NO NEED TO PUSH IT.
HA, HA, HA! WHY, PAL? LET HIM HAVE IT!
GET IN, PLEASE.
WHAT ARE THEY GOING TO DO TO US?
I IMAGINE THAT BEFORE GETTING RID OF US, THEY'LL HAVE US TALK WITH SCHMINK. HE'S THE BOSS OF THE ABWEHR HERE.
HA, HA, HA! THIS IS GOOD! I DIDN'T WANT TO BELIEVE IT, BUT IT'S TRUE THAT YOU'RE EXCEPTIONAL!
WELL, THEN. WHERE IN THE DEVIL ARE YOU TAKING US?
WELL, TO A COSTUME BALL, OF COURSE! HA, HA, HA!
47

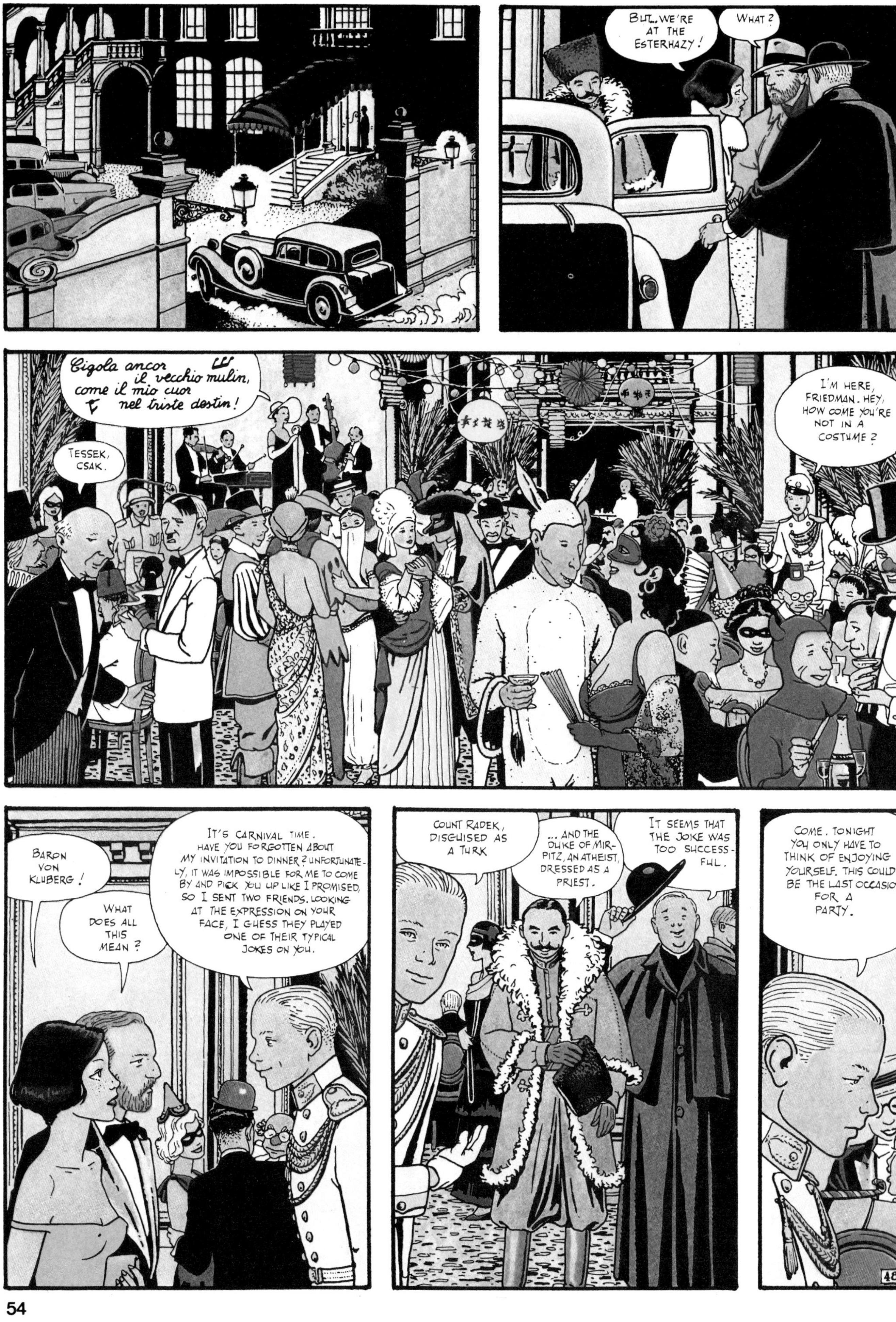
BUT... WE'RE AT THE ESTERHAZY!
WHAT?
Cigola ancor il vecchio mulin, come il mio cuor nel triste destin!
TESSEK, CSAK.
I'M HERE, FRIEDMAN. HEY, HOW COME YOU'RE NOT IN A COSTUME?
BARON VON KLUBERG!
WHAT DOES ALL THIS MEAN?
IT'S CARNIVAL TIME. HAVE YOU FORGOTTEN ABOUT MY INVITATION TO DINNER? UNFORTUNATE-LY, IT WAS IMPOSSIBLE FOR ME TO COME BY AND PICK YOU UP LIKE I PROMISED, SO I SENT TWO FRIENDS. LOOKING AT THE EXPRESSION ON YOUR FACE, I GUESS THEY PLAYED ONE OF THEIR TYPICAL JOKES ON YOU.
COUNT RADEK, DISGUISED AS A TURK
... AND THE DUKE OF MIR-PITZ, AN ATHEIST, DRESSED AS A PRIEST.
IT SEEMS THAT THE JOKE WAS TOO SUCCESS-FUL.
COME. TONIGHT YOU ONLY HAVE TO THINK OF ENJOYING YOURSELF. THIS COULD BE THE LAST OCCASION FOR A PARTY.
48

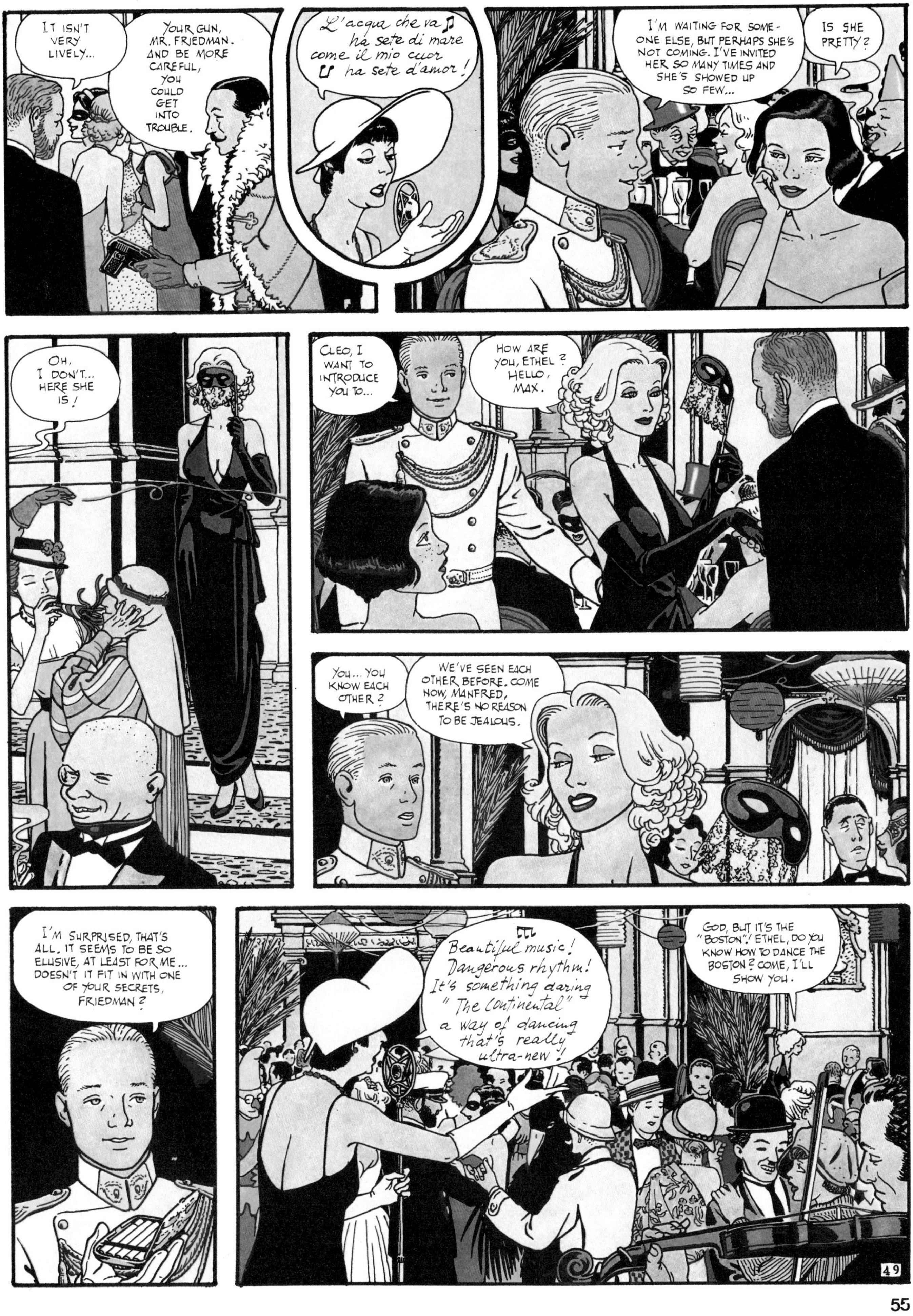

IT ISN'T VERY LIVELY...
YOUR GUN, MR. FRIEDMAN. AND BE MORE CAREFUL, YOU COULD GET INTO TROUBLE.
L'acqua che va ha sete di mare come il mio cuor ha sete d'amor!
I'M WAITING FOR SOME-ONE ELSE, BUT PERHAPS SHE'S NOT COMING. I'VE INVITED HER SO MANY TIMES AND SHE'S SHOWED UP SO FEW...
IS SHE PRETTY?
OH, I DON'T... HERE SHE IS!
CLEO, I WANT TO INTRODUCE YOU TO...
HOW ARE YOU, ETHEL? HELLO, MAX.
YOU... YOU KNOW EACH OTHER?
WE'VE SEEN EACH OTHER BEFORE. COME NOW, MANFRED, THERE'S NO REASON TO BE JEALOUS.
I'M SURPRISED, THAT'S ALL. IT SEEMS TO BE SO ELUSIVE, AT LEAST FOR ME... DOESN'T IT FIT IN WITH ONE OF YOUR SECRETS, FRIEDMAN?
Beautiful music! Dangerous rhythm! It's something daring "The Continental" a way of dancing that's really ultra-new!
GOD, BUT IT'S THE "BOSTON"! ETHEL, DO YOU KNOW HOW TO DANCE THE BOSTON? COME, I'LL SHOW YOU.
49

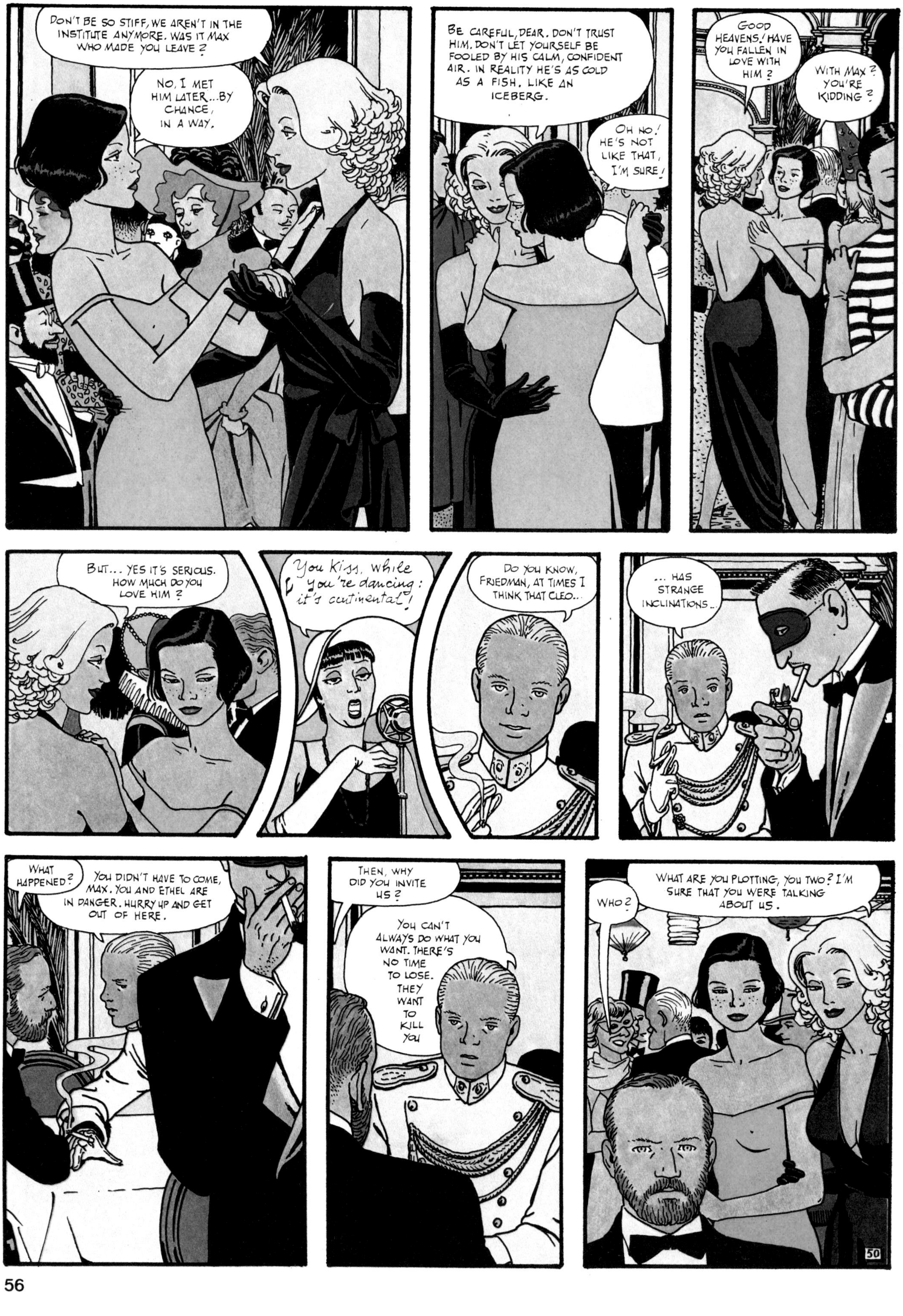

DON'T BE SO STIFF, WE AREN'T IN THE INSTITUTE ANYMORE. WAS IT MAX WHO MADE YOU LEAVE?
NO, I MET HIM LATER...BY CHANCE, IN A WAY.
BE CAREFUL, DEAR. DON'T TRUST HIM. DON'T LET YOURSELF BE FOOLED BY HIS CALM, CONFIDENT AIR. IN REALITY HE'S AS COLD AS A FISH. LIKE AN ICEBERG.
OH NO! HE'S NOT LIKE THAT, I'M SURE!
GOOD HEAVENS! HAVE YOU FALLEN IN LOVE WITH HIM?
WITH MAX? YOU'RE KIDDING?
BUT... YES IT'S SERIOUS. HOW MUCH DO YOU LOVE HIM?
You kiss, while you're dancing: it's continental!
DO YOU KNOW, FRIEDMAN, AT TIMES I THINK THAT CLEO...
... HAS STRANGE INCLINATIONS...
WHAT HAPPENED?
YOU DIDN'T HAVE TO COME, MAX. YOU AND ETHEL ARE IN DANGER. HURRY UP AND GET OUT OF HERE.
THEN, WHY DID YOU INVITE US?
YOU CAN'T ALWAYS DO WHAT YOU WANT. THERE'S NO TIME TO LOSE. THEY WANT TO KILL YOU
WHO?
WHAT ARE YOU PLOTTING, YOU TWO? I'M SURE THAT YOU WERE TALKING ABOUT US.
50

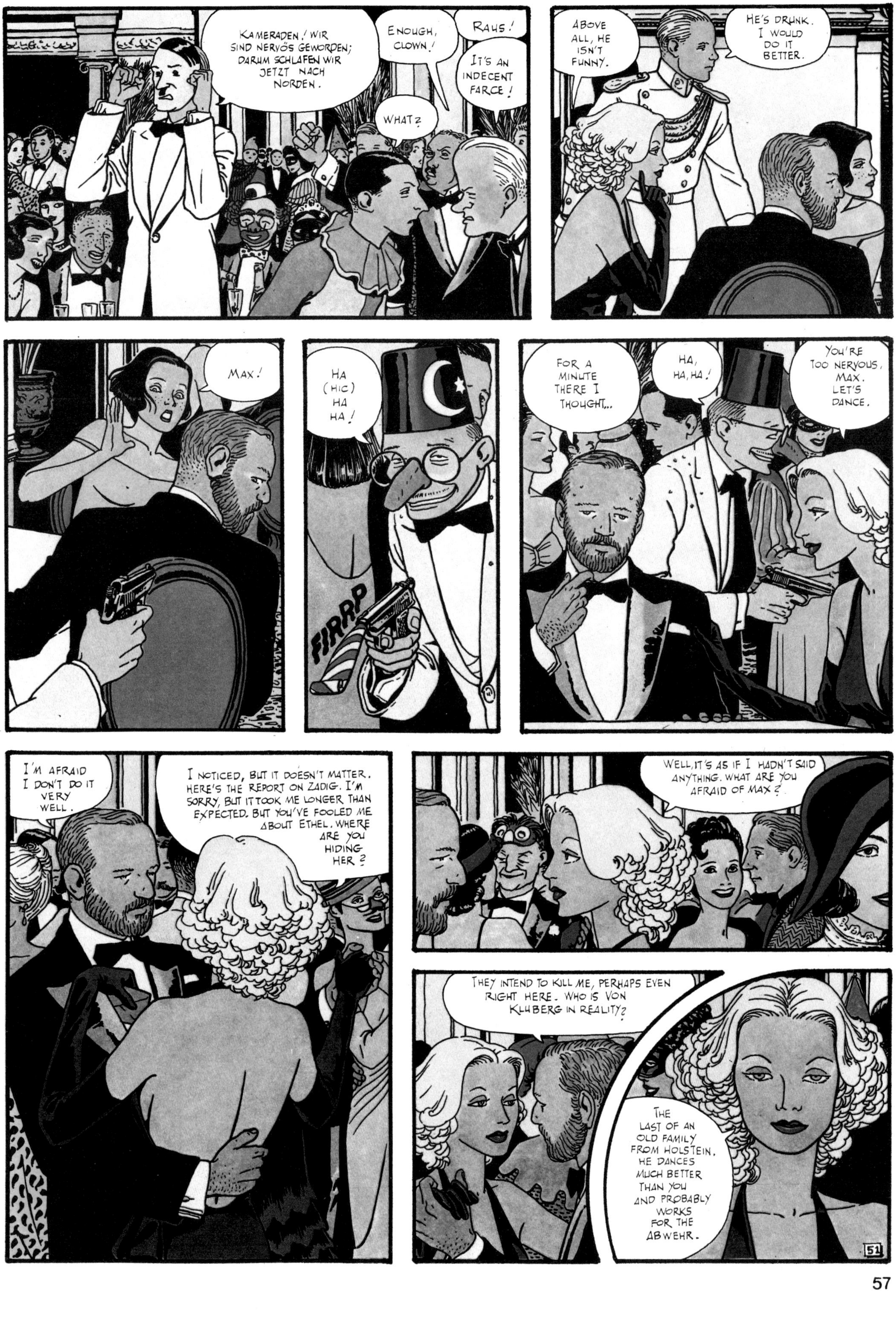
KAMERADEN! WIR SIND NERVÖS GEWORDEN; DARUM SCHLAFEN WIR JETZT NACH NORDEN.
ENOUGH, CLOWN!
RAUS!
IT'S AN INDECENT FARCE!
WHAT?
ABOVE ALL, HE ISN'T FUNNY.
HE'S DRUNK. I WOULD DO IT BETTER.
MAX!
HA (HIC) HA HA!
FIRRP
FOR A MINUTE THERE I THOUGHT...
HA, HA, HA!
YOU'RE TOO NERVOUS, MAX. LET'S DANCE.
I'M AFRAID I DON'T DO IT VERY WELL.
I NOTICED, BUT IT DOESN'T MATTER. HERE'S THE REPORT ON ZADIG. I'M SORRY, BUT IT TOOK ME LONGER THAN EXPECTED. BUT YOU'VE FOOLED ME ABOUT ETHEL. WHERE ARE YOU HIDING HER?
WELL, IT'S AS IF I HADN'T SAID ANYTHING. WHAT ARE YOU AFRAID OF MAX?
THEY INTEND TO KILL ME, PERHAPS EVEN RIGHT HERE. WHO IS VON KLUBERG IN REALITY?
THE LAST OF AN OLD FAMILY FROM HOLSTEIN. HE DANCES MUCH BETTER THAN YOU AND PROBABLY WORKS FOR THE ABWEHR.
51

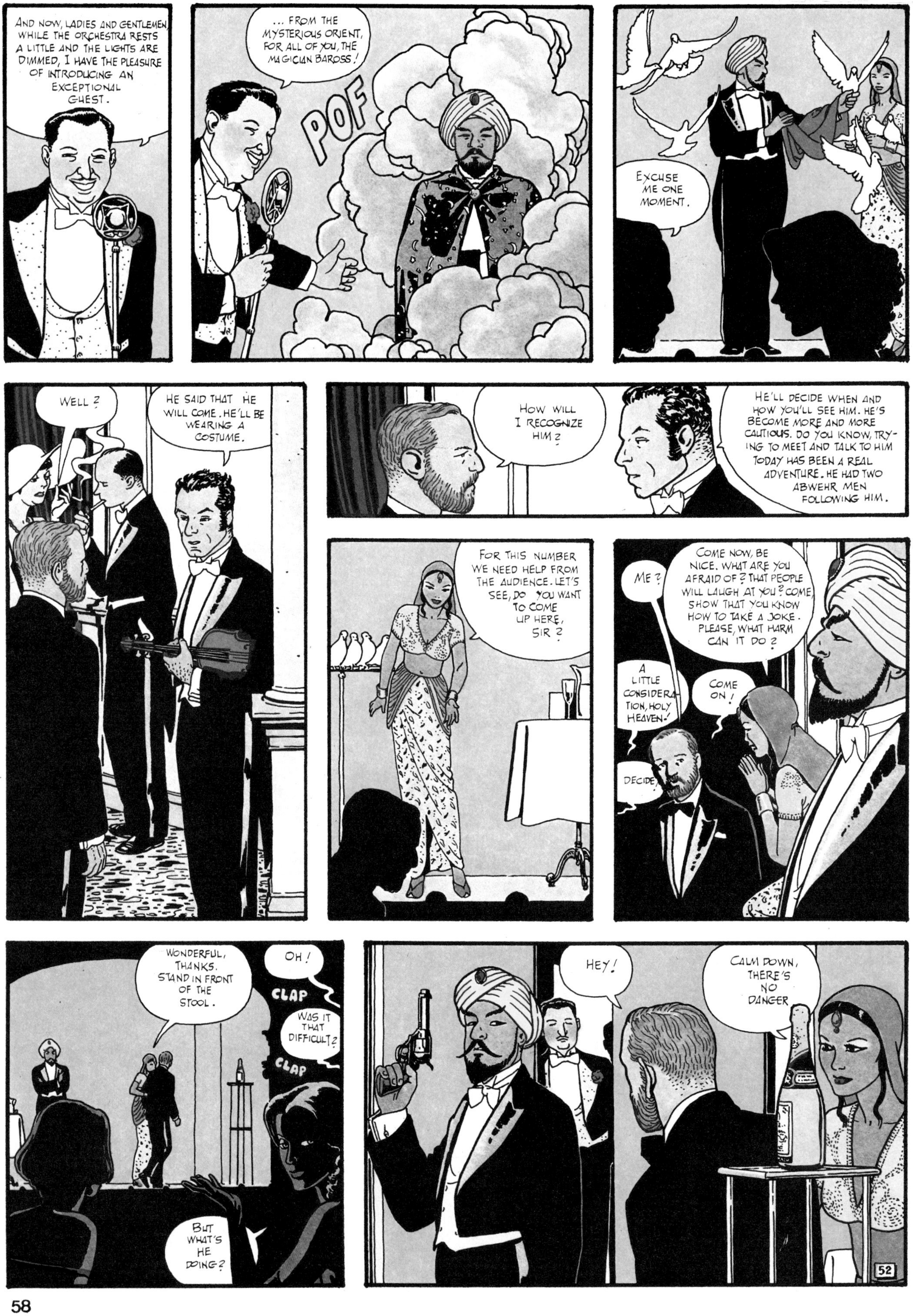

AND NOW, LADIES AND GENTLEMEN, WHILE THE ORCHESTRA RESTS A LITTLE AND THE LIGHTS ARE DIMMED, I HAVE THE PLEASURE OF INTRODUCING AN EXCEPTIONAL GUEST.
... FROM THE MYSTERIOUS ORIENT, FOR ALL OF YOU, THE MAGICIAN BAROSS!
POF
EXCUSE ME ONE MOMENT.
WELL?
HE SAID THAT HE WILL COME. HE'LL BE WEARING A COSTUME.
HOW WILL I RECOGNIZE HIM?
HE'LL DECIDE WHEN AND HOW YOU'LL SEE HIM. HE'S BECOME MORE AND MORE CAUTIOUS. DO YOU KNOW, TRYING TO MEET AND TALK TO HIM TODAY HAS BEEN A REAL ADVENTURE. HE HAD TWO ABWEHR MEN FOLLOWING HIM.
FOR THIS NUMBER WE NEED HELP FROM THE AUDIENCE. LET'S SEE, DO YOU WANT TO COME UP HERE, SIR?
ME?
COME NOW, BE NICE. WHAT ARE YOU AFRAID OF? THAT PEOPLE WILL LAUGH AT YOU? COME, SHOW THAT YOU KNOW HOW TO TAKE A JOKE. PLEASE, WHAT HARM CAN IT DO?
A LITTLE CONSIDERATION, HOLY HEAVEN!
COME ON!
DECIDE!
WONDERFUL, THANKS. STAND IN FRONT OF THE STOOL.
OH!
CLAP
WAS IT THAT DIFFICULT?
CLAP
BUT WHAT'S HE DOING?
HEY!
CALM DOWN, THERE'S NO DANGER
52

PANG

OOOH!

BRAVO!

CLAP CLAP CLAP CLAP CLAP CLAP

AAAH!

LUCI! LUCI!

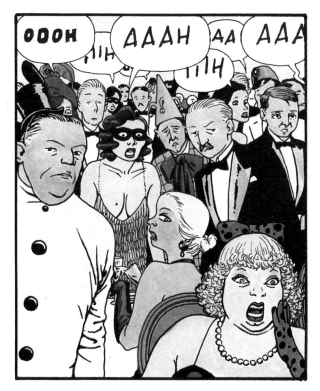

OOOH AAAH AA AAA IIIH IIIH

MAX!

LET'S FIND THE SERVICE EXIT.

QUICKLY! AND THIS TIME DON'T MISS!

53

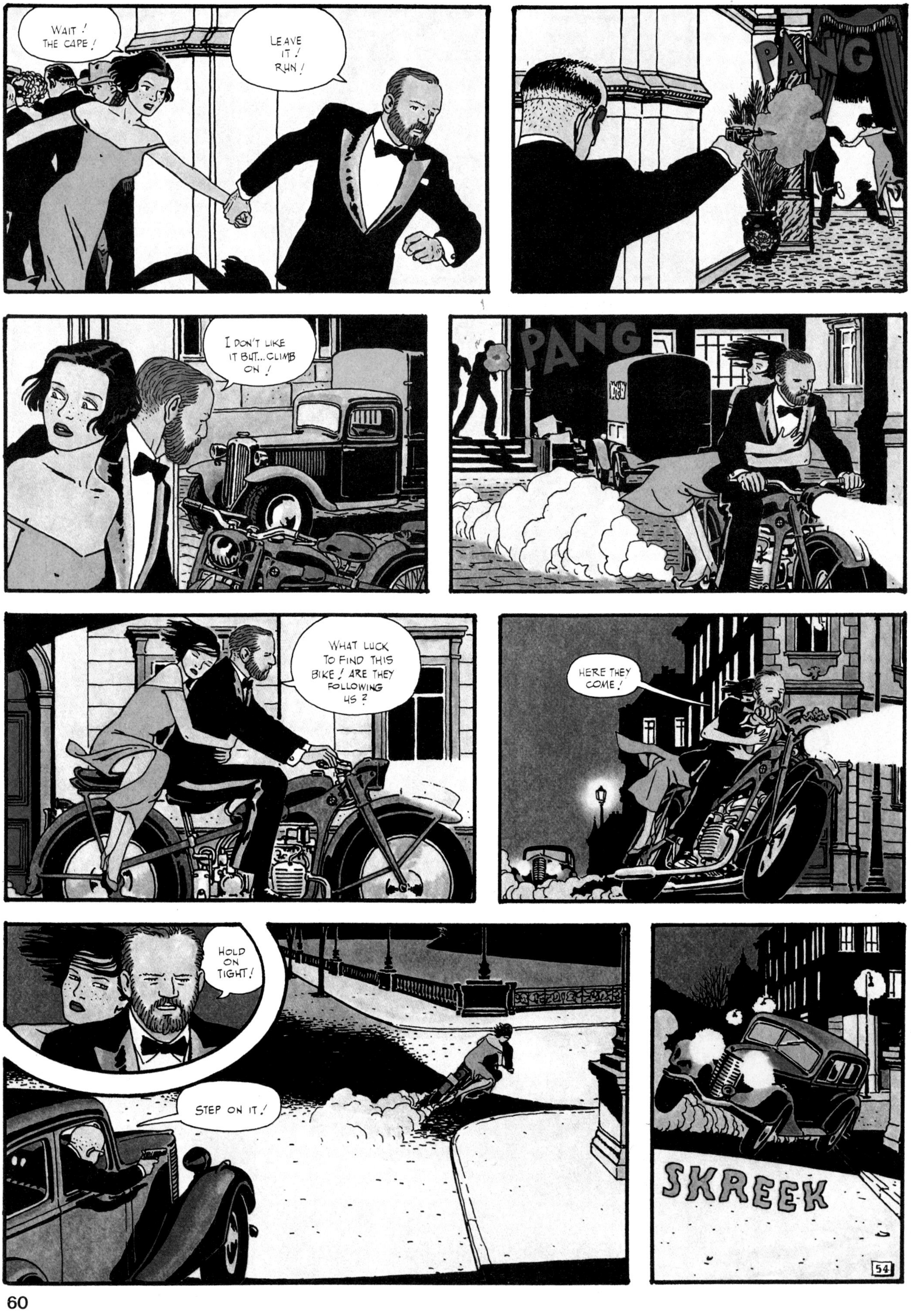
WAIT ! THE CAPE !
LEAVE IT ! RUN !
PANG
I DON'T LIKE IT BUT... CLIMB ON !
PANG
WHAT LUCK TO FIND THIS BIKE ! ARE THEY FOLLOWING US ?
HERE THEY COME !
HOLD ON TIGHT !
STEP ON IT !
SKREEK
54

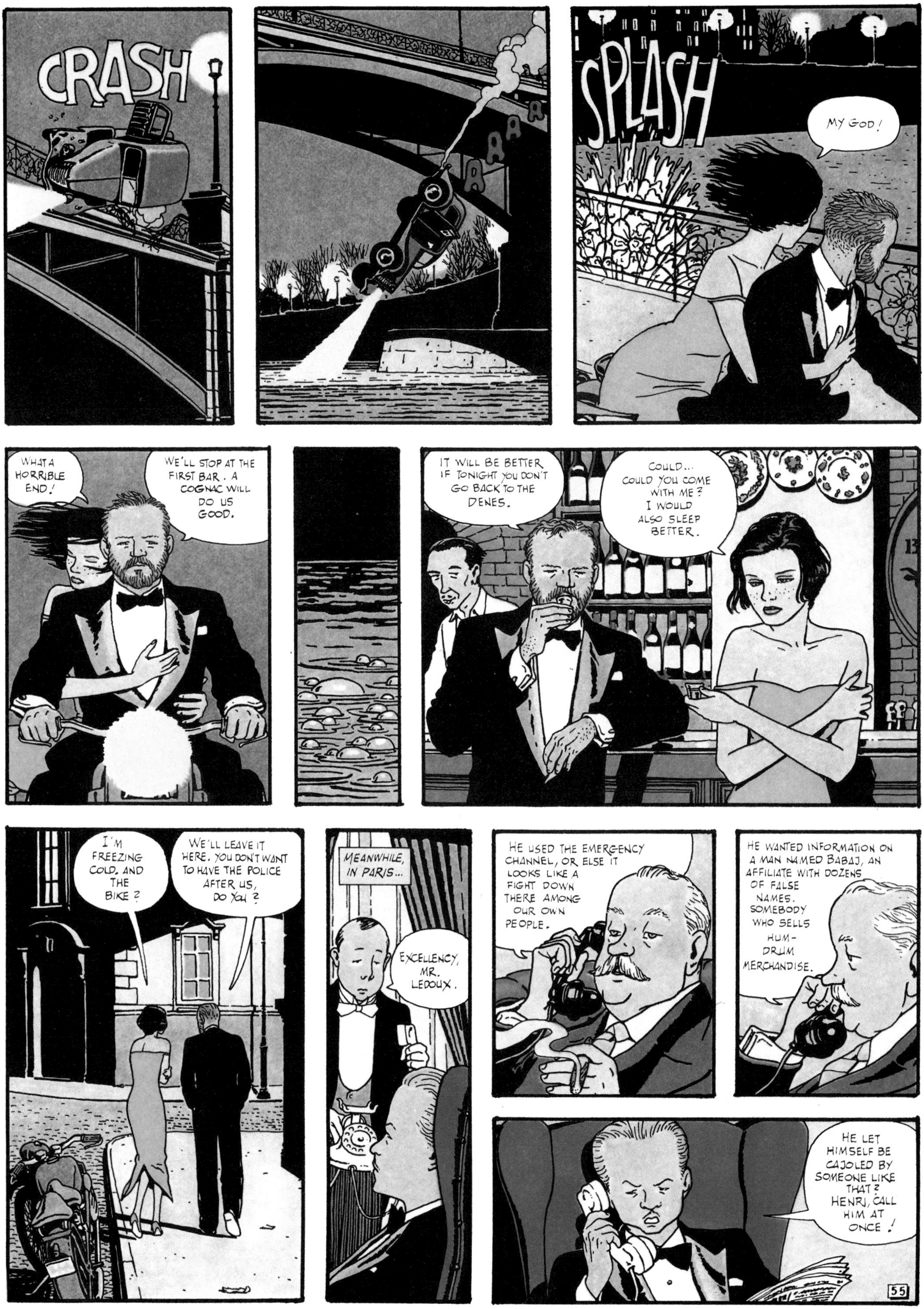
CRASH
SPLASH
MY GOD!
WHAT A HORRIBLE END!
WE'LL STOP AT THE FIRST BAR. A COGNAC WILL DO US GOOD.
IT WILL BE BETTER IF TONIGHT YOU DON'T GO BACK TO THE DENES.
COULD... COULD YOU COME WITH ME? I WOULD ALSO SLEEP BETTER.
I'M FREEZING COLD. AND THE BIKE?
WE'LL LEAVE IT HERE. YOU DON'T WANT TO HAVE THE POLICE AFTER US, DO YOU?
MEANWHILE, IN PARIS...
EXCELLENCY, MR. LEDOUX.
HE USED THE EMERGENCY CHANNEL, OR ELSE IT LOOKS LIKE A FIGHT DOWN THERE AMONG OUR OWN PEOPLE.
HE WANTED INFORMATION ON A MAN NAMED BABAJ, AN AFFILIATE WITH DOZENS OF FALSE NAMES. SOMEBODY WHO SELLS HUM-DRUM MERCHANDISE.
HE LET HIMSELF BE CAJOLED BY SOMEONE LIKE THAT? HENRI, CALL HIM AT ONCE!
55

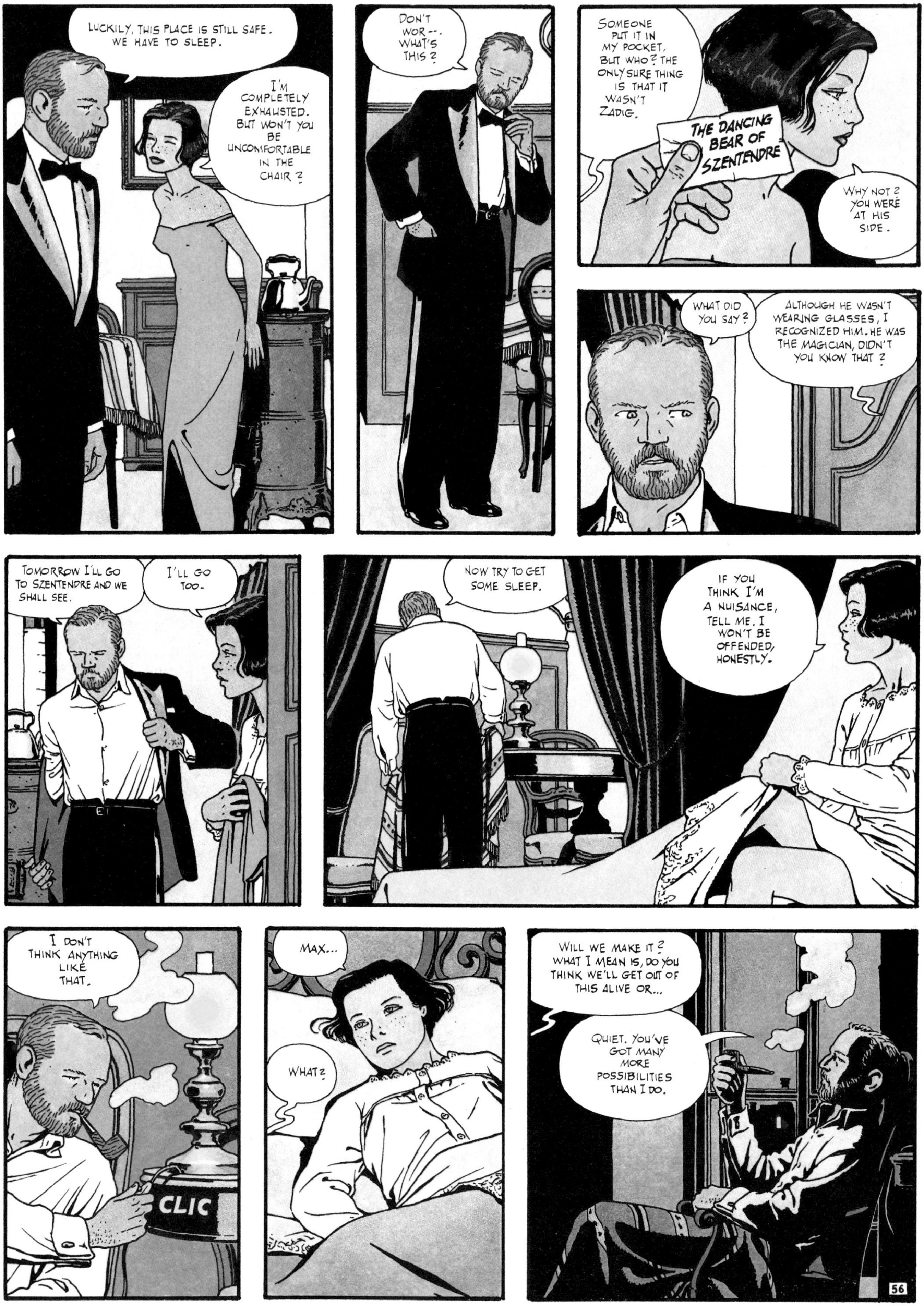
LUCKILY, THIS PLACE IS STILL SAFE. WE HAVE TO SLEEP.
I'M COMPLETELY EXHAUSTED. BUT WON'T YOU BE UNCOMFORTABLE IN THE CHAIR?
DON'T WOR--. WHAT'S THIS?
SOMEONE PUT IT IN MY POCKET, BUT WHO? THE ONLY SURE THING IS THAT IT WASN'T ZADIG.
THE DANCING BEAR OF SZENTENDRE
WHY NOT? YOU WERE AT HIS SIDE.
WHAT DID YOU SAY?
ALTHOUGH HE WASN'T WEARING GLASSES, I RECOGNIZED HIM. HE WAS THE MAGICIAN, DIDN'T YOU KNOW THAT?
TOMORROW I'LL GO TO SZENTENDRE AND WE SHALL SEE.
I'LL GO TOO.
NOW TRY TO GET SOME SLEEP.
IF YOU THINK I'M A NUISANCE, TELL ME. I WON'T BE OFFENDED, HONESTLY.
I DON'T THINK ANYTHING LIKE THAT.
CLIC
MAX...
WHAT?
WILL WE MAKE IT? WHAT I MEAN IS, DO YOU THINK WE'LL GET OUT OF THIS ALIVE OR...
QUIET. YOU'VE GOT MANY MORE POSSIBILITIES THAN I DO.
56

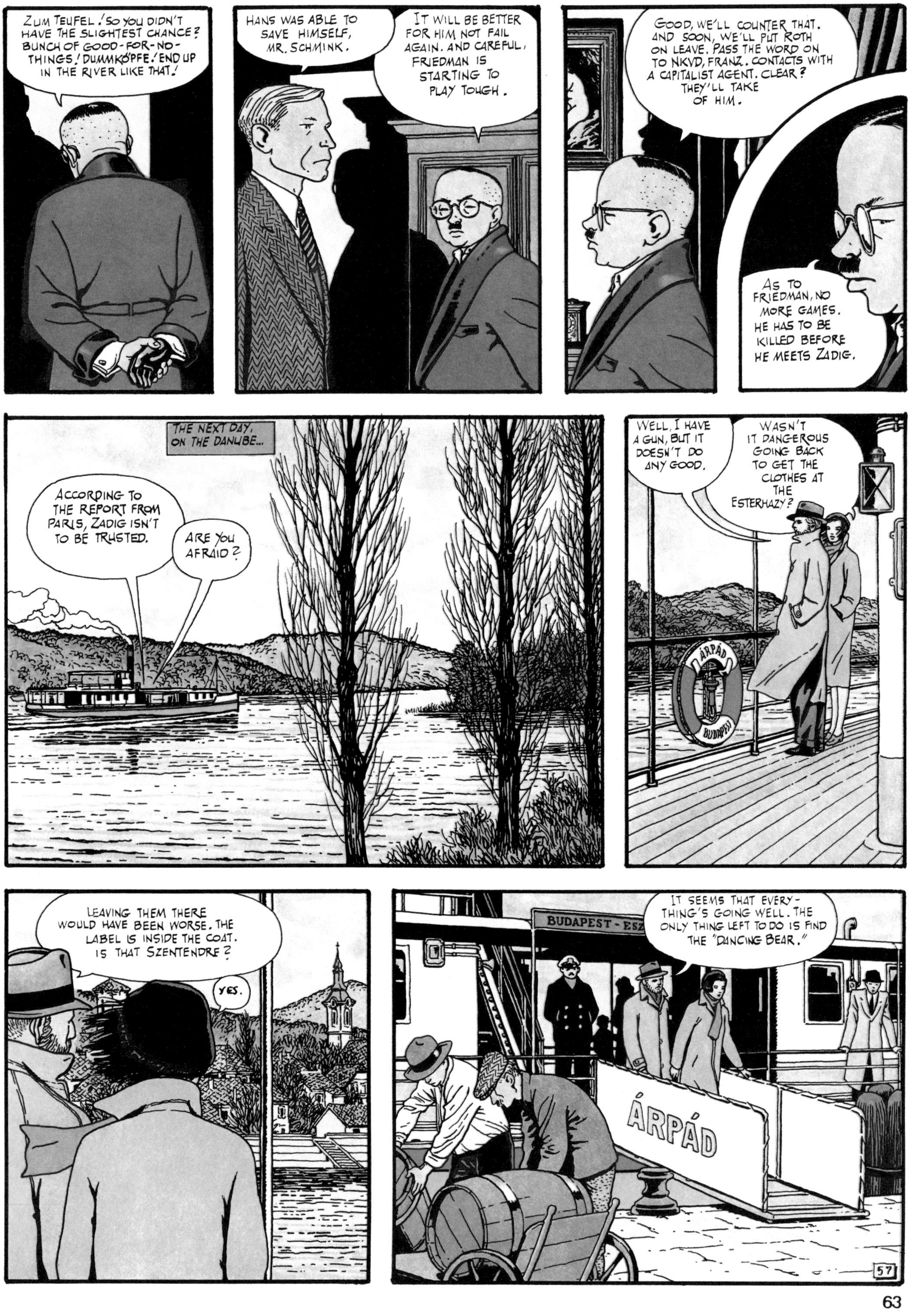
ZUM TEUFEL! SO YOU DIDN'T HAVE THE SLIGHTEST CHANCE? BUNCH OF GOOD-FOR-NO-THINGS! DUMMKÖPFE! END UP IN THE RIVER LIKE THAT!
HANS WAS ABLE TO SAVE HIMSELF, MR. SCHMINK.
IT WILL BE BETTER FOR HIM NOT FAIL AGAIN. AND CAREFUL, FRIEDMAN IS STARTING TO PLAY TOUGH.
GOOD, WE'LL COUNTER THAT. AND SOON, WE'LL PUT ROTH ON LEAVE. PASS THE WORD ON TO NKVD, FRANZ. CONTACTS WITH A CAPITALIST AGENT. CLEAR? THEY'LL TAKE OF HIM.
AS TO FRIEDMAN, NO MORE GAMES. HE HAS TO BE KILLED BEFORE HE MEETS ZADIG.
THE NEXT DAY, ON THE DANUBE...
ACCORDING TO THE REPORT FROM PARIS, ZADIG ISN'T TO BE TRUSTED.
ARE YOU AFRAID?
WELL, I HAVE A GUN, BUT IT DOESN'T DO ANY GOOD.
WASN'T IT DANGEROUS GOING BACK TO GET THE CLOTHES AT THE ESTERHAZY?
ÁRPÁD
BUDAPEST
LEAVING THEM THERE WOULD HAVE BEEN WORSE. THE LABEL IS INSIDE THE COAT. IS THAT SZENTENDRE?
YES.
BUDAPEST - ESZ
IT SEEMS THAT EVERY-THING'S GOING WELL. THE ONLY THING LEFT TO DO IS FIND THE "DANCING BEAR."
ÁRPÁD
57

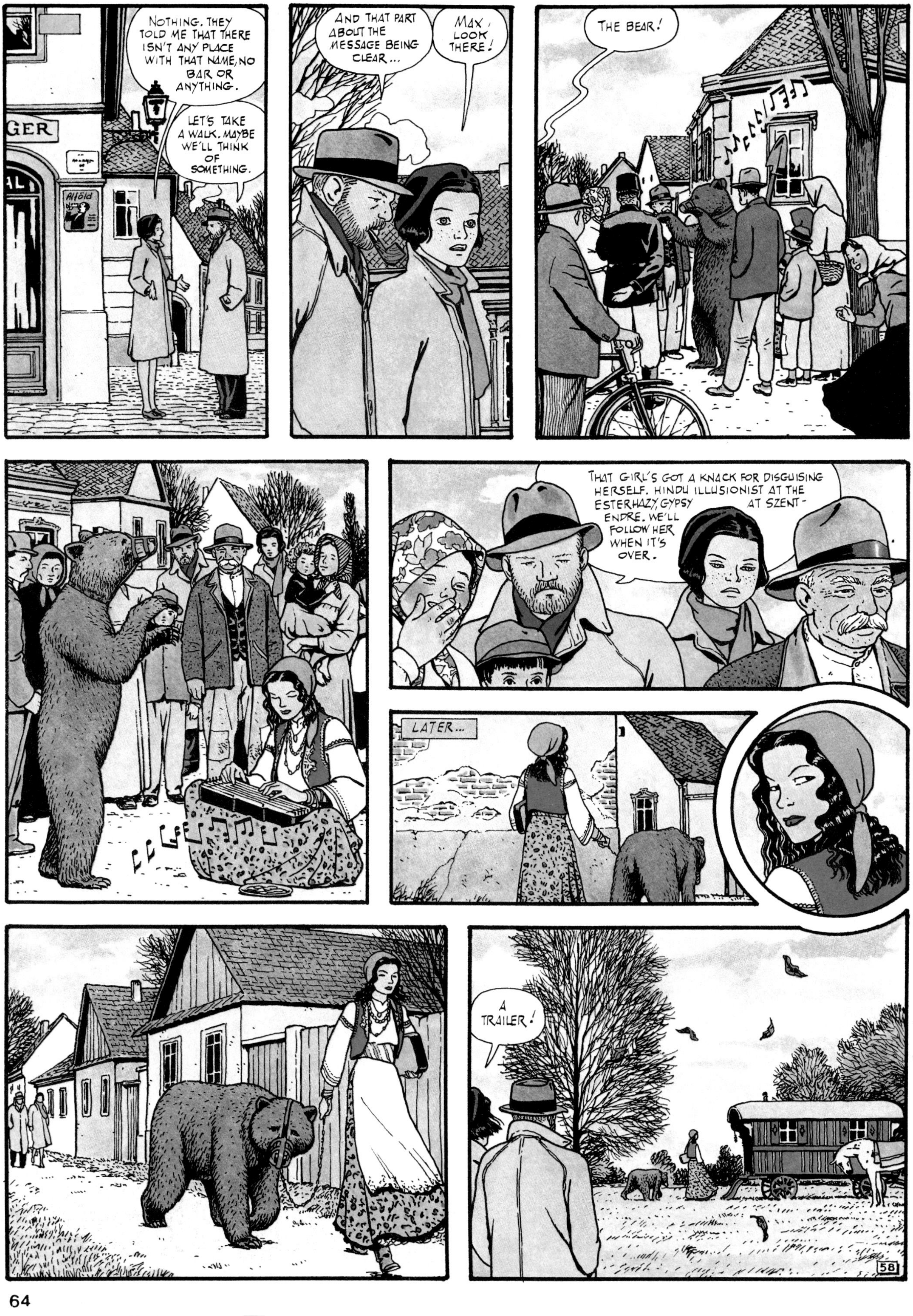

NOTHING. THEY TOLD ME THAT THERE ISN'T ANY PLACE WITH THAT NAME, NO BAR OR ANYTHING.
LET'S TAKE A WALK. MAYBE WE'LL THINK OF SOMETHING.
GER
AND THAT PART ABOUT THE MESSAGE BEING CLEAR...
MAX, LOOK THERE!
THE BEAR!
THAT GIRL'S GOT A KNACK FOR DISGUISING HERSELF. HINDU ILLUSIONIST AT THE ESTERHAZY, GYPSY AT SZENT-ENDRE. WE'LL FOLLOW HER WHEN IT'S OVER.
LATER...
A TRAILER!
58

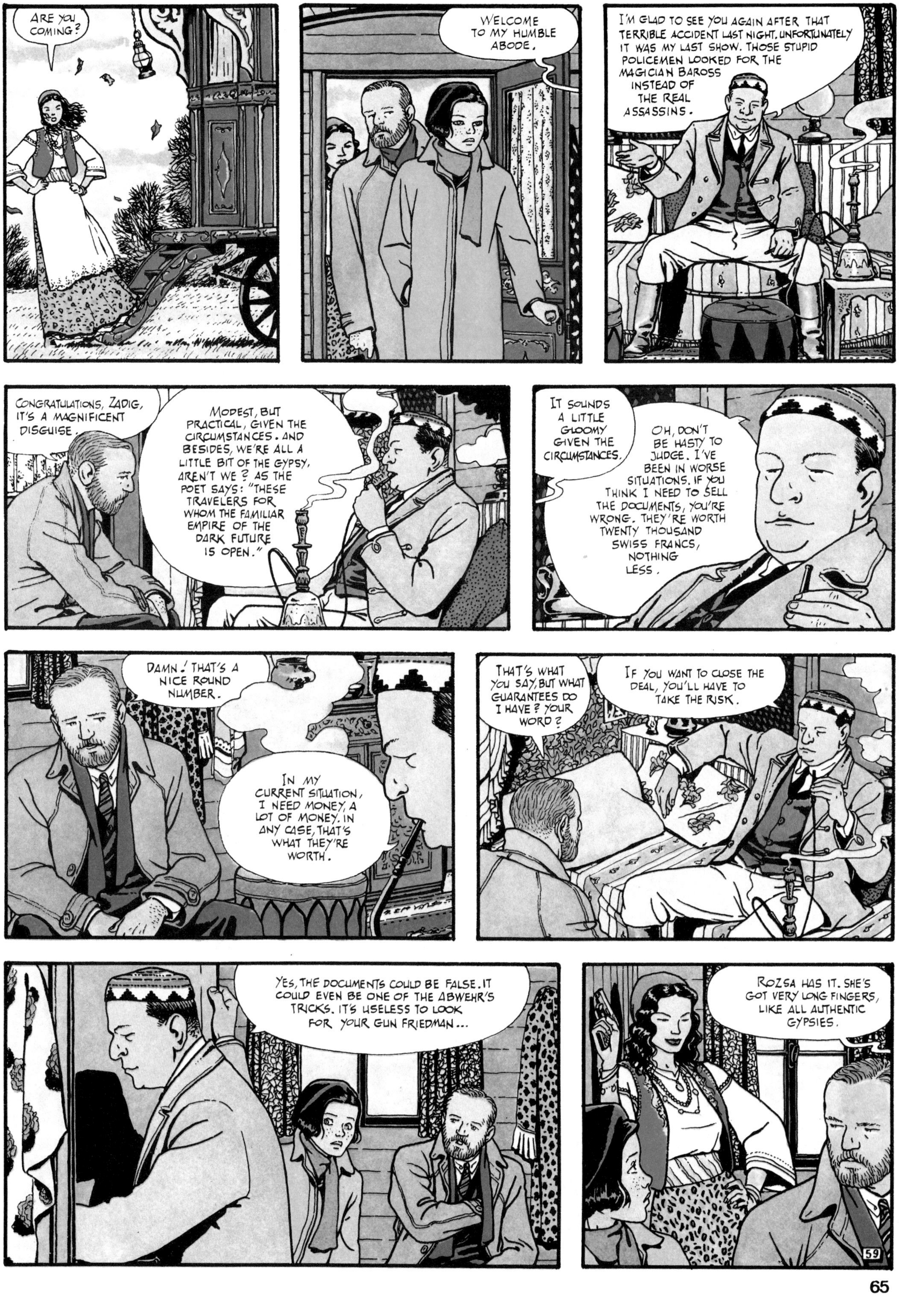
ARE YOU COMING?
WELCOME TO MY HUMBLE ABODE.
I'M GLAD TO SEE YOU AGAIN AFTER THAT TERRIBLE ACCIDENT LAST NIGHT. UNFORTUNATELY IT WAS MY LAST SHOW. THOSE STUPID POLICEMEN LOOKED FOR THE MAGICIAN BAROSS INSTEAD OF THE REAL ASSASSINS.
CONGRATULATIONS, ZADIG, IT'S A MAGNIFICENT DISGUISE.
MODEST, BUT PRACTICAL, GIVEN THE CIRCUMSTANCES. AND BESIDES, WE'RE ALL A LITTLE BIT OF THE GYPSY, AREN'T WE? AS THE POET SAYS: "THESE TRAVELERS FOR WHOM THE FAMILIAR EMPIRE OF THE DARK FUTURE IS OPEN."
IT SOUNDS A LITTLE GLOOMY GIVEN THE CIRCUMSTANCES.
OH, DON'T BE HASTY TO JUDGE. I'VE BEEN IN WORSE SITUATIONS. IF YOU THINK I NEED TO SELL THE DOCUMENTS, YOU'RE WRONG. THEY'RE WORTH TWENTY THOUSAND SWISS FRANCS, NOTHING LESS.
DAMN! THAT'S A NICE ROUND NUMBER.
IN MY CURRENT SITUATION, I NEED MONEY, A LOT OF MONEY. IN ANY CASE, THAT'S WHAT THEY'RE WORTH.
THAT'S WHAT YOU SAY, BUT WHAT GUARANTEES DO I HAVE? YOUR WORD?
IF YOU WANT TO CLOSE THE DEAL, YOU'LL HAVE TO TAKE THE RISK.
YES, THE DOCUMENTS COULD BE FALSE. IT COULD EVEN BE ONE OF THE ABWEHR'S TRICKS. IT'S USELESS TO LOOK FOR YOUR GUN FRIEDMAN...
ROZSA HAS IT. SHE'S GOT VERY LONG FINGERS, LIKE ALL AUTHENTIC GYPSIES.
59

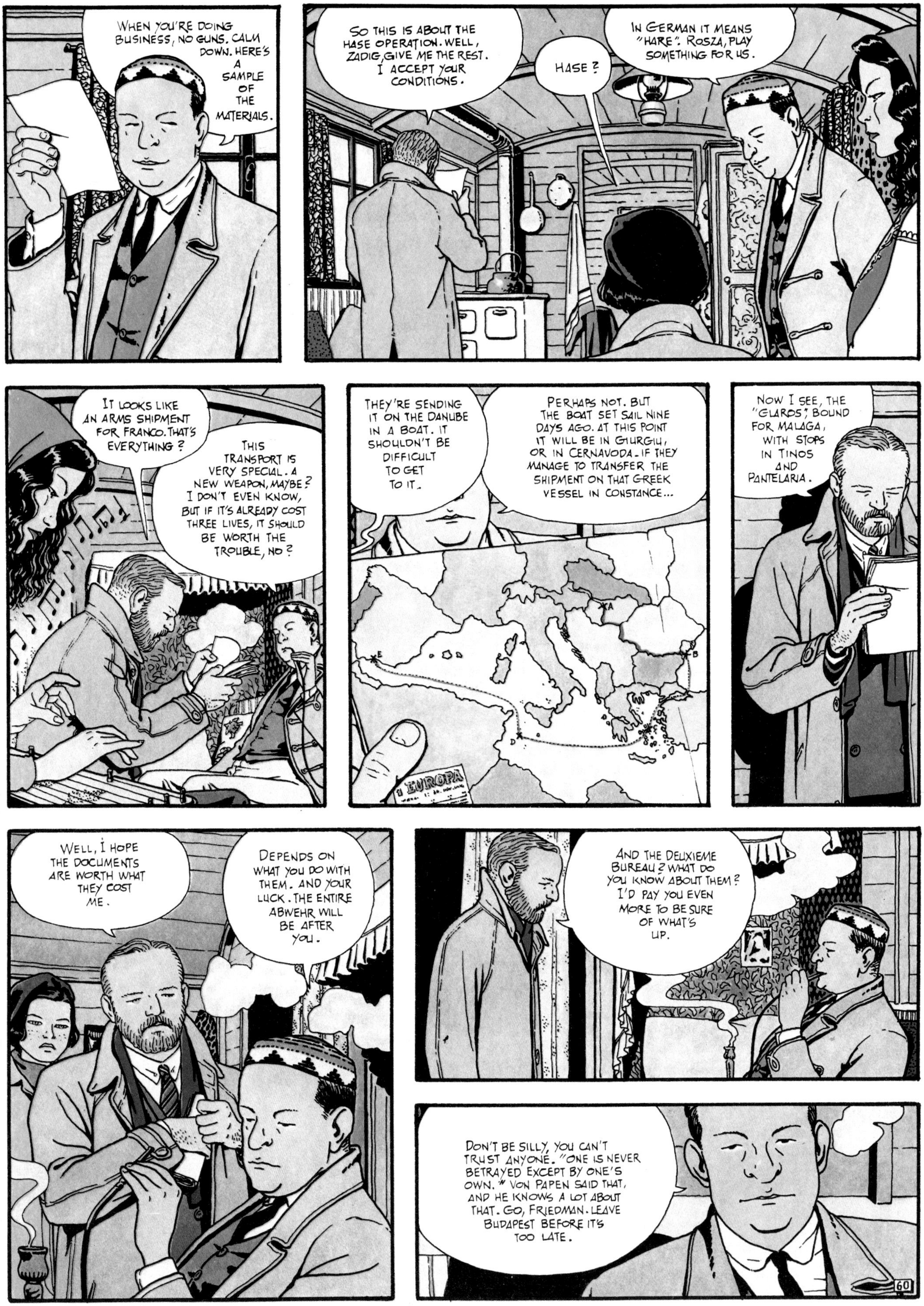
WHEN YOU'RE DOING BUSINESS, NO GUNS. CALM DOWN. HERE'S A SAMPLE OF THE MATERIALS.
SO THIS IS ABOUT THE HASE OPERATION. WELL, ZADIG, GIVE ME THE REST. I ACCEPT YOUR CONDITIONS.
HASE?
IN GERMAN IT MEANS "HARE". ROSZA, PLAY SOMETHING FOR US.
IT LOOKS LIKE AN ARMS SHIPMENT FOR FRANCO. THAT'S EVERYTHING?
THIS TRANSPORT IS VERY SPECIAL. A NEW WEAPON, MAYBE? I DON'T EVEN KNOW, BUT IF IT'S ALREADY COST THREE LIVES, IT SHOULD BE WORTH THE TROUBLE, NO?
THEY'RE SENDING IT ON THE DANUBE IN A BOAT. IT SHOULDN'T BE DIFFICULT TO GET TO IT.
PERHAPS NOT. BUT THE BOAT SET SAIL NINE DAYS AGO. AT THIS POINT IT WILL BE IN GIURGIU, OR IN CERNAVODA. IF THEY MANAGE TO TRANSFER THE SHIPMENT ON THAT GREEK VESSEL IN CONSTANCE...
EUROPA
NOW I SEE, THE "GLAROS", BOUND FOR MALAGA, WITH STOPS IN TINOS AND PANTELARIA.
WELL, I HOPE THE DOCUMENTS ARE WORTH WHAT THEY COST ME.
DEPENDS ON WHAT YOU DO WITH THEM. AND YOUR LUCK. THE ENTIRE ABWEHR WILL BE AFTER YOU.
AND THE DEUXIEME BUREAU? WHAT DO YOU KNOW ABOUT THEM? I'D PAY YOU EVEN MORE TO BE SURE OF WHAT'S UP.
DON'T BE SILLY, YOU CAN'T TRUST ANYONE. "ONE IS NEVER BETRAYED EXCEPT BY ONE'S OWN." VON PAPEN SAID THAT, AND HE KNOWS A LOT ABOUT THAT. GO, FRIEDMAN. LEAVE BUDAPEST BEFORE IT'S TOO LATE.
60

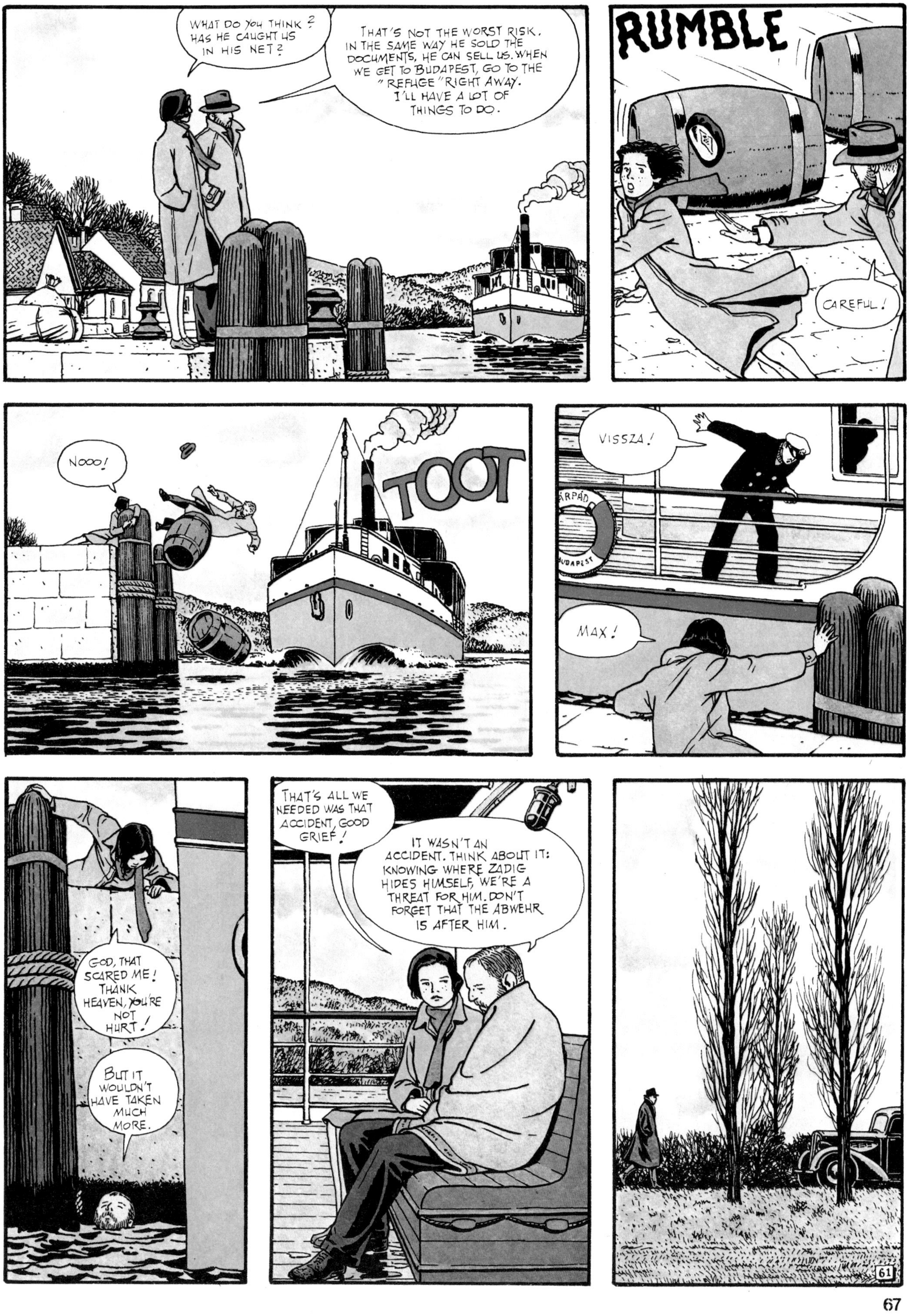
WHAT DO YOU THINK? HAS HE CAUGHT US IN HIS NET?
THAT'S NOT THE WORST RISK. IN THE SAME WAY HE SOLD THE DOCUMENTS, HE CAN SELL US. WHEN WE GET TO BUDAPEST, GO TO THE "REFUGE" RIGHT AWAY. I'LL HAVE A LOT OF THINGS TO DO.
RUMBLE
CAREFUL!
NOOO!
TOOT
VISSZA!
MAX!
GOD, THAT SCARED ME! THANK HEAVEN, YOU'RE NOT HURT!
BUT IT WOULDN'T HAVE TAKEN MUCH MORE.
THAT'S ALL WE NEEDED WAS THAT ACCIDENT, GOOD GRIEF!
IT WASN'T AN ACCIDENT. THINK ABOUT IT: KNOWING WHERE ZADIG HIDES HIMSELF, WE'RE A THREAT FOR HIM. DON'T FORGET THAT THE ABWEHR IS AFTER HIM.
61

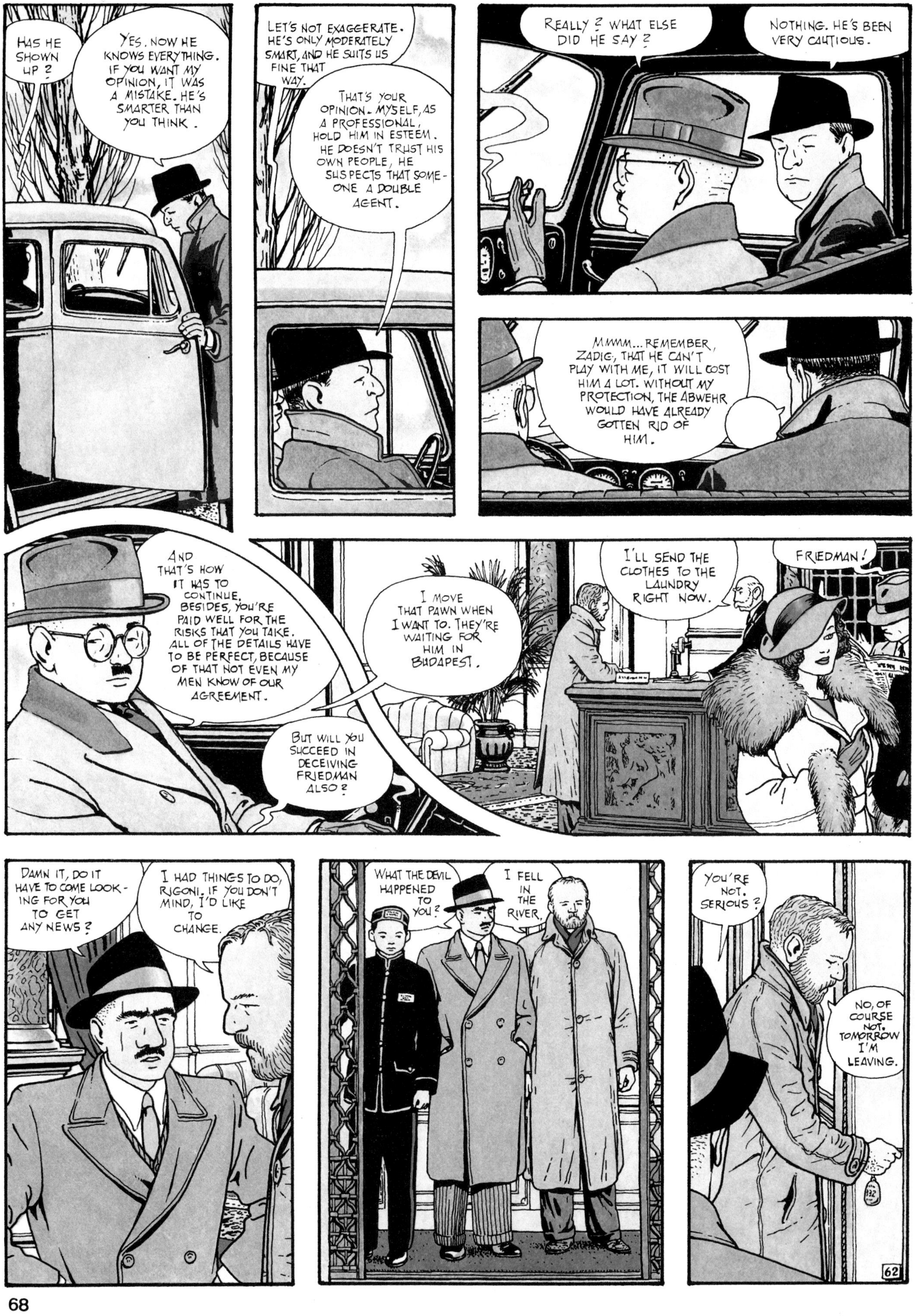
HAS HE SHOWN UP ?
YES. NOW HE KNOWS EVERYTHING. IF YOU WANT MY OPINION, IT WAS A MISTAKE. HE'S SMARTER THAN YOU THINK.
LET'S NOT EXAGGERATE. HE'S ONLY MODERATELY SMART, AND HE SUITS US FINE THAT WAY.
THAT'S YOUR OPINION. MYSELF, AS A PROFESSIONAL, HOLD HIM IN ESTEEM. HE DOESN'T TRUST HIS OWN PEOPLE, HE SUSPECTS THAT SOMEONE A DOUBLE AGENT.
REALLY ? WHAT ELSE DID HE SAY ?
NOTHING. HE'S BEEN VERY CAUTIOUS.
MMMM... REMEMBER, ZADIG, THAT HE CAN'T PLAY WITH ME, IT WILL COST HIM A LOT. WITHOUT MY PROTECTION, THE ABWEHR WOULD HAVE ALREADY GOTTEN RID OF HIM.
AND THAT'S HOW IT HAS TO CONTINUE. BESIDES, YOU'RE PAID WELL FOR THE RISKS THAT YOU TAKE. ALL OF THE DETAILS HAVE TO BE PERFECT, BECAUSE OF THAT NOT EVEN MY MEN KNOW OF OUR AGREEMENT.
I MOVE THAT PAWN WHEN I WANT TO. THEY'RE WAITING FOR HIM IN BUDAPEST.
BUT WILL YOU SUCCEED IN DECEIVING FRIEDMAN ALSO ?
I'LL SEND THE CLOTHES TO THE LAUNDRY RIGHT NOW.
FRIEDMAN!
DAMN IT, DO IT HAVE TO COME LOOKING FOR YOU TO GET ANY NEWS ?
I HAD THINGS TO DO, RIGONI. IF YOU DON'T MIND, I'D LIKE TO CHANGE.
WHAT THE DEVIL HAPPENED TO YOU ?
I FELL IN THE RIVER.
YOU'RE NOT. SERIOUS ?
NO, OF COURSE NOT. TOMORROW I'M LEAVING.
132
62

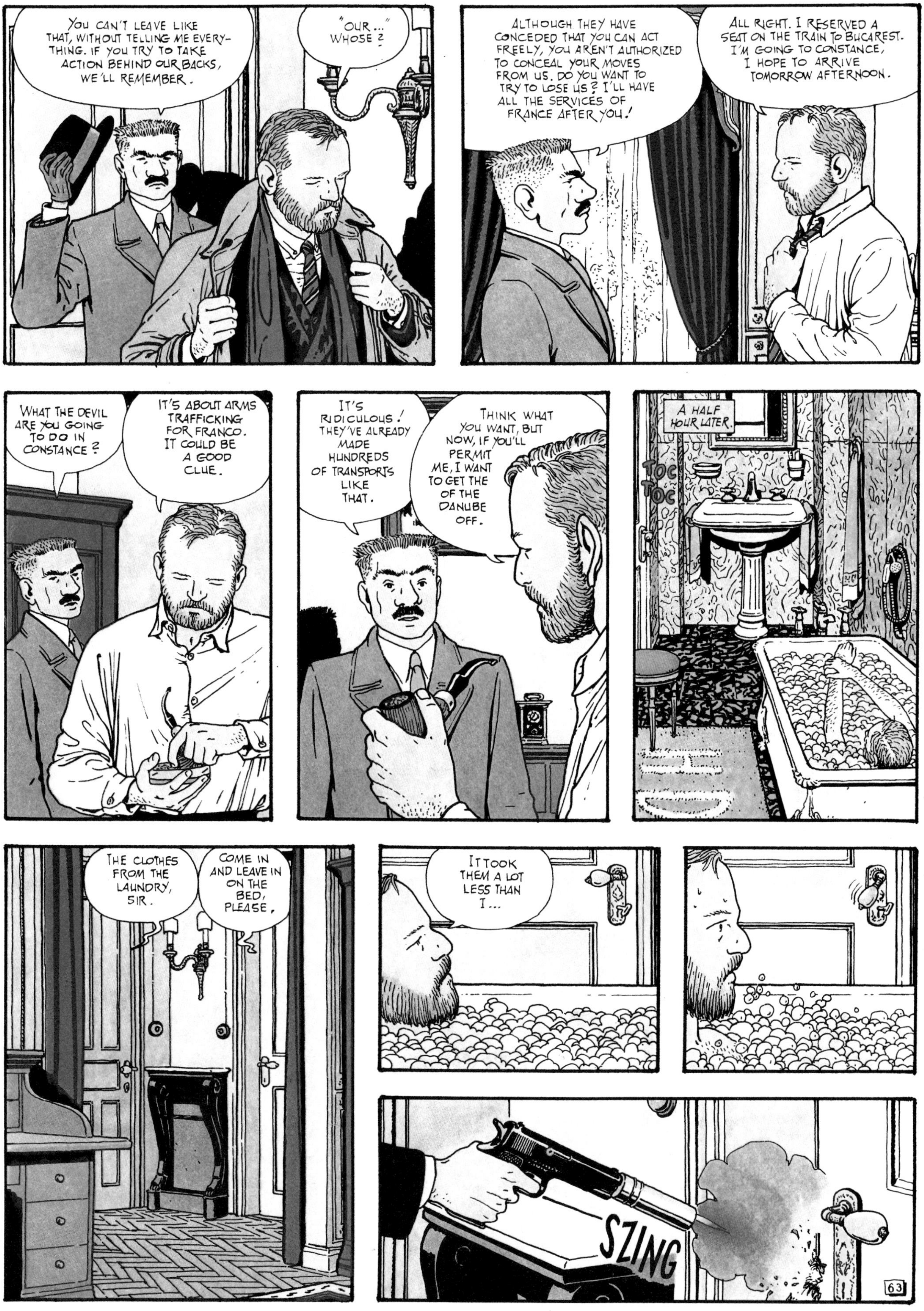

YOU CAN'T LEAVE LIKE THAT, WITHOUT TELLING ME EVERYTHING. IF YOU TRY TO TAKE ACTION BEHIND OUR BACKS, WE'LL REMEMBER.
"OUR..." WHOSE?
ALTHOUGH THEY HAVE CONCEDED THAT YOU CAN ACT FREELY, YOU AREN'T AUTHORIZED TO CONCEAL YOUR MOVES FROM US. DO YOU WANT TO TRY TO LOSE US? I'LL HAVE ALL THE SERVICES OF FRANCE AFTER YOU!
ALL RIGHT. I RESERVED A SEAT ON THE TRAIN TO BUCAREST. I'M GOING TO CONSTANCE, I HOPE TO ARRIVE TOMORROW AFTERNOON.
WHAT THE DEVIL ARE YOU GOING TO DO IN CONSTANCE?
IT'S ABOUT ARMS TRAFFICKING FOR FRANCO. IT COULD BE A GOOD CLUE.
IT'S RIDICULOUS! THEY'VE ALREADY MADE HUNDREDS OF TRANSPORTS LIKE THAT.
THINK WHAT YOU WANT, BUT NOW, IF YOU'LL PERMIT ME, I WANT TO GET THE OF THE DANUBE OFF.
A HALF HOUR LATER.
TOC TOC
THE CLOTHES FROM THE LAUNDRY, SIR.
COME IN AND LEAVE IN ON THE BED, PLEASE.
IT TOOK THEM A LOT LESS THAN I...
SZING
63

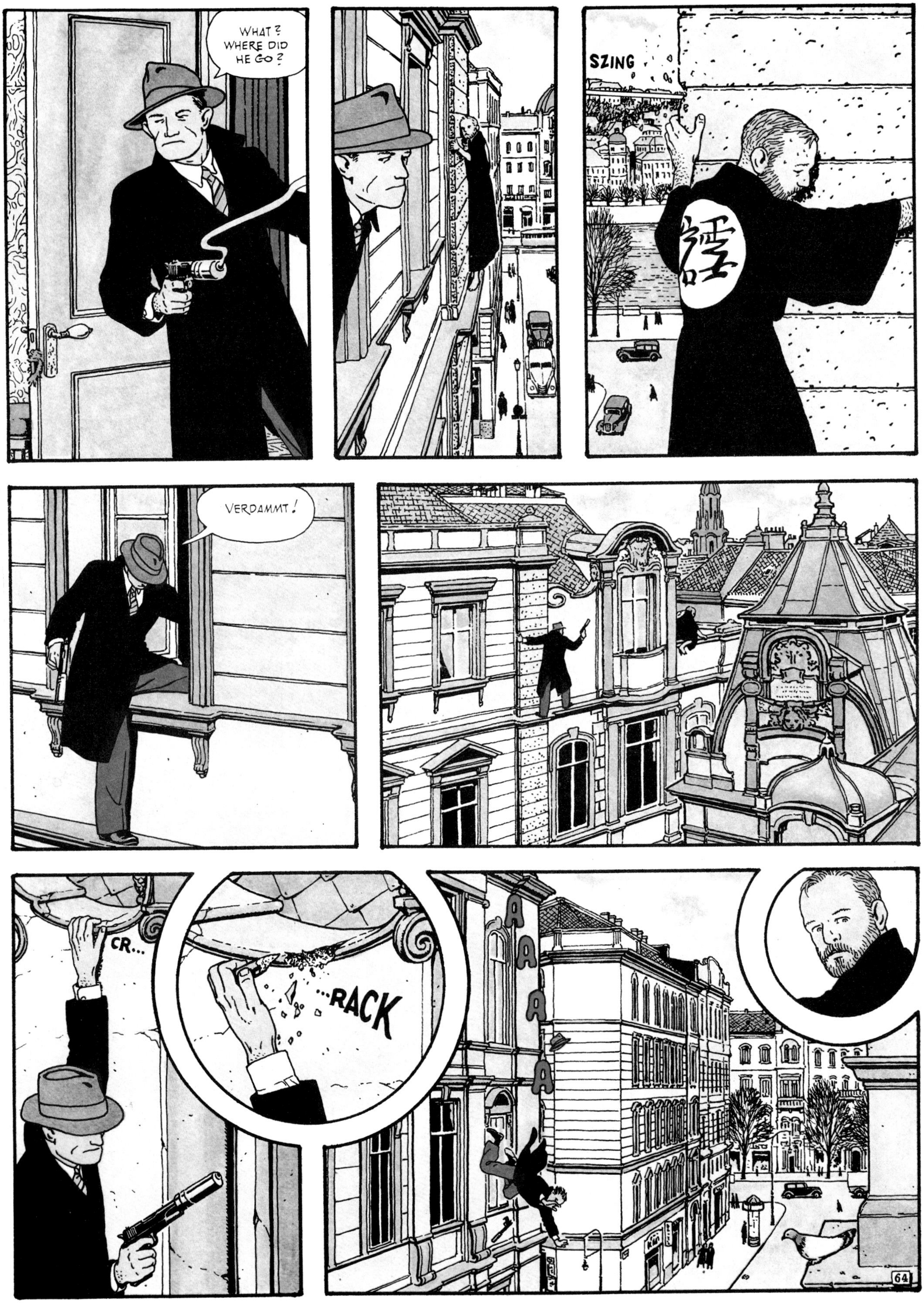
WHAT? WHERE DID HE GO?
SZING
VERDAMMT!
CR...
...RACK
AAAAA
64

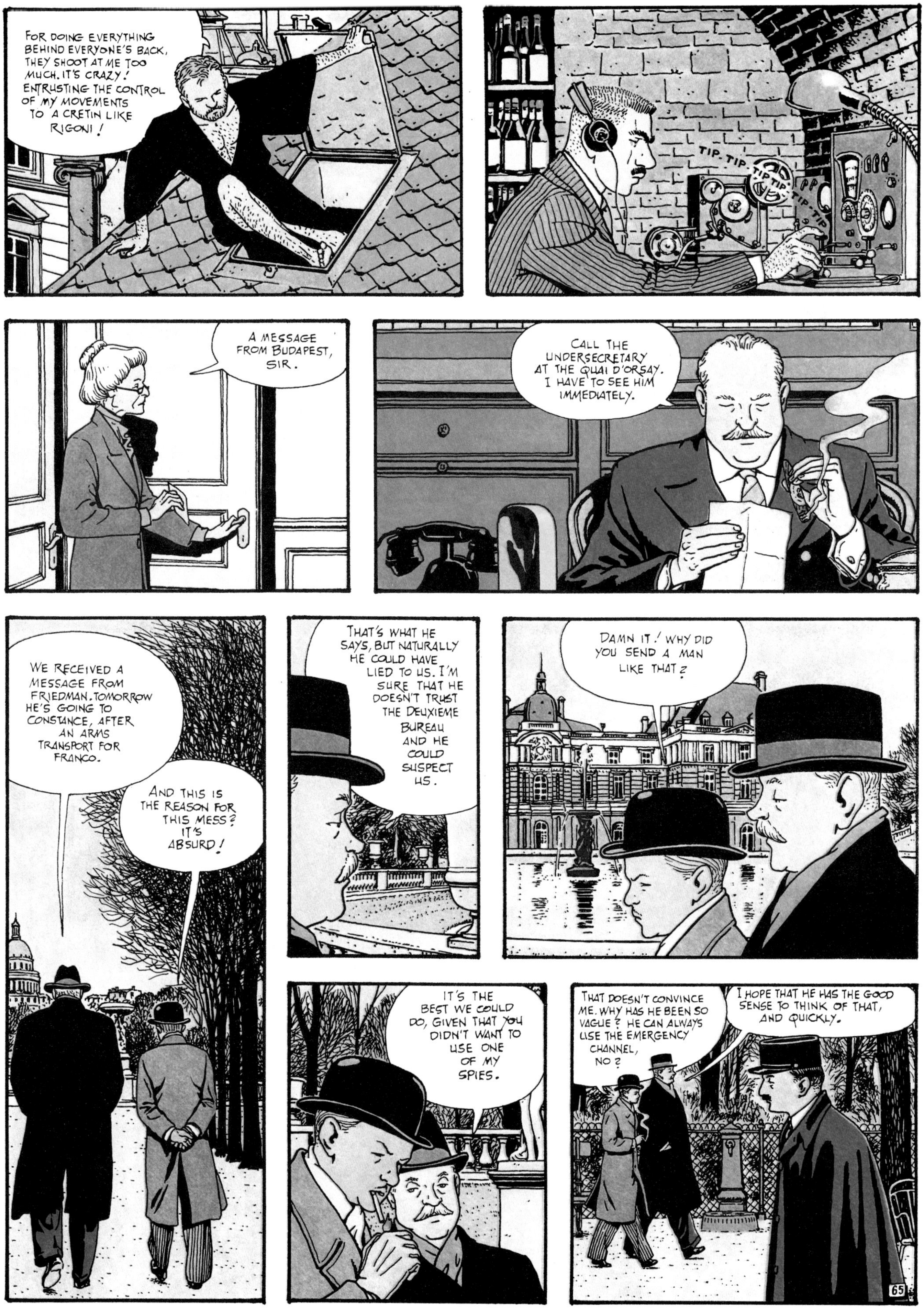
FOR DOING EVERYTHING BEHIND EVERYONE'S BACK, THEY SHOOT AT ME TOO MUCH. IT'S CRAZY! ENTRUSTING THE CONTROL OF MY MOVEMENTS TO A CRETIN LIKE RIGONI!
TIP-TIP-TIP-TIP-TIP-TIP
A MESSAGE FROM BUDAPEST, SIR.
CALL THE UNDERSECRETARY AT THE QUAI D'ORSAY. I HAVE TO SEE HIM IMMEDIATELY.
WE RECEIVED A MESSAGE FROM FRIEDMAN. TOMORROW HE'S GOING TO CONSTANCE, AFTER AN ARMS TRANSPORT FOR FRANCO.
AND THIS IS THE REASON FOR THIS MESS? IT'S ABSURD!
THAT'S WHAT HE SAYS, BUT NATURALLY HE COULD HAVE LIED TO US. I'M SURE THAT HE DOESN'T TRUST THE DEUXIEME BUREAU AND HE COULD SUSPECT US.
DAMN IT! WHY DID YOU SEND A MAN LIKE THAT?
IT'S THE BEST WE COULD DO, GIVEN THAT YOU DIDN'T WANT TO USE ONE OF MY SPIES.
THAT DOESN'T CONVINCE ME. WHY HAS HE BEEN SO VAGUE? HE CAN ALWAYS USE THE EMERGENCY CHANNEL, NO?
I HOPE THAT HE HAS THE GOOD SENSE TO THINK OF THAT, AND QUICKLY.
65

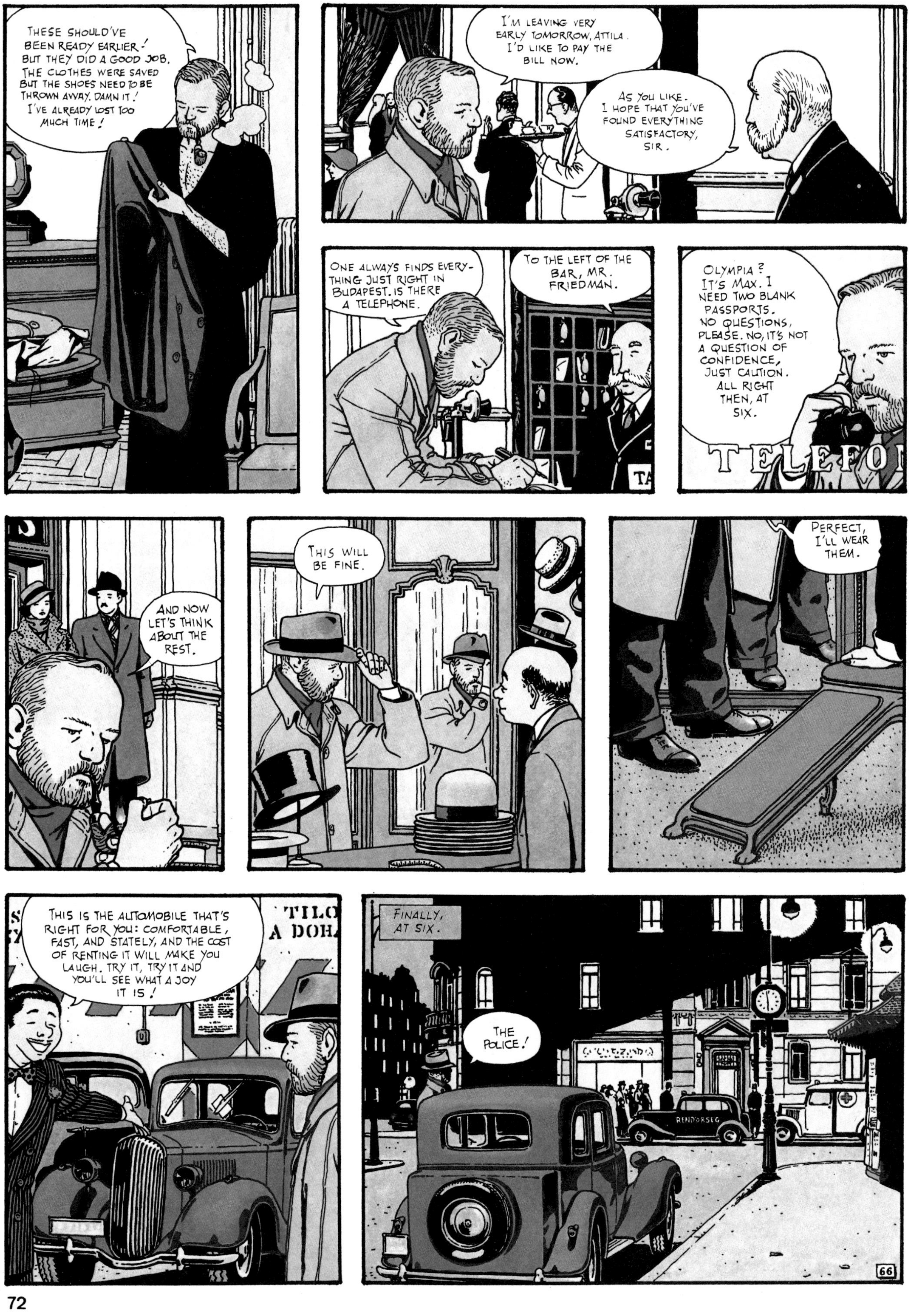

THESE SHOULD'VE BEEN READY EARLIER! BUT THEY DID A GOOD JOB. THE CLOTHES WERE SAVED BUT THE SHOES NEED TO BE THROWN AWAY. DAMN IT! I'VE ALREADY LOST TOO MUCH TIME!
I'M LEAVING VERY EARLY TOMORROW, ATTILA. I'D LIKE TO PAY THE BILL NOW.
AS YOU LIKE. I HOPE THAT YOU'VE FOUND EVERYTHING SATISFACTORY, SIR.
ONE ALWAYS FINDS EVERYTHING JUST RIGHT IN BUDAPEST. IS THERE A TELEPHONE.
TO THE LEFT OF THE BAR, MR. FRIEDMAN.
OLYMPIA? IT'S MAX. I NEED TWO BLANK PASSPORTS. NO QUESTIONS, PLEASE. NO, IT'S NOT A QUESTION OF CONFIDENCE, JUST CAUTION. ALL RIGHT THEN, AT SIX.
TELEFO
AND NOW LET'S THINK ABOUT THE REST.
THIS WILL BE FINE.
PERFECT, I'LL WEAR THEM.
THIS IS THE AUTOMOBILE THAT'S RIGHT FOR YOU: COMFORTABLE, FAST, AND STATELY, AND THE COST OF RENTING IT WILL MAKE YOU LAUGH. TRY IT, TRY IT AND YOU'LL SEE WHAT A JOY IT IS!
TILO
A DOHA
FINALLY, AT SIX.
THE POLICE!
RENDŐRSÉG
66

URAM! ALLJON MEG!

MY GOD!

WHO ARE YOU? HOW DID YOU GET IN HERE?

I'M LOOKING FOR OLYMPIA. WHAT HAPPENED?

THE DEVIL! WHY DID THEY LET YOU IN? PAPERS, PLEASE.

MMMM, MAX FRIEDMAN, I DON'T REMEMBER VERY WELL BUT IT SEEMS I'VE ALREADY HEARD THAT NAME. LET'S GO, AND DON'T TELL ME THAT THE "GREEN MOON" IS KNOWN EVEN IN FRANCE. WERE YOU A CLIENT?

IN A CERTAIN SENSE, YES.

NOW THAT YOU'RE HERE, COME ON.

WHAT A MESS!

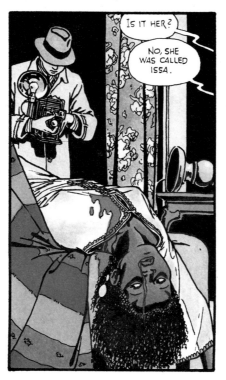

IS IT HER?

NO, SHE WAS CALLED ISSA.

ONE MOMENT... DID YOU BY CHANCE COME TO HUNGARY ON THE EXPRESS TRAIN FROM PARIS? WHEN EXACTLY, MR. FRIEDMAN?

THE SEVENTH.

AH, SO IT HAS TO DO WITH THAT TRAIN. I SAW YOUR NAME ON THE LIST OF PASSENGERS. STRANGE COINCIDENCE, NO?

67

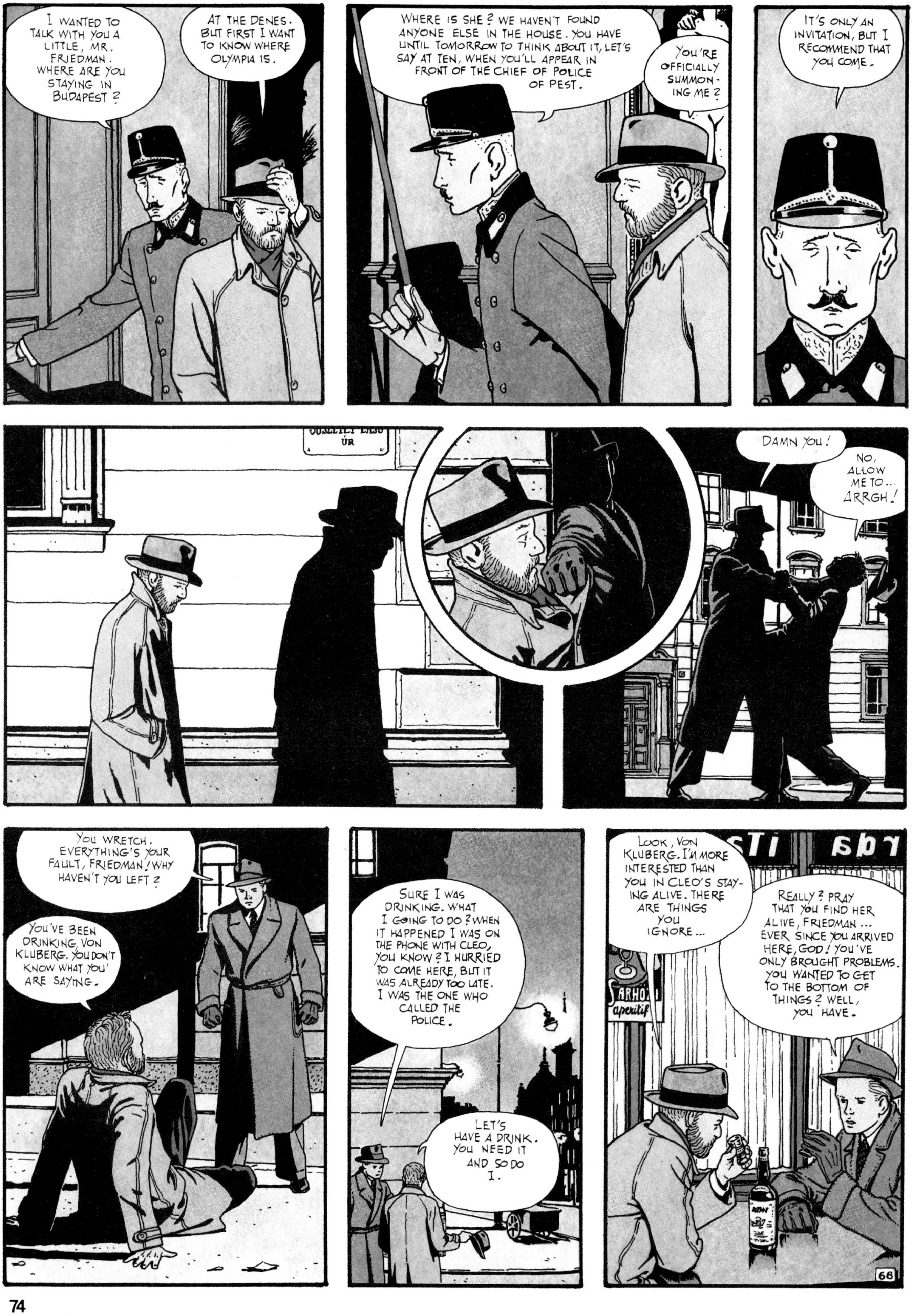
I WANTED TO TALK WITH YOU A LITTLE, MR. FRIEDMAN. WHERE ARE YOU STAYING IN BUDAPEST?
AT THE DENES. BUT FIRST I WANT TO KNOW WHERE OLYMPIA IS.
WHERE IS SHE? WE HAVEN'T FOUND ANYONE ELSE IN THE HOUSE. YOU HAVE UNTIL TOMORROW TO THINK ABOUT IT, LET'S SAY AT TEN, WHEN YOU'LL APPEAR IN FRONT OF THE CHIEF OF POLICE OF PEST.
YOU'RE OFFICIALLY SUMMONING ME?
IT'S ONLY AN INVITATION, BUT I RECOMMEND THAT YOU COME.
ÚR
DAMN YOU!
NO, ALLOW ME TO... ARRGH!
YOU WRETCH. EVERYTHING'S YOUR FAULT, FRIEDMAN! WHY HAVEN'T YOU LEFT?
YOU'VE BEEN DRINKING, VON KLUBERG. YOU DON'T KNOW WHAT YOU' ARE SAYING.
SURE I WAS DRINKING. WHAT I GOING TO DO? WHEN IT HAPPENED I WAS ON THE PHONE WITH CLEO, YOU KNOW? I HURRIED TO COME HERE, BUT IT WAS ALREADY TOO LATE. I WAS THE ONE WHO CALLED THE POLICE.
LET'S HAVE A DRINK. YOU NEED IT AND SO DO I.
LOOK, VON KLUBERG. I'M MORE INTERESTED THAN YOU IN CLEO'S STAYING ALIVE. THERE ARE THINGS YOU IGNORE...
REALLY? PRAY THAT YOU FIND HER ALIVE, FRIEDMAN... EVER SINCE YOU ARRIVED HERE, GOD! YOU'VE ONLY BROUGHT PROBLEMS. YOU WANTED TO GET TO THE BOTTOM OF THINGS? WELL, YOU HAVE.
aperitif
68

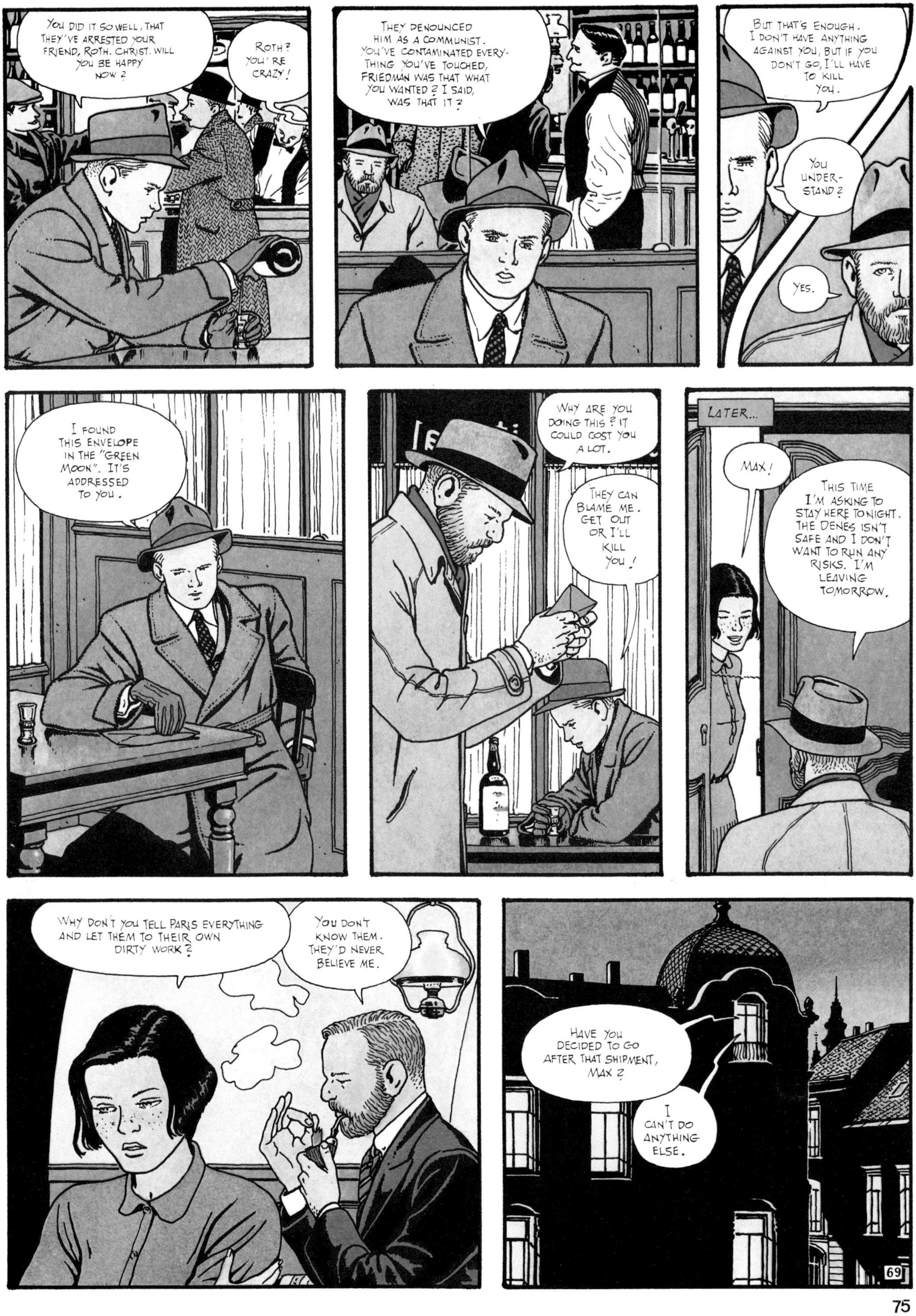
You did it so well, that they've arrested your friend, Roth. Christ. Will you be happy now?
Roth? You're crazy!
They denounced him as a communist. You've contaminated everything you've touched, Friedman was that what you wanted? I said, was that it?
But that's enough. I don't have anything against you, but if you don't go, I'll have to kill you.
You understand?
Yes.
I found this envelope in the "Green Moon". It's addressed to you.
Why are you doing this? It could cost you a lot.
They can blame me. Get out or I'll kill you!
Later...
Max!
This time I'm asking to stay here tonight. The Denes isn't safe and I don't want to run any risks. I'm leaving tomorrow.
Why don't you tell Paris everything and let them to their own dirty work?
You don't know them. They'd never believe me.
Have you decided to go after that shipment, Max?
I can't do anything else.
69

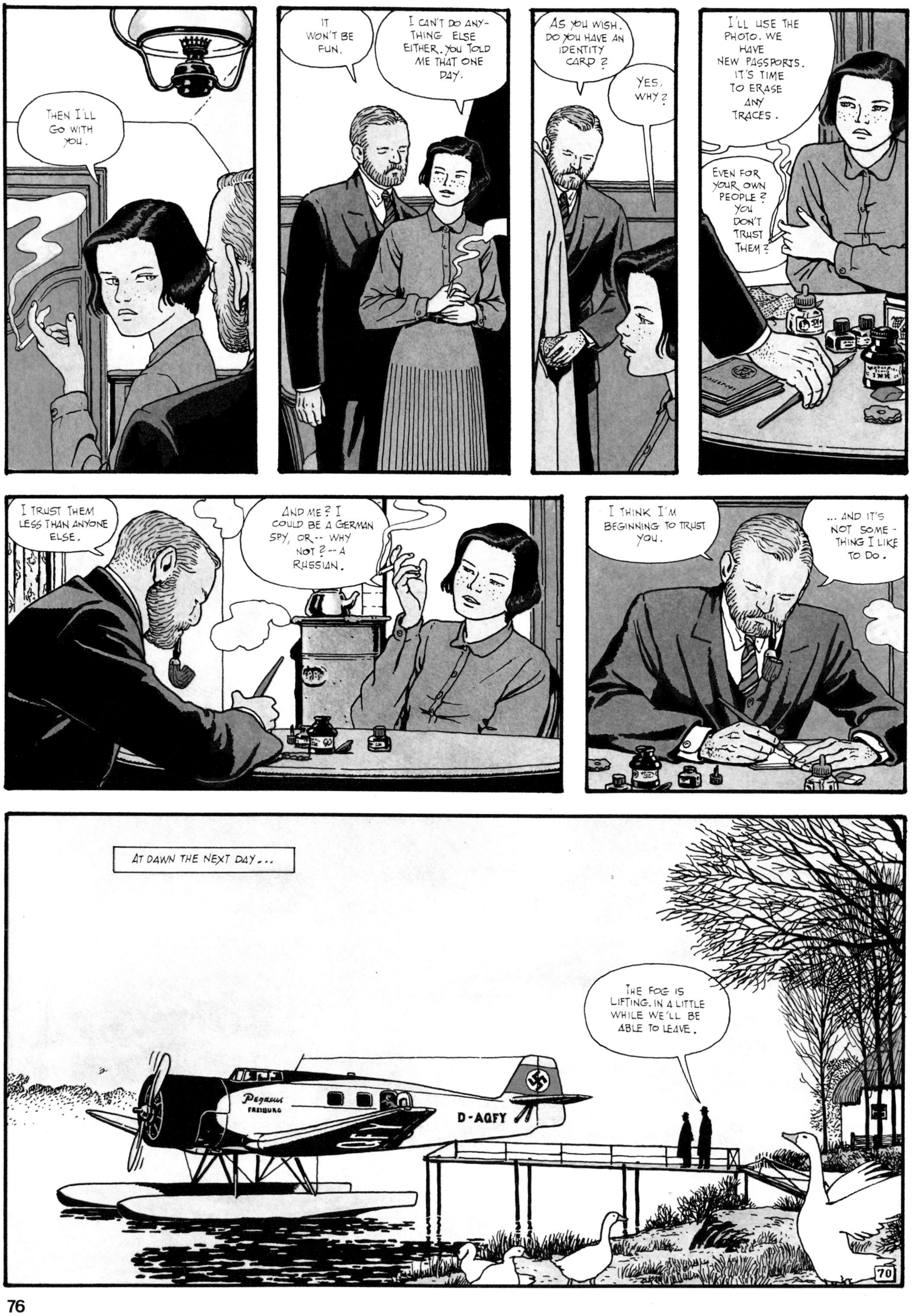
THEN I'LL GO WITH YOU.
IT WON'T BE FUN.
I CAN'T DO ANYTHING ELSE EITHER. YOU TOLD ME THAT ONE DAY.
AS YOU WISH. DO YOU HAVE AN IDENTITY CARD?
YES, WHY?
I'LL USE THE PHOTO. WE HAVE NEW PASSPORTS. IT'S TIME TO ERASE ANY TRACES.
EVEN FOR YOUR OWN PEOPLE? YOU DON'T TRUST THEM?
I TRUST THEM LESS THAN ANYONE ELSE.
AND ME? I COULD BE A GERMAN SPY, OR -- WHY NOT? -- A RUSSIAN.
I THINK I'M BEGINNING TO TRUST YOU.
... AND IT'S NOT SOMETHING I LIKE TO DO.
AT DAWN THE NEXT DAY...
THE FOG IS LIFTING. IN A LITTLE WHILE WE'LL BE ABLE TO LEAVE.
Pegasus
FREIBURG
D-AGFY
70

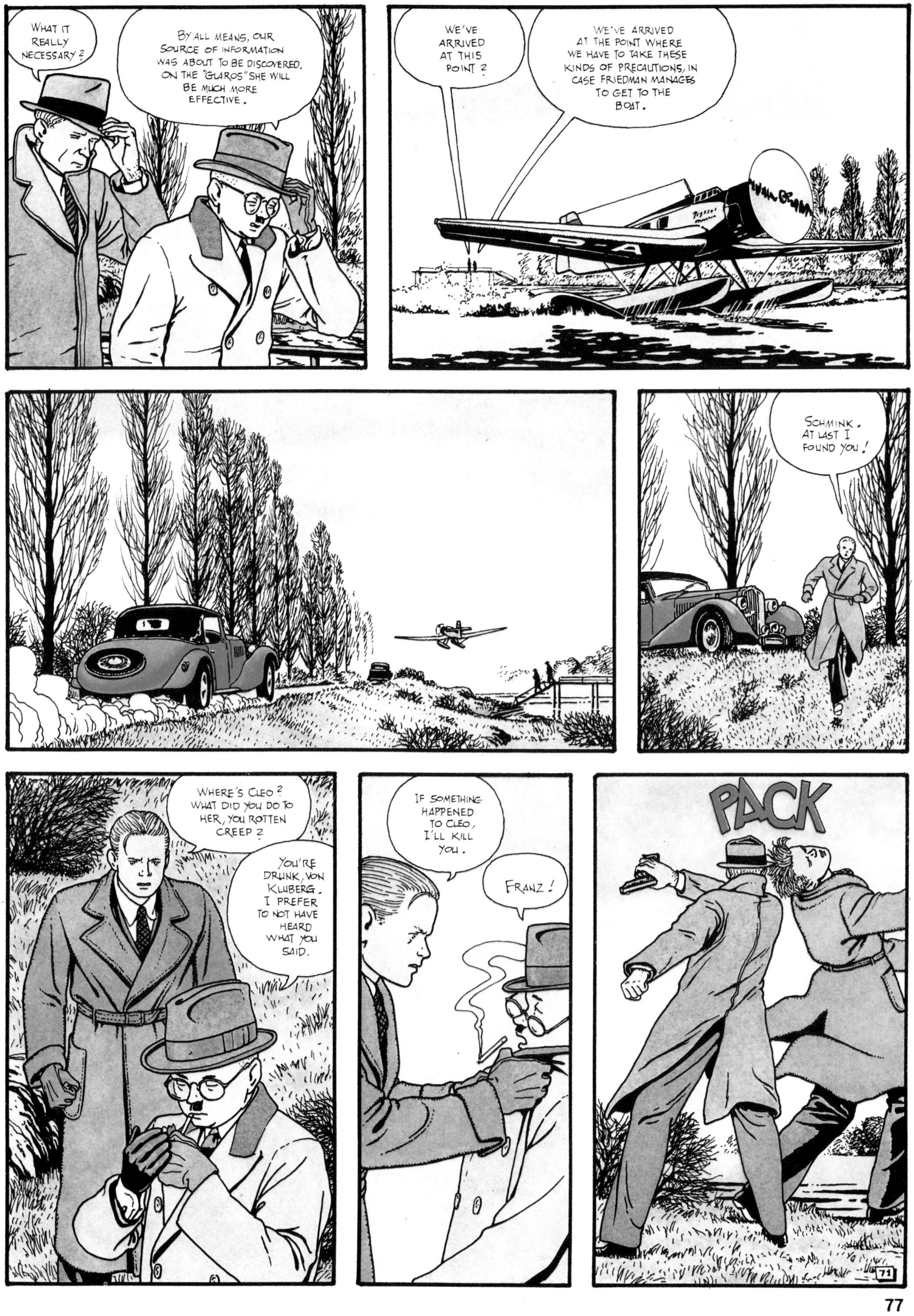
WHAT IT REALLY NECESSARY ?
BY ALL MEANS, OUR SOURCE OF INFORMATION WAS ABOUT TO BE DISCOVERED. ON THE "GLAROS" SHE WILL BE MUCH MORE EFFECTIVE.
WE'VE ARRIVED AT THIS POINT ?
WE'VE ARRIVED AT THE POINT WHERE WE HAVE TO TAKE THESE KINDS OF PRECAUTIONS, IN CASE FRIEDMAN MANAGES TO GET TO THE BOAT.
SCHMINK. AT LAST I FOUND YOU!
WHERE'S CLEO ? WHAT DID YOU DO TO HER, YOU ROTTEN CREEP ?
YOU'RE DRUNK, VON KLUBERG. I PREFER TO NOT HAVE HEARD WHAT YOU SAID.
IF SOMETHING HAPPENED TO CLEO, I'LL KILL YOU.
FRANZ!
PACK
71

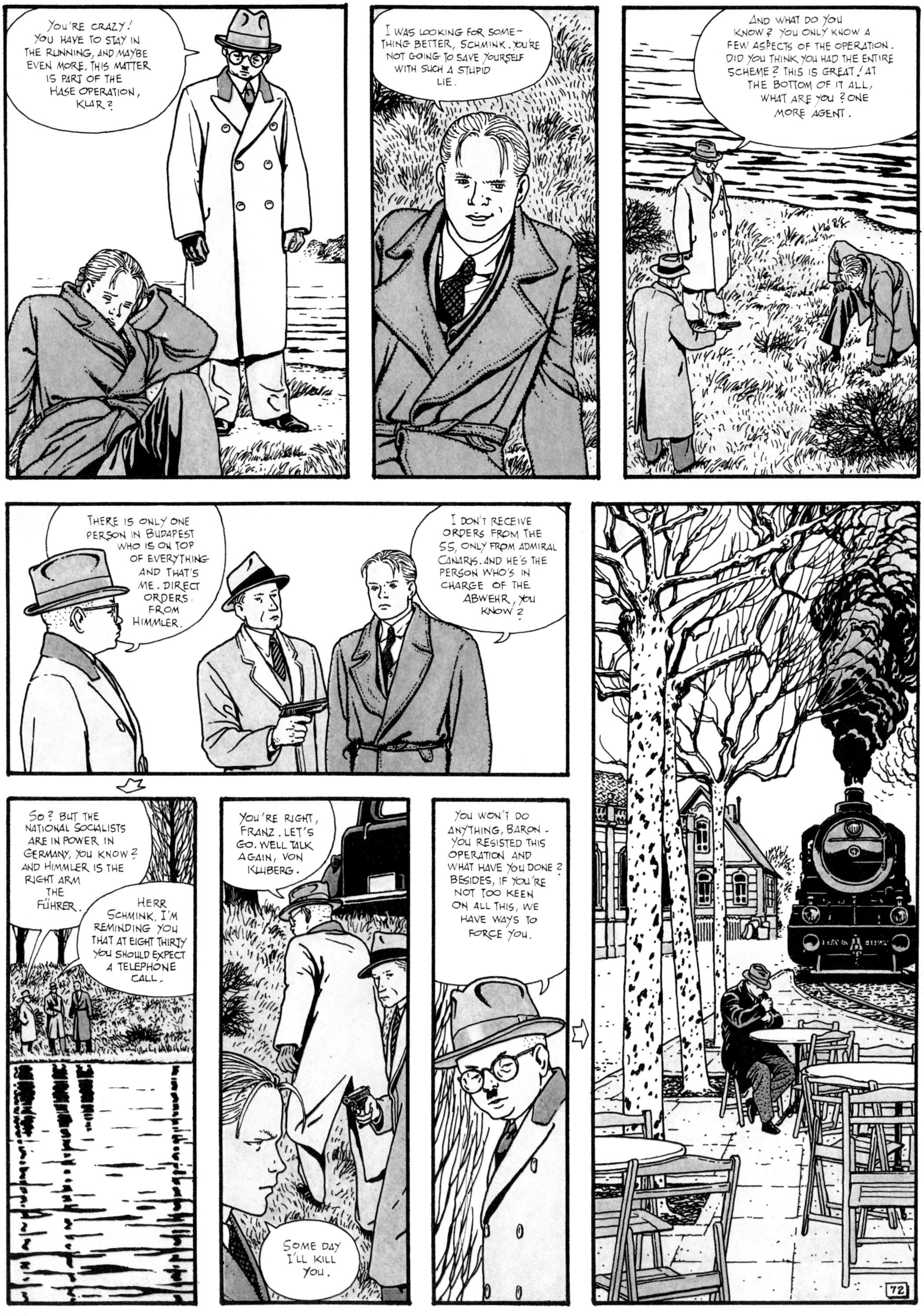

YOU'RE CRAZY! YOU HAVE TO STAY IN THE RUNNING, AND MAYBE EVEN MORE. THIS MATTER IS PART OF THE HASE OPERATION, KLAR?
I WAS LOOKING FOR SOMETHING BETTER, SCHMINK. YOU'RE NOT GOING TO SAVE YOURSELF WITH SUCH A STUPID LIE.
AND WHAT DO YOU KNOW? YOU ONLY KNOW A FEW ASPECTS OF THE OPERATION. DID YOU THINK YOU HAD THE ENTIRE SCHEME? THIS IS GREAT! AT THE BOTTOM OF IT ALL, WHAT ARE YOU? ONE MORE AGENT.
THERE IS ONLY ONE PERSON IN BUDAPEST WHO IS ON TOP OF EVERYTHING AND THAT'S ME. DIRECT ORDERS FROM HIMMLER.
I DON'T RECEIVE ORDERS FROM THE SS, ONLY FROM ADMIRAL CANARIS. AND HE'S THE PERSON WHO'S IN CHARGE OF THE ABWEHR, YOU KNOW?
SO? BUT THE NATIONAL SOCIALISTS ARE IN POWER IN GERMANY, YOU KNOW? AND HIMMLER IS THE RIGHT ARM THE FÜHRER.
HERR SCHMINK, I'M REMINDING YOU THAT AT EIGHT THIRTY YOU SHOULD EXPECT A TELEPHONE CALL.
YOU'RE RIGHT, FRANZ. LET'S GO. WELL TALK AGAIN, VON KLUBERG.
SOME DAY I'LL KILL YOU.
YOU WON'T DO ANYTHING, BARON. YOU RESISTED THIS OPERATION AND WHAT HAVE YOU DONE? BESIDES, IF YOU'RE NOT TOO KEEN ON ALL THIS, WE HAVE WAYS TO FORCE YOU.
72

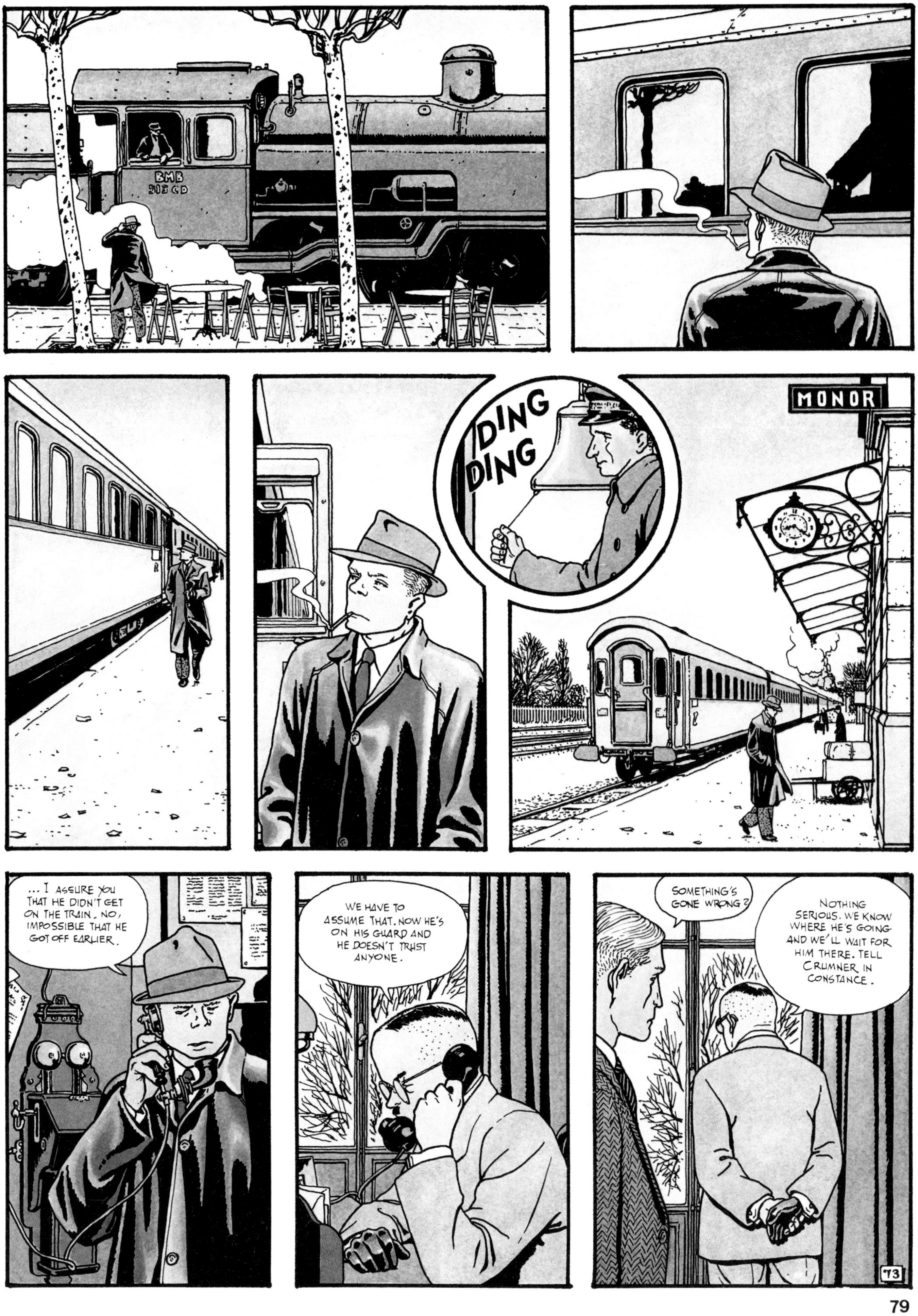
BMB
513 GD
DING
DING
MONOR
... I ASSURE YOU THAT HE DIDN'T GET ON THE TRAIN. NO, IMPOSSIBLE THAT HE GOT OFF EARLIER.
WE HAVE TO ASSUME THAT. NOW HE'S ON HIS GUARD AND HE DOESN'T TRUST ANYONE.
SOMETHING'S GONE WRONG?
NOTHING SERIOUS. WE KNOW WHERE HE'S GOING AND WE'LL WAIT FOR HIM THERE. TELL CRUMNER IN CONSTANCE.
73

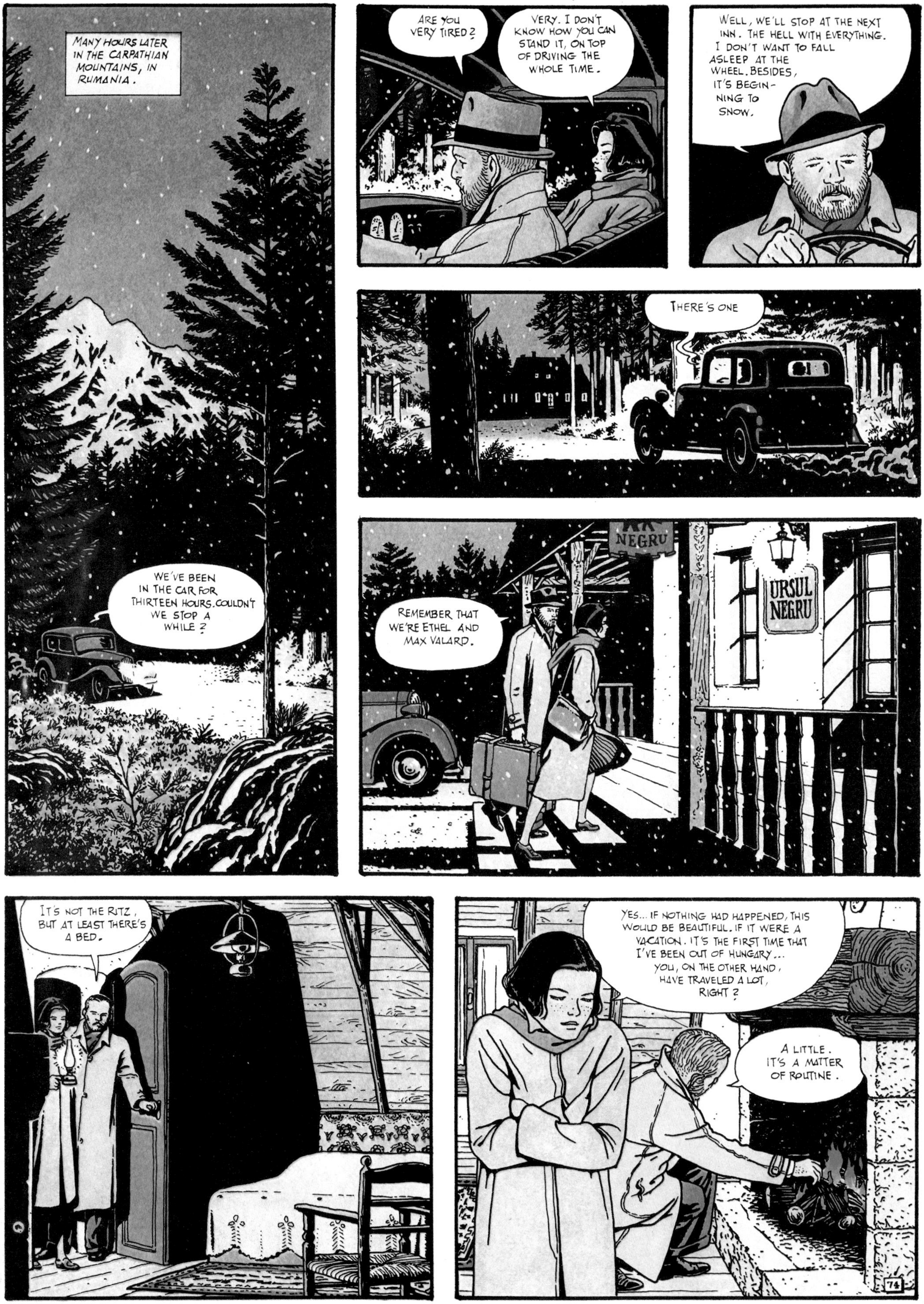
MANY HOURS LATER IN THE CARPATHIAN MOUNTAINS, IN RUMANIA.
WE'VE BEEN IN THE CAR FOR THIRTEEN HOURS. COULDN'T WE STOP A WHILE?
ARE YOU VERY TIRED?
VERY. I DON'T KNOW HOW YOU CAN STAND IT, ON TOP OF DRIVING THE WHOLE TIME.
WELL, WE'LL STOP AT THE NEXT INN. THE HELL WITH EVERYTHING. I DON'T WANT TO FALL ASLEEP AT THE WHEEL. BESIDES, IT'S BEGIN-NING TO SNOW.
THERE'S ONE
NEGRU
URSUL NEGRU
REMEMBER THAT WE'RE ETHEL AND MAX VALARD.
IT'S NOT THE RITZ, BUT AT LEAST THERE'S A BED.
YES... IF NOTHING HAD HAPPENED, THIS WOULD BE BEAUTIFUL. IF IT WERE A VACATION. IT'S THE FIRST TIME THAT I'VE BEEN OUT OF HUNGARY... YOU, ON THE OTHER HAND, HAVE TRAVELED A LOT, RIGHT?
A LITTLE. IT'S A MATTER OF ROUTINE.
74

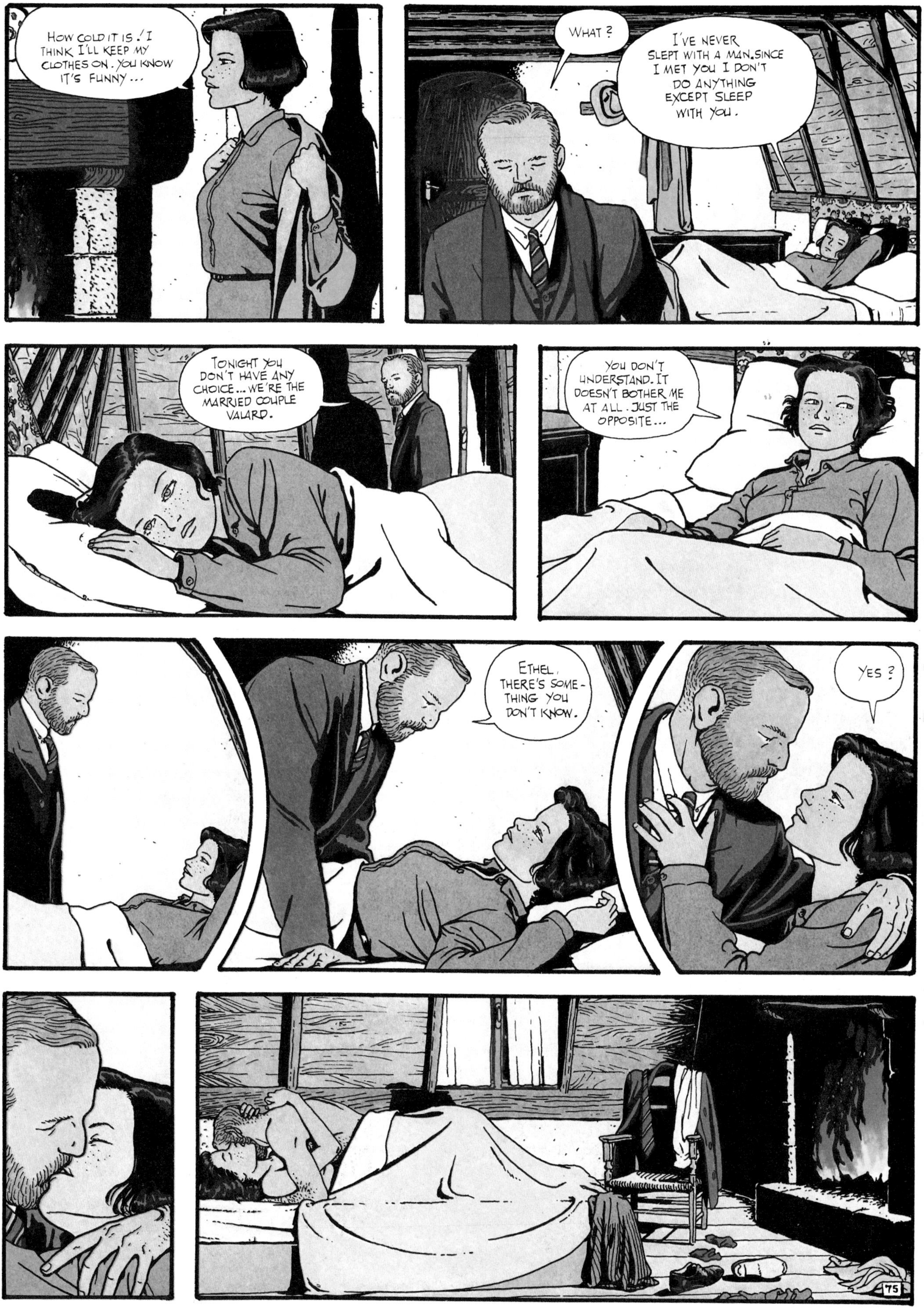
HOW COLD IT IS! I THINK I'LL KEEP MY CLOTHES ON. YOU KNOW IT'S FUNNY...
WHAT?
I'VE NEVER SLEPT WITH A MAN. SINCE I MET YOU I DON'T DO ANYTHING EXCEPT SLEEP WITH YOU.
TONIGHT YOU DON'T HAVE ANY CHOICE... WE'RE THE MARRIED COUPLE VALARD.
YOU DON'T UNDERSTAND. IT DOESN'T BOTHER ME AT ALL. JUST THE OPPOSITE...
ETHEL, THERE'S SOMETHING YOU DON'T KNOW.
YES?
75

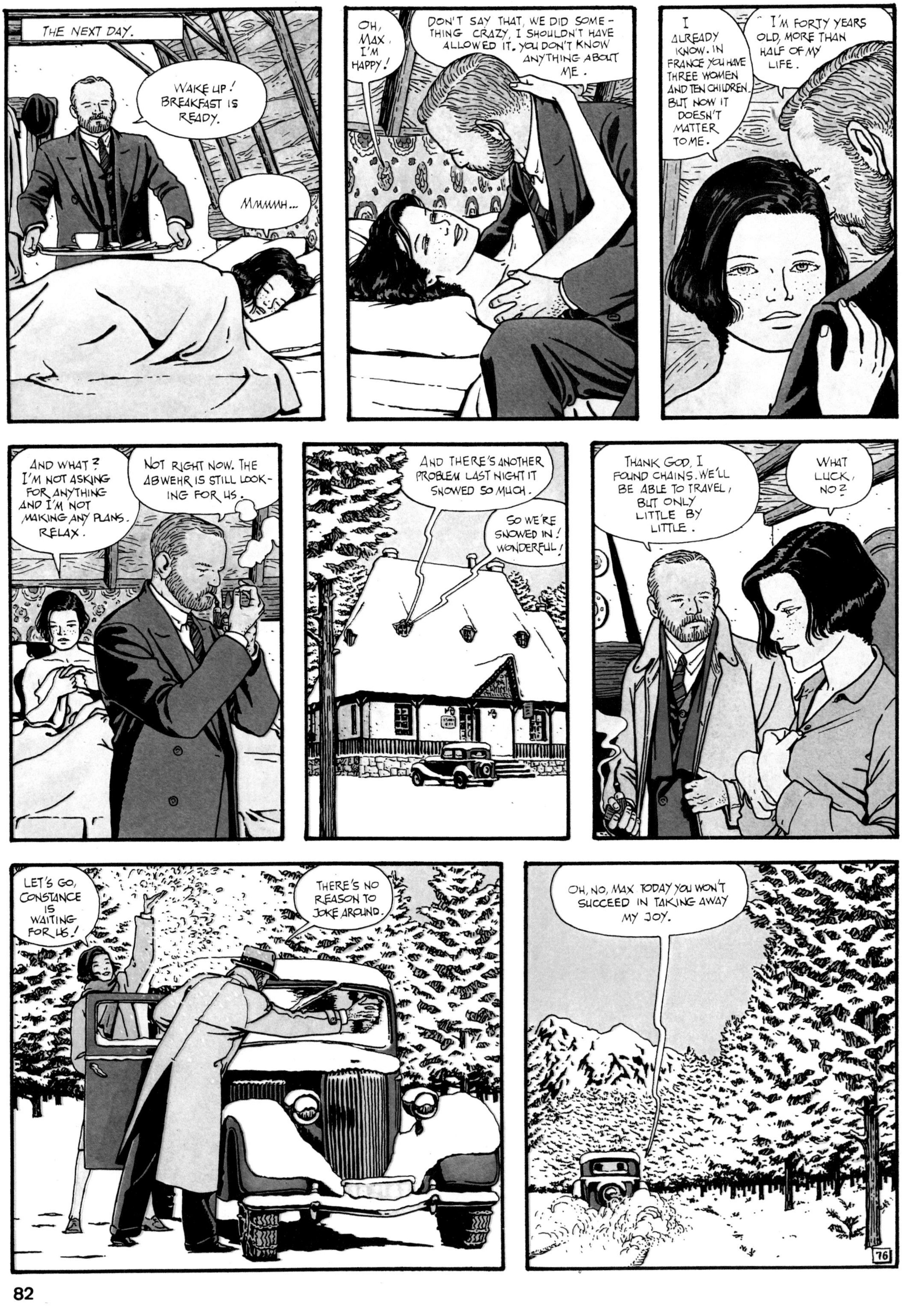
THE NEXT DAY.
WAKE UP! BREAKFAST IS READY.
MMMMH...
OH, MAX, I'M HAPPY!
DON'T SAY THAT, WE DID SOMETHING CRAZY, I SHOULDN'T HAVE ALLOWED IT. YOU DON'T KNOW ANYTHING ABOUT ME.
I'M FORTY YEARS OLD, MORE THAN HALF OF MY LIFE.
I ALREADY KNOW. IN FRANCE YOU HAVE THREE WOMEN AND TEN CHILDREN. BUT NOW IT DOESN'T MATTER TO ME.
AND WHAT? I'M NOT ASKING FOR ANYTHING AND I'M NOT MAKING ANY PLANS. RELAX.
NOT RIGHT NOW. THE ABWEHR IS STILL LOOKING FOR US.
AND THERE'S ANOTHER PROBLEM LAST NIGHT IT SNOWED SO MUCH.
SO WE'RE SNOWED IN! WONDERFUL!
THANK GOD, I FOUND CHAINS. WE'LL BE ABLE TO TRAVEL, BUT ONLY LITTLE BY LITTLE.
WHAT LUCK, NO?
LET'S GO, CONSTANCE IS WAITING FOR US!
THERE'S NO REASON TO JOKE AROUND.
OH, NO, MAX. TODAY YOU WON'T SUCCEED IN TAKING AWAY MY JOY.
76

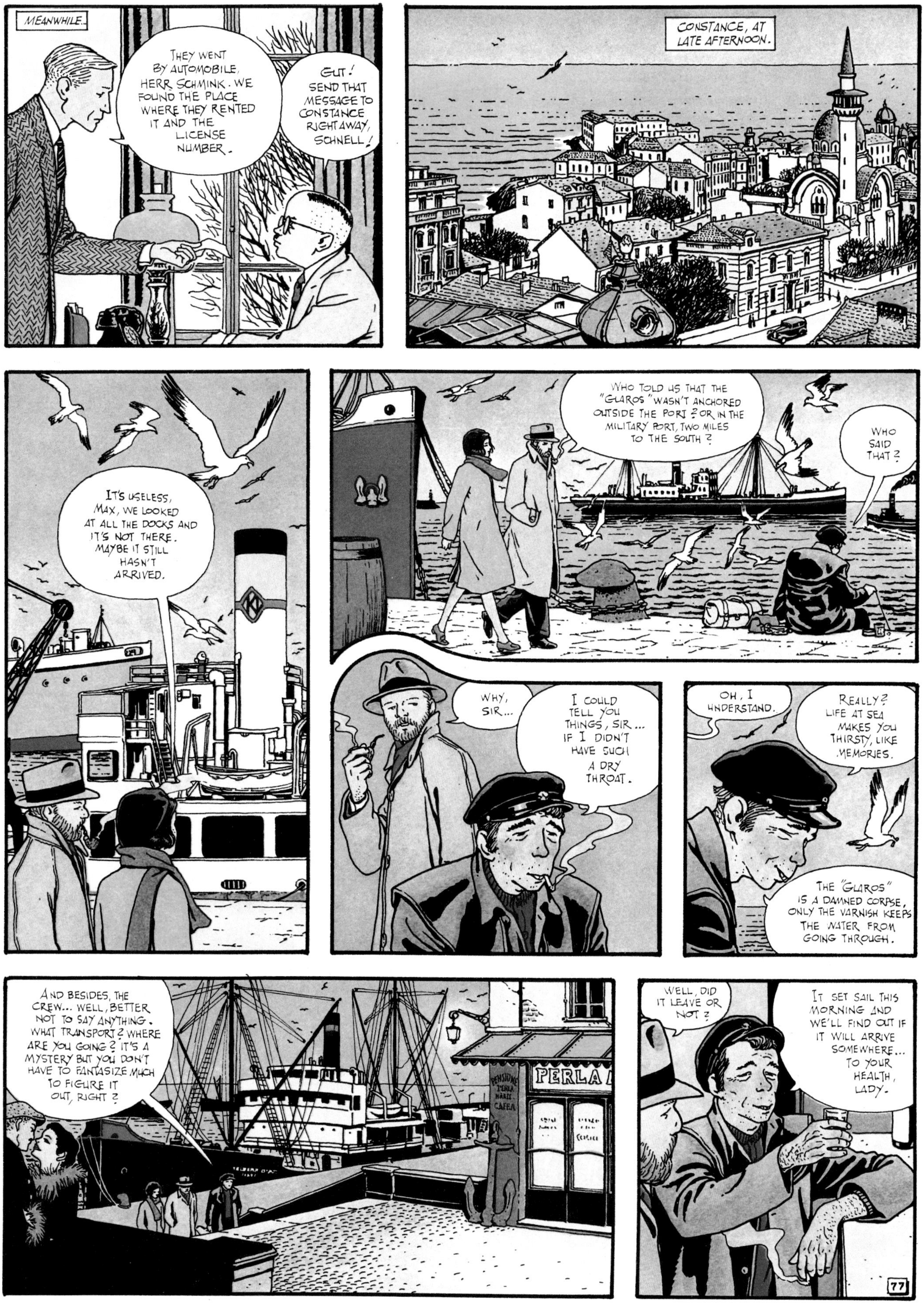
MEANWHILE...
THEY WENT BY AUTOMOBILE, HERR SCHMINK. WE FOUND THE PLACE WHERE THEY RENTED IT AND THE LICENSE NUMBER.
GUT! SEND THAT MESSAGE TO CONSTANCE RIGHT AWAY, SCHNELL!
CONSTANCE, AT LATE AFTERNOON.
IT'S USELESS, MAX, WE LOOKED AT ALL THE DOCKS AND IT'S NOT THERE. MAYBE IT STILL HASN'T ARRIVED.
WHO TOLD US THAT THE "GLAROS" WASN'T ANCHORED OUTSIDE THE PORT? OR IN THE MILITARY PORT, TWO MILES TO THE SOUTH?
WHO SAID THAT?
WHY, SIR...
I COULD TELL YOU THINGS, SIR... IF I DIDN'T HAVE SUCH A DRY THROAT.
OH, I UNDERSTAND.
REALLY? LIFE AT SEA MAKES YOU THIRSTY, LIKE MEMORIES.
THE "GLAROS" IS A DAMNED CORPSE, ONLY THE VARNISH KEEPS THE WATER FROM GOING THROUGH.
AND BESIDES, THE CREW... WELL, BETTER NOT TO SAY ANYTHING. WHAT TRANSPORT? WHERE ARE YOU GOING? IT'S A MYSTERY BUT YOU DON'T HAVE TO FANTASIZE MUCH TO FIGURE IT OUT, RIGHT?
PERLA
WELL, DID IT LEAVE OR NOT?
IT SET SAIL THIS MORNING AND WE'LL FIND OUT IF IT WILL ARRIVE SOMEWHERE... TO YOUR HEALTH, LADY.
77

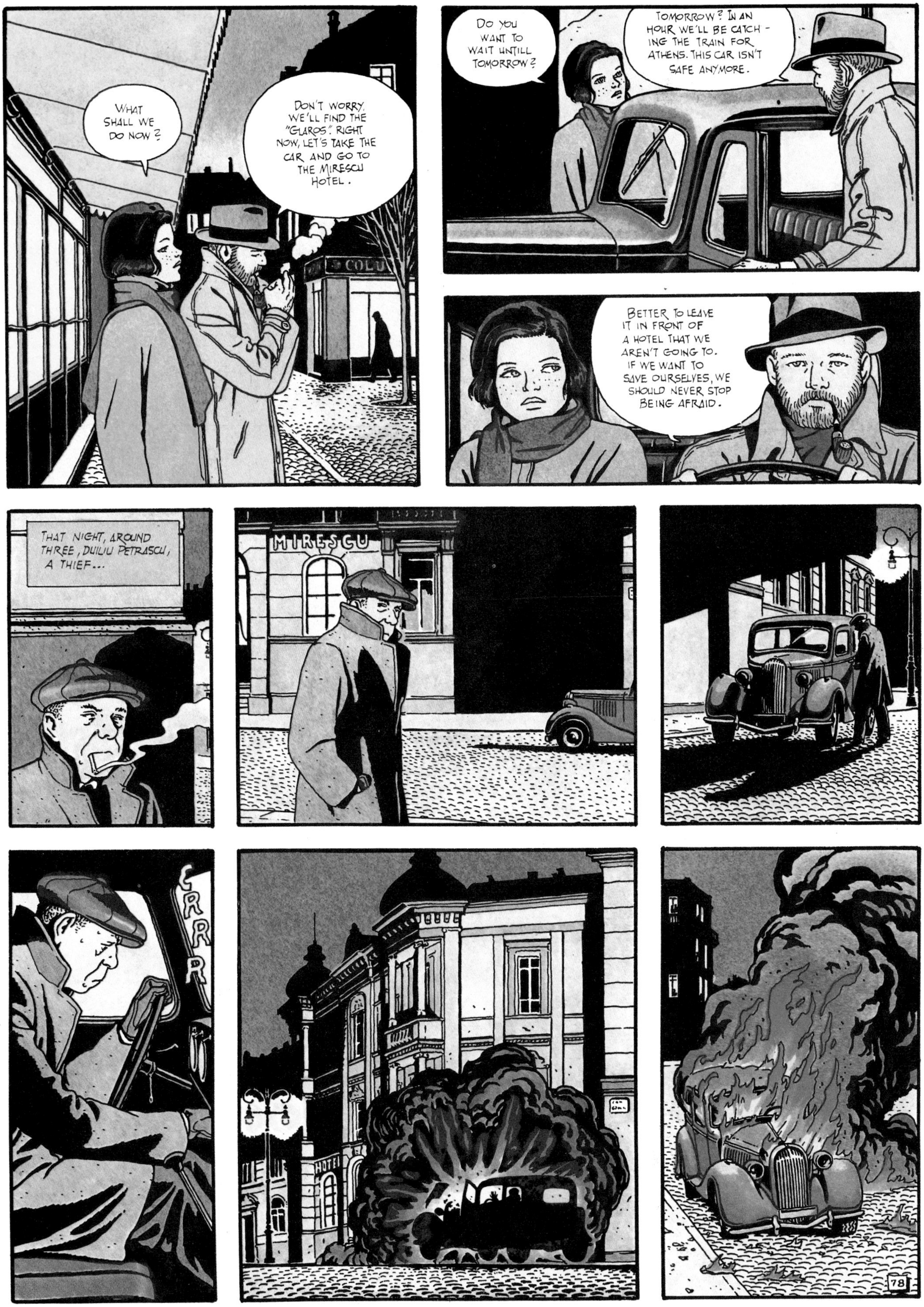
WHAT SHALL WE DO NOW?
DON'T WORRY, WE'LL FIND THE "GLAROS". RIGHT NOW, LET'S TAKE THE CAR AND GO TO THE MIRESCU HOTEL.
DO YOU WANT TO WAIT UNTILL TOMORROW?
TOMORROW? IN AN HOUR WE'LL BE CATCH - ING THE TRAIN FOR ATHENS. THIS CAR ISN'T SAFE ANYMORE.
BETTER TO LEAVE IT IN FRONT OF A HOTEL THAT WE AREN'T GOING TO. IF WE WANT TO SAVE OURSELVES, WE SHOULD NEVER STOP BEING AFRAID.
THAT NIGHT, AROUND THREE, DUILIU PETRASCU, A THIEF...
MIRESCU
CRRR
HOTEL
78

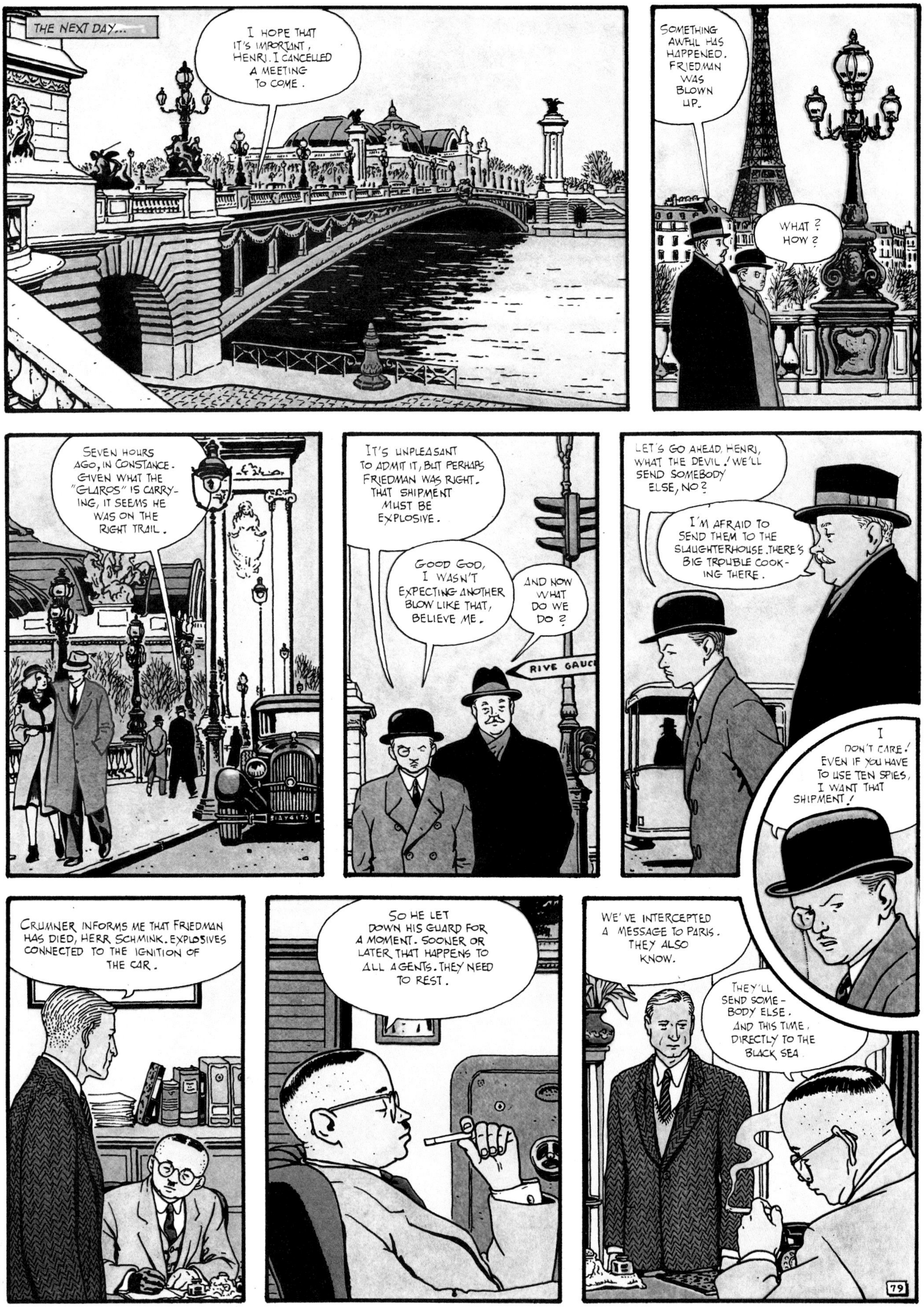
THE NEXT DAY...
I HOPE THAT IT'S IMPORTANT, HENRI. I CANCELLED A MEETING TO COME.
SOMETHING AWFUL HAS HAPPENED. FRIEDMAN WAS BLOWN UP.
WHAT? HOW?
SEVEN HOURS AGO, IN CONSTANCE. GIVEN WHAT THE "GLAROS" IS CARRYING, IT SEEMS HE WAS ON THE RIGHT TRAIL.
IT'S UNPLEASANT TO ADMIT IT, BUT PERHAPS FRIEDMAN WAS RIGHT. THAT SHIPMENT MUST BE EXPLOSIVE.
GOOD GOD, I WASN'T EXPECTING ANOTHER BLOW LIKE THAT, BELIEVE ME.
AND NOW WHAT DO WE DO?
RIVE GAUC
LET'S GO AHEAD, HENRI, WHAT THE DEVIL! WE'LL SEND SOMEBODY ELSE, NO?
I'M AFRAID TO SEND THEM TO THE SLAUGHTERHOUSE. THERE'S BIG TROUBLE COOKING THERE.
I DON'T CARE! EVEN IF YOU HAVE TO USE TEN SPIES, I WANT THAT SHIPMENT!
CRUMNER INFORMS ME THAT FRIEDMAN HAS DIED, HERR SCHMINK. EXPLOSIVES CONNECTED TO THE IGNITION OF THE CAR.
SO HE LET DOWN HIS GUARD FOR A MOMENT. SOONER OR LATER THAT HAPPENS TO ALL AGENTS. THEY NEED TO REST.
WE'VE INTERCEPTED A MESSAGE TO PARIS. THEY ALSO KNOW.
THEY'LL SEND SOMEBODY ELSE. AND THIS TIME, DIRECTLY TO THE BLACK SEA.
79

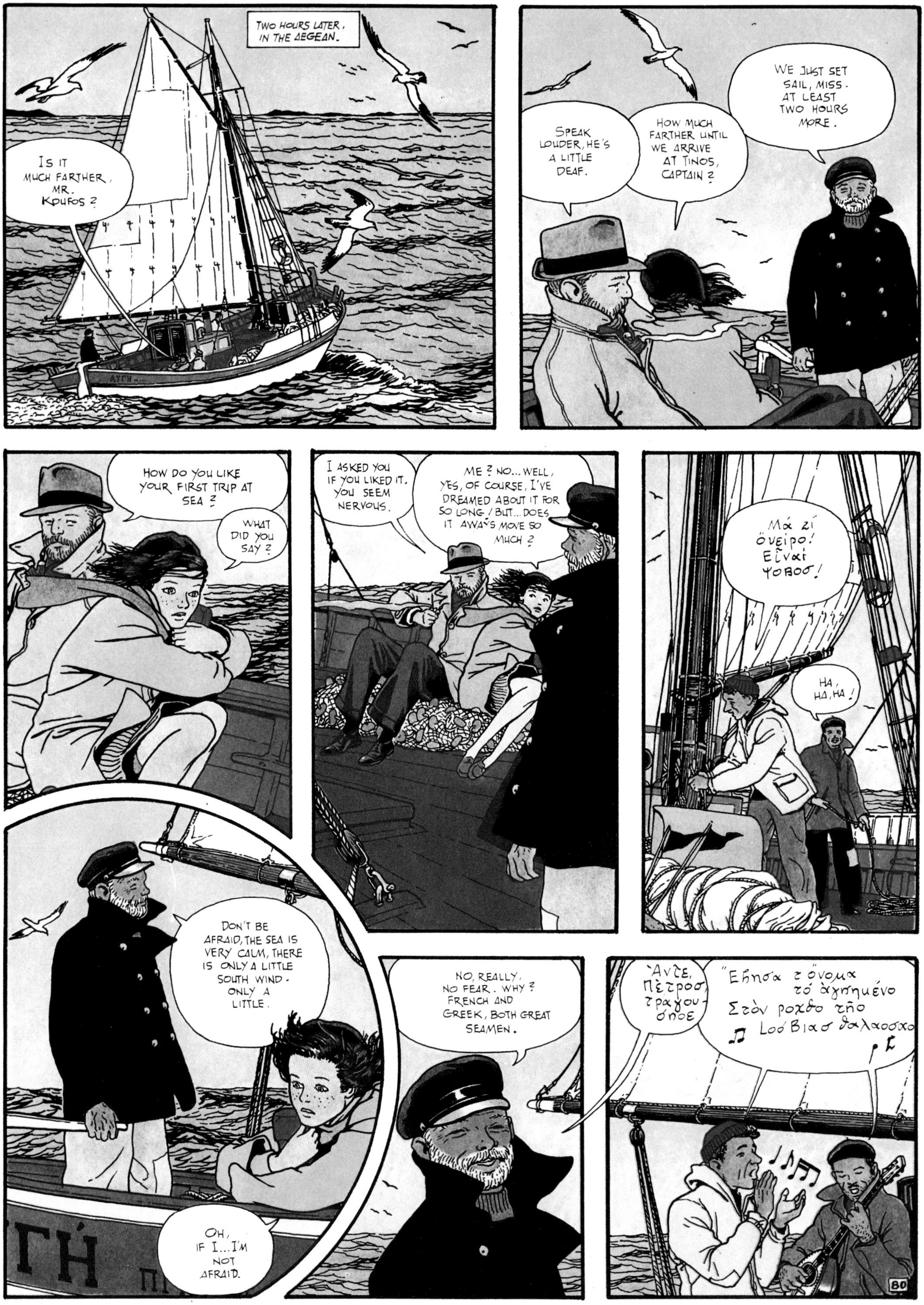
TWO HOURS LATER, IN THE AEGEAN.
IS IT MUCH FARTHER, MR. KRUFOS ?
SPEAK LOUDER, HE'S A LITTLE DEAF.
HOW MUCH FARTHER UNTIL WE ARRIVE AT TINOS, CAPTAIN ?
WE JUST SET SAIL, MISS. AT LEAST TWO HOURS MORE.
HOW DO YOU LIKE YOUR FIRST TRIP AT SEA ?
WHAT DID YOU SAY ?
I ASKED YOU IF YOU LIKED IT. YOU SEEM NERVOUS.
ME ? NO... WELL, YES, OF COURSE, I'VE DREAMED ABOUT IT FOR SO LONG ! BUT... DOES IT ALWAYS MOVE SO MUCH ?
Μά zί ὄνειρο! Εἶναί ΨΟΒΟσ!
HA, HA, HA !
DON'T BE AFRAID, THE SEA IS VERY CALM, THERE IS ONLY A LITTLE SOUTH WIND. ONLY A LITTLE.
OH, IF I... I'M NOT AFRAID.
NO, REALLY, NO FEAR. WHY ? FRENCH AND GREEK, BOTH GREAT SEAMEN.
Ἀντε, Πὲτροσ, τραγου-όποε
"Εḣησα τ ὄνομα τό ἀγνημένο Στὸν ροχθο τῆο Loό Βιασ θαλασσχο
80

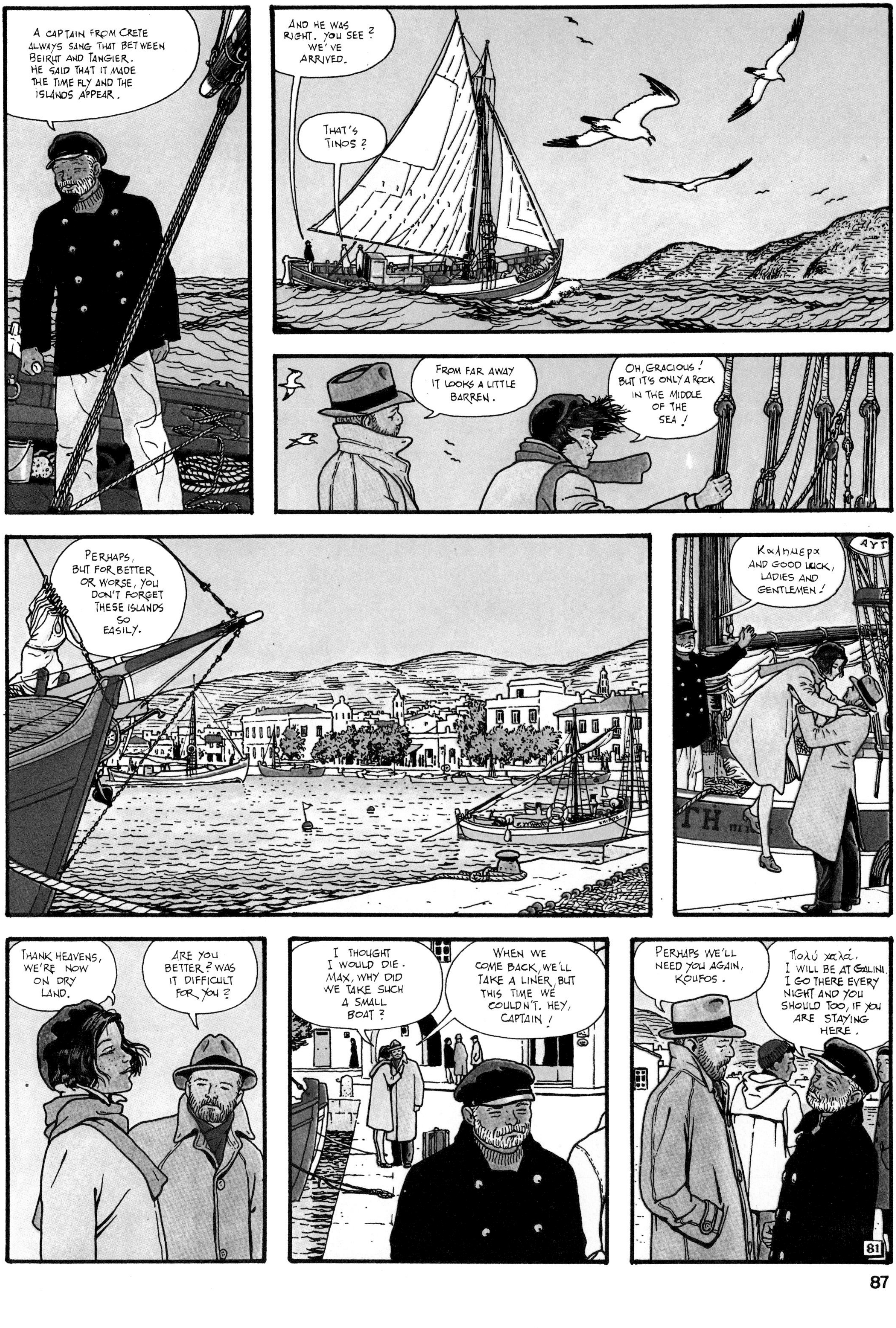
A CAPTAIN FROM CRETE ALWAYS SANG THAT BETWEEN BEIRUT AND TANGIER. HE SAID THAT IT MADE THE TIME FLY AND THE ISLANDS APPEAR.
AND HE WAS RIGHT. YOU SEE ? WE'VE ARRIVED.
THAT'S TINOS ?
FROM FAR AWAY IT LOOKS A LITTLE BARREN.
OH, GRACIOUS ! BUT IT'S ONLY A ROCK IN THE MIDDLE OF THE SEA !
PERHAPS, BUT FOR BETTER OR WORSE, YOU DON'T FORGET THESE ISLANDS SO EASILY.
Καλημερα AND GOOD LUCK, LADIES AND GENTLEMEN !
THANK HEAVENS, WE'RE NOW ON DRY LAND.
ARE YOU BETTER ? WAS IT DIFFICULT FOR YOU ?
I THOUGHT I WOULD DIE. MAX, WHY DID WE TAKE SUCH A SMALL BOAT ?
WHEN WE COME BACK, WE'LL TAKE A LINER, BUT THIS TIME WE COULDN'T. HEY, CAPTAIN !
PERHAPS WE'LL NEED YOU AGAIN, KOUFOS.
Πολύ καλά, I WILL BE AT GALINI. I GO THERE EVERY NIGHT AND YOU SHOULD TOO, IF YOU ARE STAYING HERE.
81

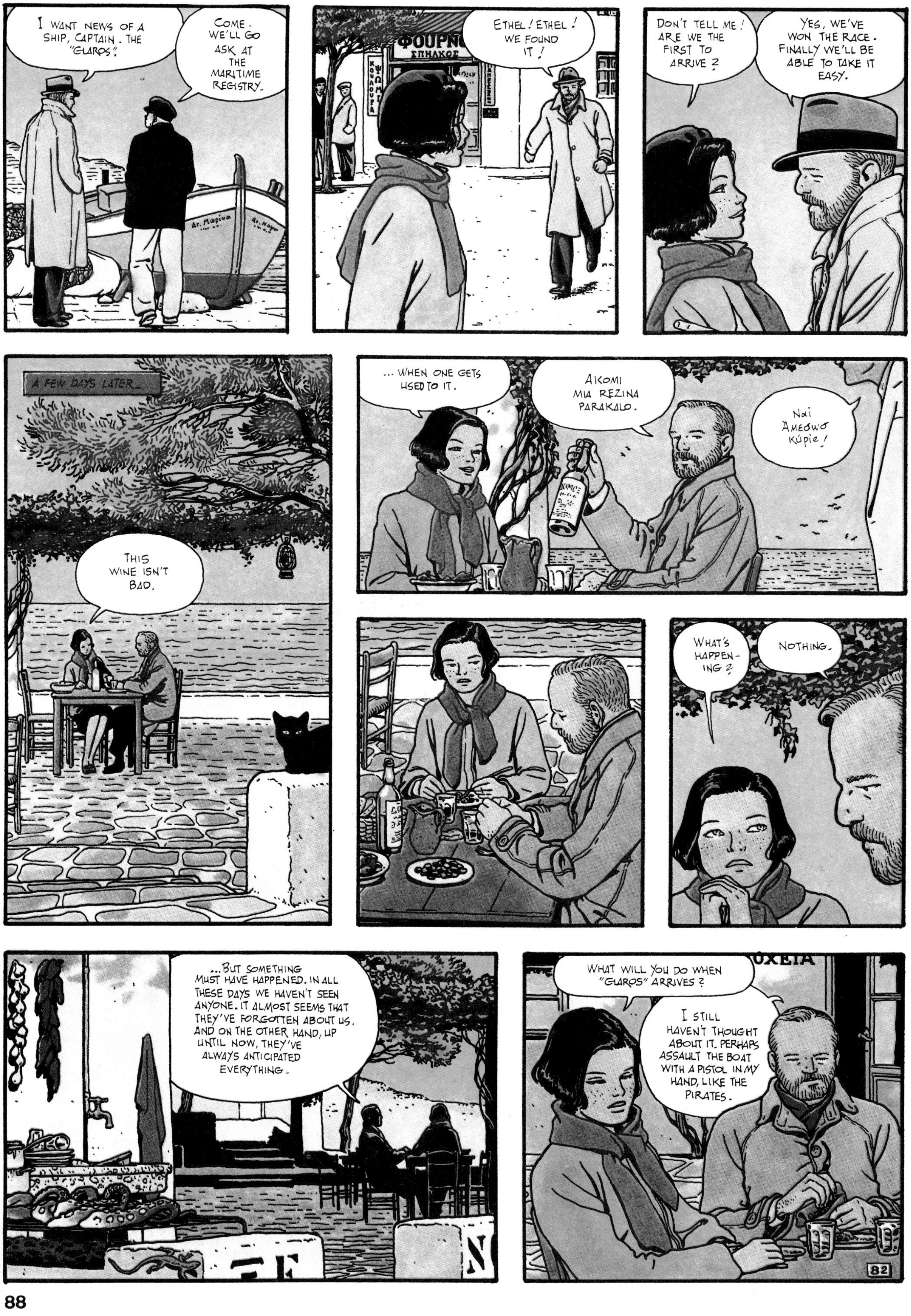

I WANT NEWS OF A SHIP, CAPTAIN. THE "GLAROS".
COME. WE'LL GO ASK AT THE MARITIME REGISTRY.
ETHEL! ETHEL! WE FOUND IT!
DON'T TELL ME! ARE WE THE FIRST TO ARRIVE?
YES, WE'VE WON THE RACE. FINALLY WE'LL BE ABLE TO TAKE IT EASY.
A FEW DAYS LATER...
THIS WINE ISN'T BAD.
... WHEN ONE GETS USED TO IT.
AKOMI MIA REZINA PARAKALO.
Ναί Άμεσως Κύριε!
WHAT'S HAPPENING?
NOTHING.
...BUT SOMETHING MUST HAVE HAPPENED. IN ALL THESE DAYS WE HAVEN'T SEEN ANYONE. IT ALMOST SEEMS THAT THEY'VE FORGOTTEN ABOUT US. AND ON THE OTHER HAND, UP UNTIL NOW, THEY'VE ALWAYS ANTICIPATED EVERYTHING.
WHAT WILL YOU DO WHEN "GLAROS" ARRIVES?
I STILL HAVEN'T THOUGHT ABOUT IT. PERHAPS ASSAULT THE BOAT WITH A PISTOL IN MY HAND, LIKE THE PIRATES.
82

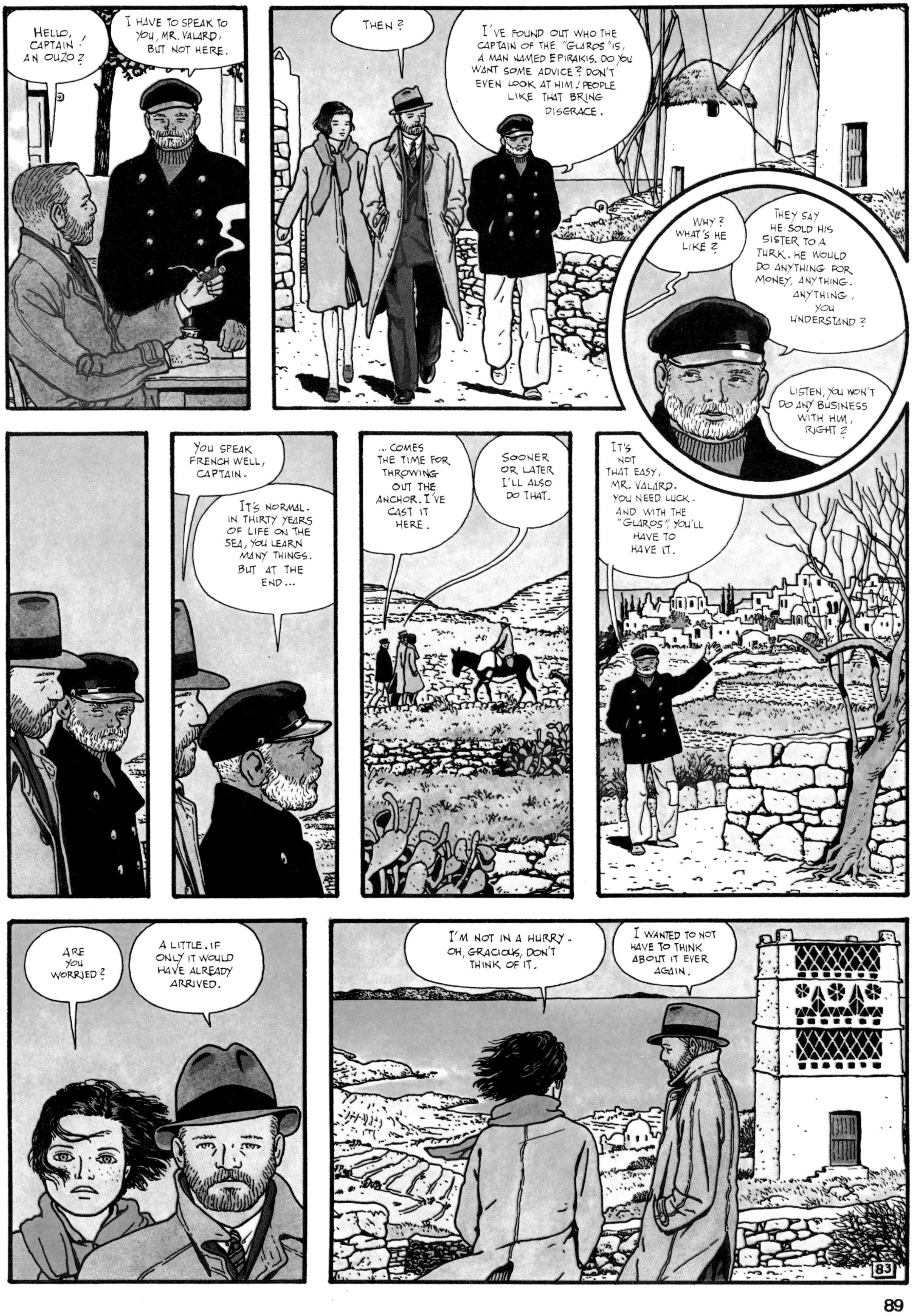
HELLO, CAPTAIN! AN OUZO?
I HAVE TO SPEAK TO YOU, MR. VALARD, BUT NOT HERE.
THEN?
I'VE FOUND OUT WHO THE CAPTAIN OF THE "GLAROS" IS, A MAN NAMED EPIRAKIS. DO YOU WANT SOME ADVICE? DON'T EVEN LOOK AT HIM! PEOPLE LIKE THAT BRING DISGRACE.
WHY? WHAT'S HE LIKE?
THEY SAY HE SOLD HIS SISTER TO A TURK. HE WOULD DO ANYTHING FOR MONEY, ANYTHING. ANYTHING, YOU UNDERSTAND?
LISTEN, YOU WON'T DO ANY BUSINESS WITH HIM, RIGHT?
YOU SPEAK FRENCH WELL, CAPTAIN.
IT'S NORMAL. IN THIRTY YEARS OF LIFE ON THE SEA, YOU LEARN MANY THINGS. BUT AT THE END...
...COMES THE TIME FOR THROWING OUT THE ANCHOR. I'VE CAST IT HERE.
SOONER OR LATER I'LL ALSO DO THAT.
IT'S NOT THAT EASY, MR. VALARD. YOU NEED LUCK. AND WITH THE "GLAROS", YOU'LL HAVE TO HAVE IT.
ARE YOU WORRIED?
A LITTLE. IF ONLY IT WOULD HAVE ALREADY ARRIVED.
I'M NOT IN A HURRY. OH, GRACIOUS, DON'T THINK OF IT.
I WANTED TO NOT HAVE TO THINK ABOUT IT EVER AGAIN.
83

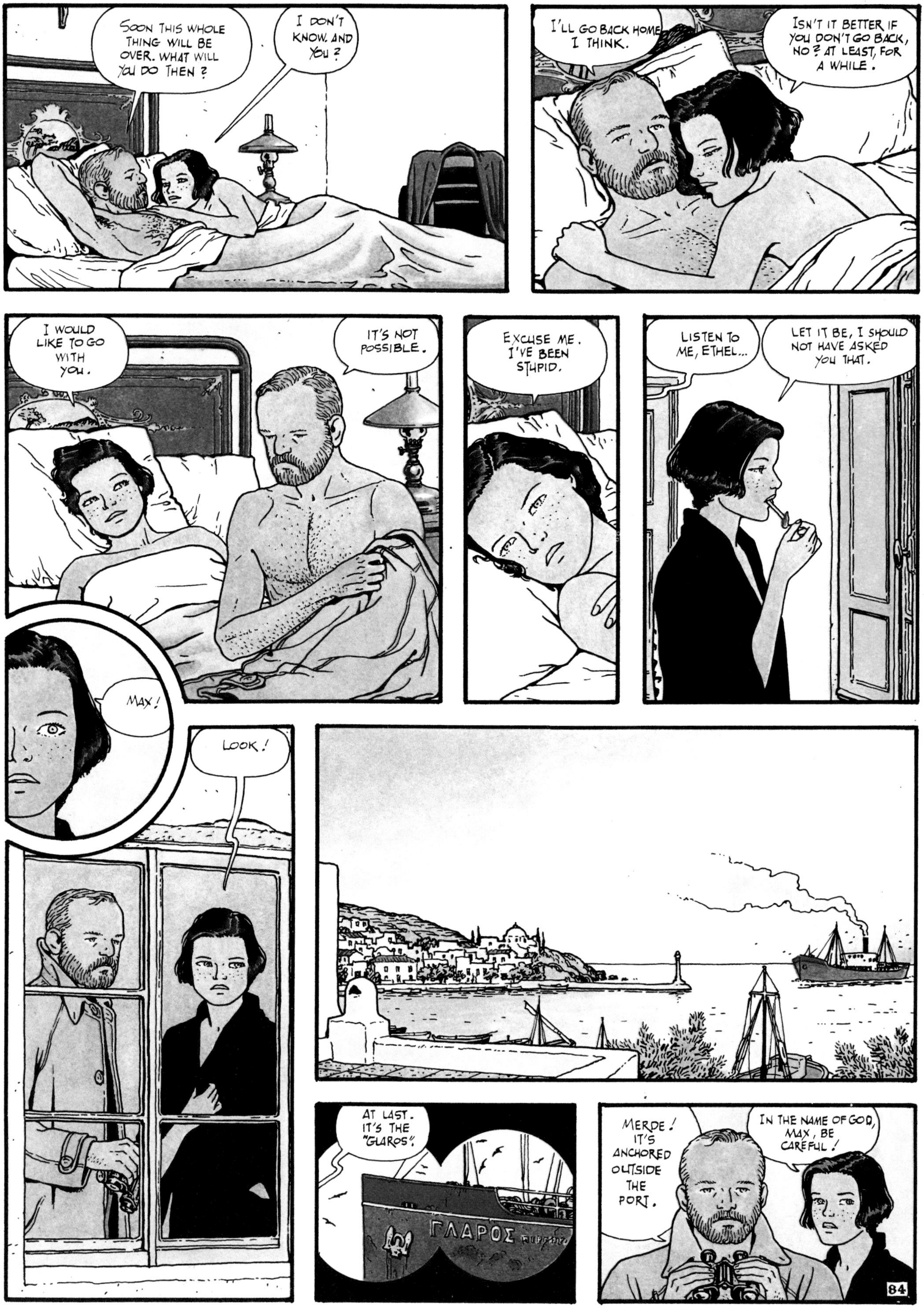
SOON THIS WHOLE THING WILL BE OVER. WHAT WILL YOU DO THEN ?
I DON'T KNOW. AND YOU ?
I'LL GO BACK HOME I THINK.
ISN'T IT BETTER IF YOU DON'T GO BACK, NO ? AT LEAST, FOR A WHILE.
I WOULD LIKE TO GO WITH YOU.
IT'S NOT POSSIBLE.
EXCUSE ME. I'VE BEEN STUPID.
LISTEN TO ME, ETHEL...
LET IT BE, I SHOULD NOT HAVE ASKED YOU THAT.
MAX!
LOOK!
AT LAST. IT'S THE "GLAROS".
ΓΛΑΡΟΣ
MERDE! IT'S ANCHORED OUTSIDE THE PORT.
IN THE NAME OF GOD, MAX, BE CAREFUL!
84

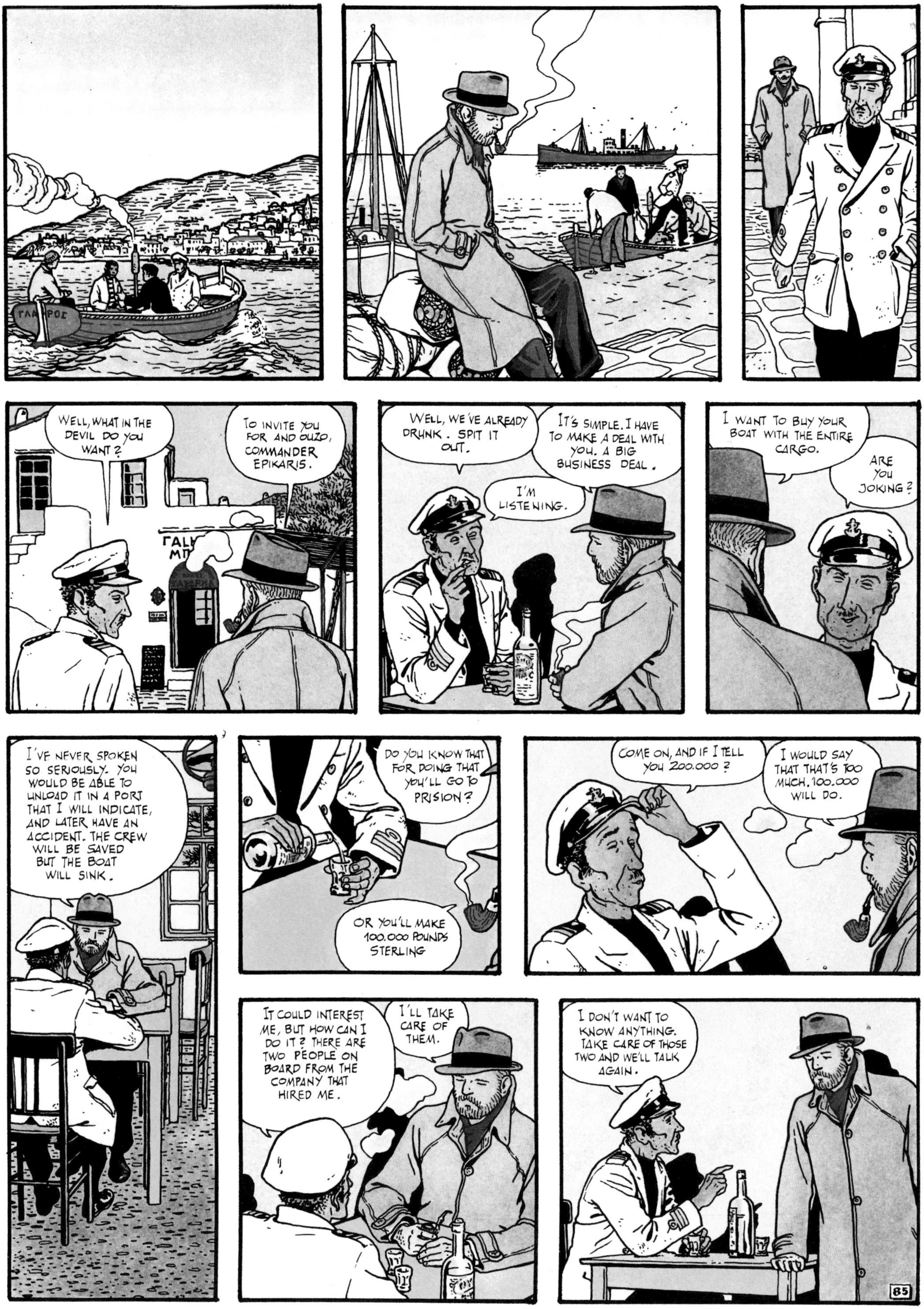
WELL, WHAT IN THE DEVIL DO YOU WANT ?
TO INVITE YOU FOR AND OUZO, COMMANDER EPIKARIS.
WELL, WE'VE ALREADY DRUNK . SPIT IT OUT.
IT'S SIMPLE. I HAVE TO MAKE A DEAL WITH YOU. A BIG BUSINESS DEAL .
I'M LISTENING.
I WANT TO BUY YOUR BOAT WITH THE ENTIRE CARGO.
ARE YOU JOKING ?
I'VE NEVER SPOKEN SO SERIOUSLY. YOU WOULD BE ABLE TO UNLOAD IT IN A PORT THAT I WILL INDICATE, AND LATER HAVE AN ACCIDENT. THE CREW WILL BE SAVED BUT THE BOAT WILL SINK.
DO YOU KNOW THAT FOR DOING THAT YOU'LL GO TO PRISION ?
OR YOU'LL MAKE 100.000 POUNDS STERLING
COME ON, AND IF I TELL YOU 200.000 ?
I WOULD SAY THAT THAT'S TOO MUCH. 100.000 WILL DO.
IT COULD INTEREST ME, BUT HOW CAN I DO IT ? THERE ARE TWO PEOPLE ON BOARD FROM THE COMPANY THAT HIRED ME.
I'LL TAKE CARE OF THEM.
I DON'T WANT TO KNOW ANYTHING. TAKE CARE OF THOSE TWO AND WE'LL TALK AGAIN.
85

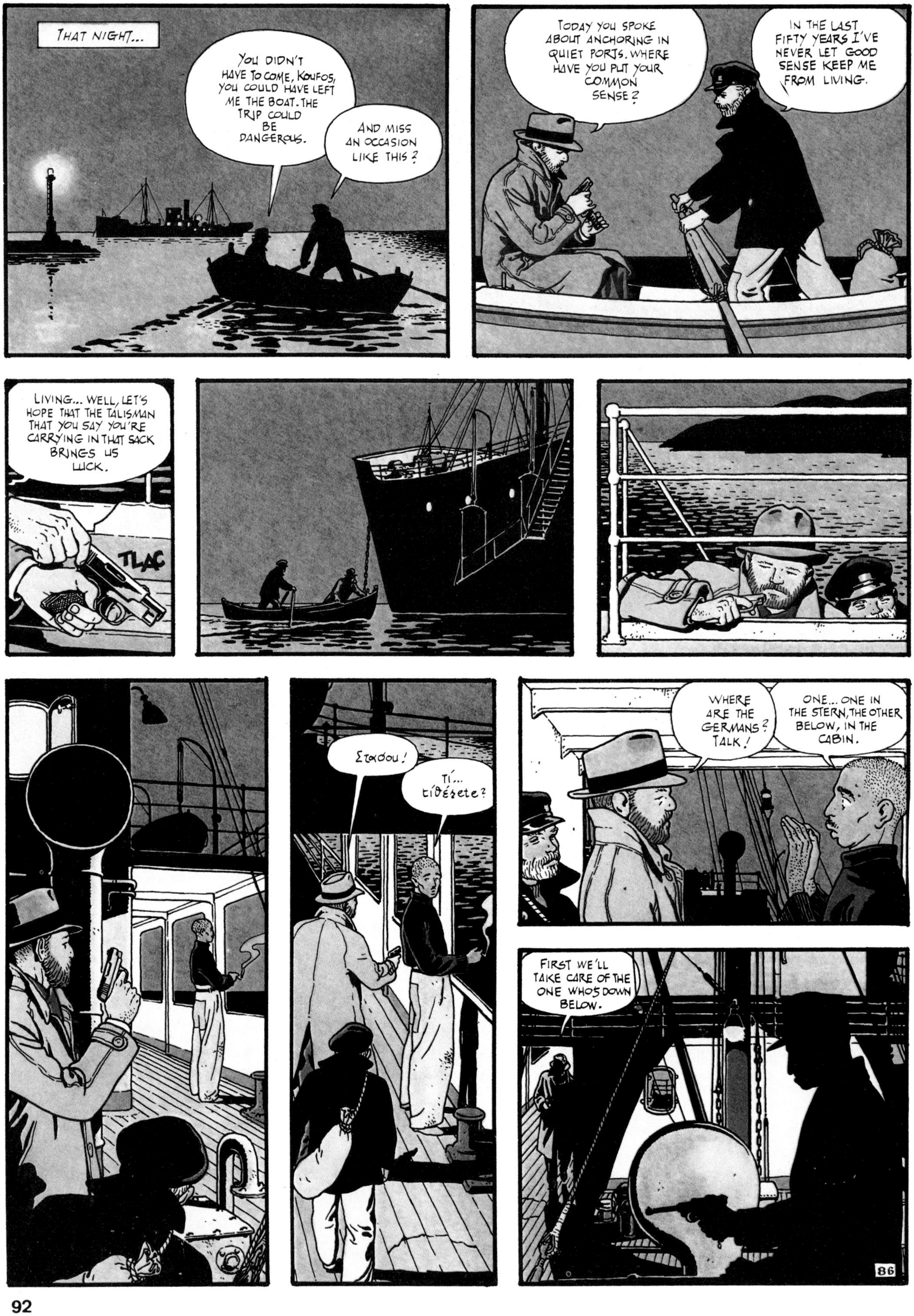
THAT NIGHT...
YOU DIDN'T HAVE TO COME, KOUFOS, YOU COULD HAVE LEFT ME THE BOAT. THE TRIP COULD BE DANGEROUS.
AND MISS AN OCCASION LIKE THIS?
TODAY YOU SPOKE ABOUT ANCHORING IN QUIET PORTS. WHERE HAVE YOU PUT YOUR COMMON SENSE?
IN THE LAST FIFTY YEARS I'VE NEVER LET GOOD SENSE KEEP ME FROM LIVING.
LIVING... WELL, LET'S HOPE THAT THE TALISMAN THAT YOU SAY YOU'RE CARRYING IN THAT SACK BRINGS US LUCK.
TLAC
Στασου!
Τί... τίθέξετe?
WHERE ARE THE GERMANS? TALK!
ONE... ONE IN THE STERN, THE OTHER BELOW, IN THE CABIN.
FIRST WE'LL TAKE CARE OF THE ONE WHO'S DOWN BELOW.
86

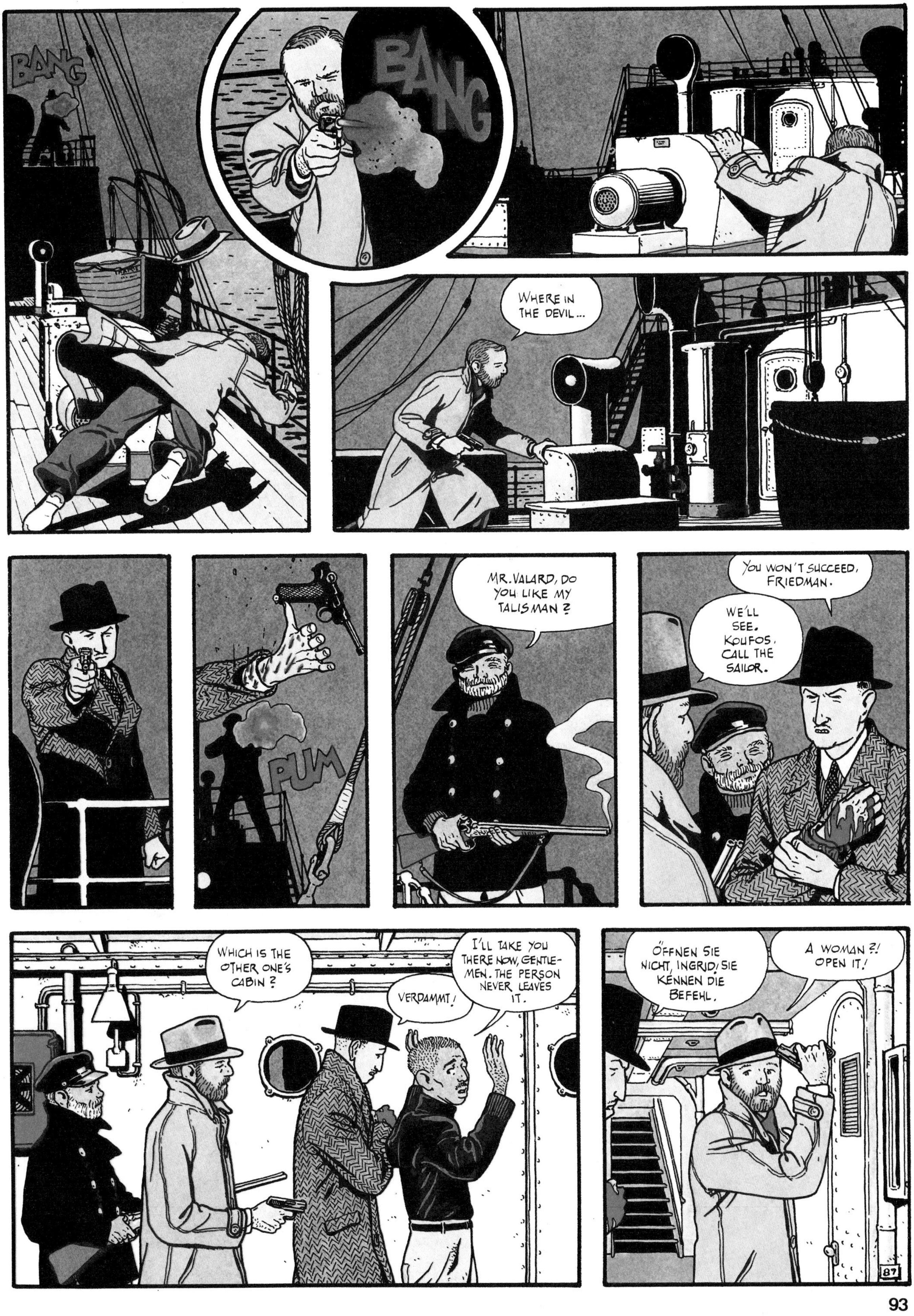
BANG
BANG
WHERE IN THE DEVIL...
PUM
MR. VALARD, DO YOU LIKE MY TALISMAN?
YOU WON'T SUCCEED, FRIEDMAN.
WE'LL SEE. KOUFOS, CALL THE SAILOR.
WHICH IS THE OTHER ONE'S CABIN?
I'LL TAKE YOU THERE NOW, GENTLEMEN. THE PERSON NEVER LEAVES IT.
VERDAMMT!
ÖFFNEN SIE NICHT, INGRID! SIE KENNEN DIE BEFEHL.
A WOMAN?! OPEN IT!
87

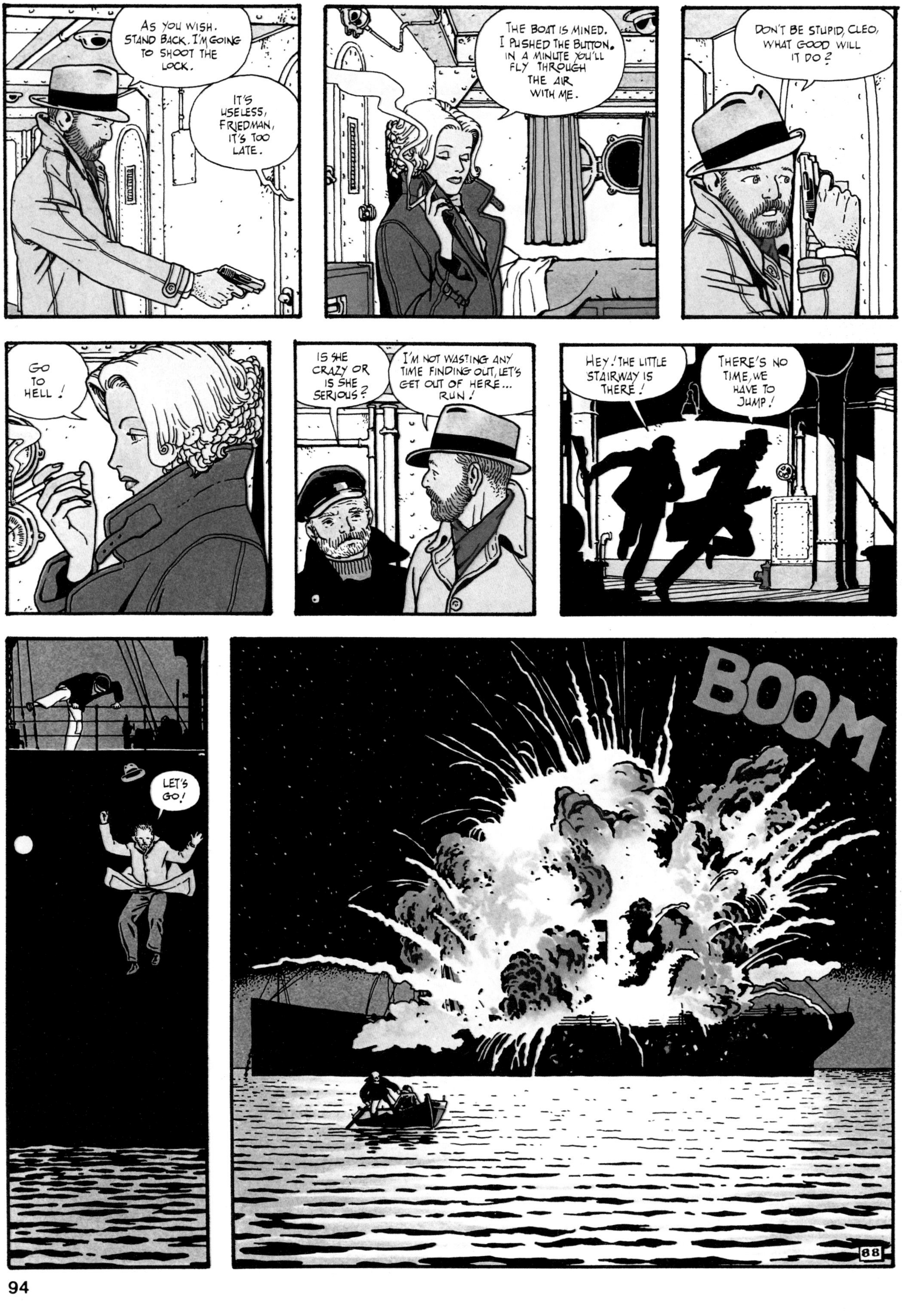

As you wish. Stand back. I'm going to shoot the lock.
It's useless, Friedman, it's too late.
The boat is mined. I pushed the button. In a minute you'll fly through the air with me.
Don't be stupid, Cleo, what good will it do?
Go to hell!
Is she crazy or is she serious?
I'm not wasting any time finding out, let's get out of here... Run!
Hey! The little stairway is there!
There's no time, we have to jump!
Let's go!
BOOM
88

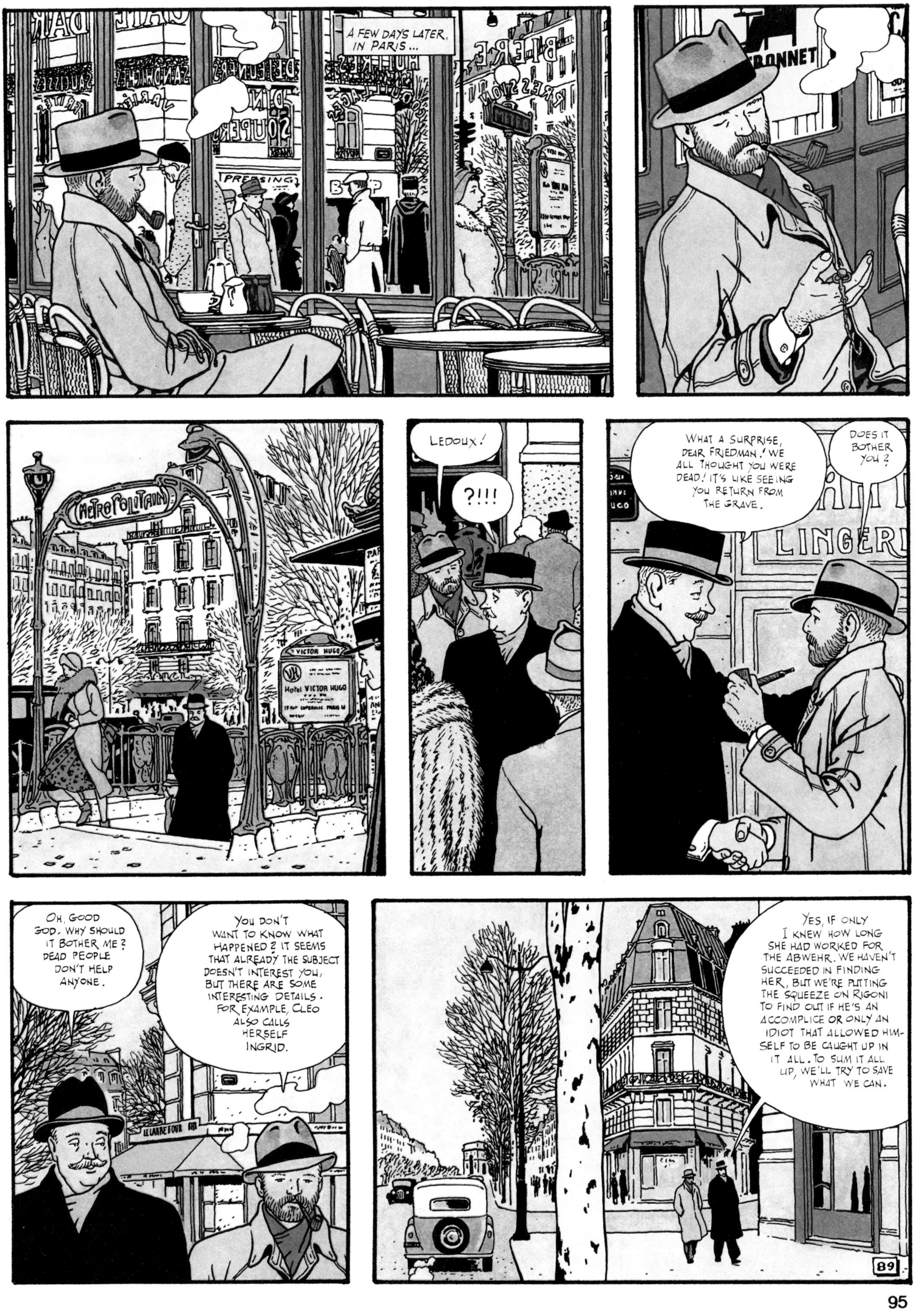
A FEW DAYS LATER, IN PARIS...
LEDOUX!
?!!!
WHAT A SURPRISE, DEAR FRIEDMAN! WE ALL THOUGHT YOU WERE DEAD! IT'S LIKE SEEING YOU RETURN FROM THE GRAVE.
DOES IT BOTHER YOU?
OH, GOOD GOD. WHY SHOULD IT BOTHER ME? DEAD PEOPLE DON'T HELP ANYONE.
YOU DON'T WANT TO KNOW WHAT HAPPENED? IT SEEMS THAT ALREADY THE SUBJECT DOESN'T INTEREST YOU, BUT THERE ARE SOME INTERESTING DETAILS. FOR EXAMPLE, CLEO ALSO CALLS HERSELF INGRID.
YES, IF ONLY I KNEW HOW LONG SHE HAD WORKED FOR THE ABWEHR. WE HAVEN'T SUCCEEDED IN FINDING HER, BUT WE'RE PUTTING THE SQUEEZE ON RIGONI TO FIND OUT IF HE'S AN ACCOMPLICE OR ONLY AN IDIOT THAT ALLOWED HIMSELF TO BE CAUGHT UP IN IT ALL. TO SUM IT ALL UP, WE'LL TRY TO SAVE WHAT WE CAN.
89

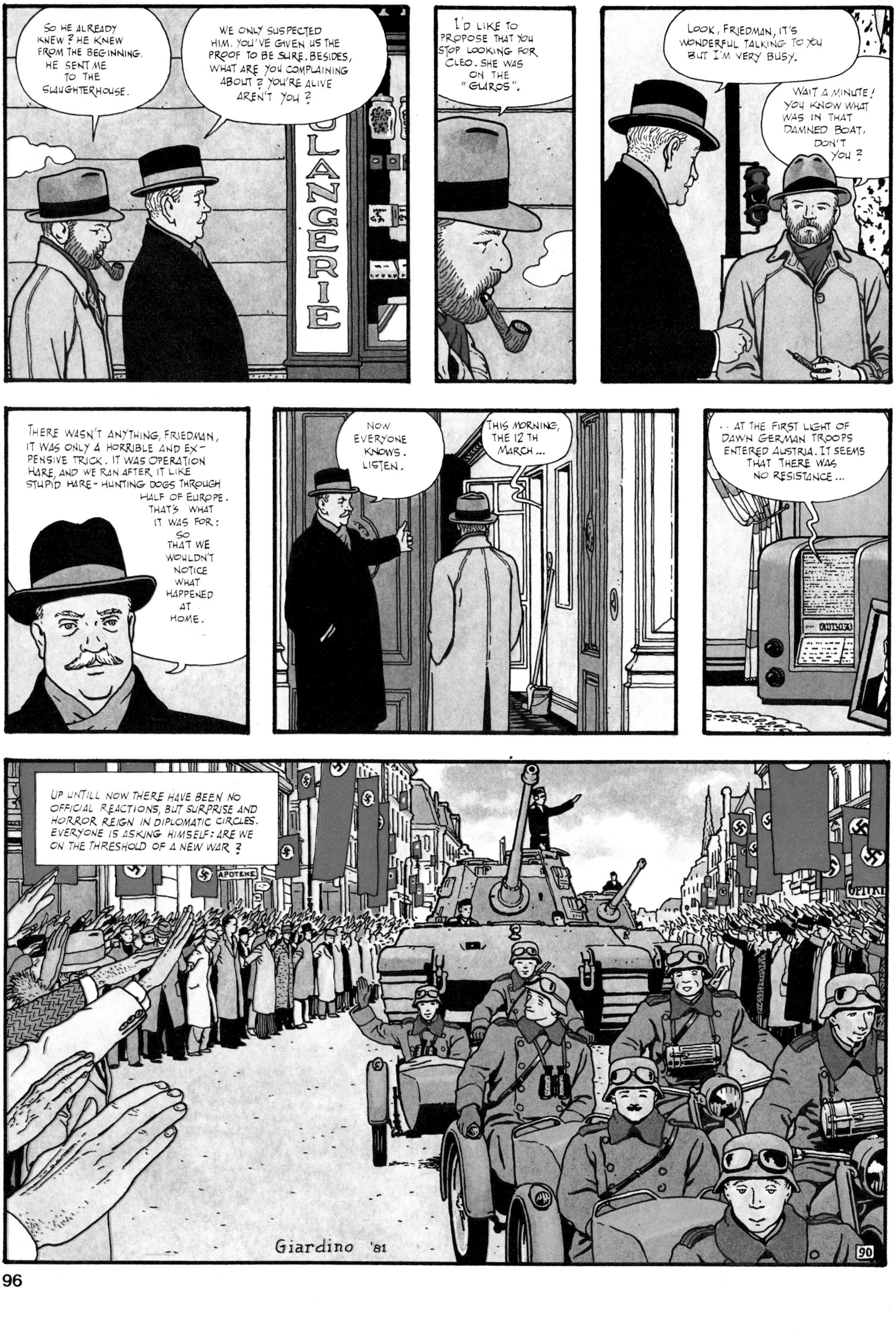
So he already knew? He knew from the beginning. He sent me to the slaughterhouse.
We only suspected him. You've given us the proof to be sure. Besides, what are you complaining about? You're alive aren't you?
LANGERIE
I'd like to propose that you stop looking for Cleo. She was on the "Gluros".
Look, Friedman, it's wonderful talking to you but I'm very busy.
Wait a minute! You know what was in that damned boat, don't you?
There wasn't anything, Friedman, it was only a horrible and expensive trick. It was Operation Hare, and we ran after it like stupid hare-hunting dogs through half of Europe. That's what it was for: so that we wouldn't notice what happened at home.
Now everyone knows. Listen.
This morning, the 12th March...
.. at the first light of dawn German troops entered Austria. It seems that there was no resistance...
Up untill now there have been no official reactions, but surprise and horror reign in diplomatic circles. Everyone is asking himself: are we on the threshold of a new war?
APOTEKE
OPTIKE
Giardino '81
90